Experiments in Rethinking History

ᴌ18·99

History is a narrative discourse, full of unfinished stories. This collection of innovative and experimental pieces of historical writing shows there are fascinating and important new ways of telling the past. The pieces illustrate the performative and fictive nature of history, and point to new ways of thinking about the past.

Fourteen engaging and thought-provoking pieces lead the reader to a deeper understanding of some of the possible responses to the question 'What is history?', and even suggest that this traditional question might be better replaced with a new question, 'How shall I engage with the past today?' The collection includes subjects as diverse as a lynching in South Carolina, the life of an eighteenth-century French marquise and a journey to a string of Pacific islands. The pieces show what is possible in doing history, and demonstrate how other factors, such as the impact of emotions, the feeling of 'otherness', the confining character of boundaries, authorial subjectivity, and even a sense of boredom with conventional ways of doing history, intrude on historical practice.

As well as being a compelling read, the book includes a thorough two-part introduction on theory and practice, as well as further introductory matter at the start of each Part to allow the reader to engage fully with the theoretical aspects of each section of the book. This book should be read by all those with an interest in history and its theory.

Alun Munslow is Professor of History and Historical Theory at Staffordshire University. He is the author of *Deconstructing History* (1997), *The Routledge Companion to Historical Studies* (2000) and most recently *The New History* (2003) and is the UK Editor of *Rethinking History: The Journal of Theory and Practice*.

Robert A. Rosenstone, Professor of History at the California Institute of Technology, is author of six books, including *Romantic Revolutionary: A Biography of John Reed* (1975), *Mirror in the Shrine: American Encounters with Meiji Japan* (1988), *Visions of the Past: The Challenge of Film to Our Idea of History* (1995) and *King of Odessa* (2003). Currently he serves as Founding Editor of *Rethinking History: The Journal of Theory and Practice*.

Experiments in Rethinking History

Edited by Alun Munslow
and Robert A. Rosenstone

Routledge
Taylor & Francis Group

NEW YORK AND LONDON

First published 2004
by Routledge
29 West 35th Street, New York, NY 10001

Simultaneously published in the UK
by Routledge
2 Park Square, Milton Park, Abingdon,
Oxfordshire OX14 4RN

Routledge is an imprint of the Taylor & Francis Group

Typeset in Garamond by
Keystroke, Jacaranda Lodge, Wolverhampton
Printed and bound in Great Britain by
The Cromwell Press, Trowbridge, Wiltshire

British Library Cataloguing in Publication Data
A catalogue record for this book is available from the British Library

Library of Congress Cataloging in Publication Data
Experiments in rethinking history / [edited by] Alun Munslow and Robert
Rosenstone.
    p. cm.
Includes bibliographical references.
1. History–Philosophy. 2. History–Methodology. 3. Historiography.
I. Munslow, Alun, 1947– II. Rosenstone, Robert A.
    D16.E89 2004
    901–dc22   2003027159

ISBN 0–415–30145–9 (hbk)
ISBN 0–415–30146–7 (pbk)

Contents

List of figures

Notes on contributors

Marjorie Becker is an Associate Professor of Latin American history at the University of Southern California. A former Peace Corps volunteer in rural Paraguay, she has lived and conducted research in rural Michoacán villages and towns, and in Mexico City. She has written extensively on the Mexican revolution, its masculinization, about the invention of the Mexican Indian, about race and gender and the relationships between peasants and Lázaro Cárdenas in the making of the post-revolutionary Mexican government.

Jesse Berrett is the chair of the History Department at University High School in San Francisco. He has written about history, literature, television and music for a variety of publications.

Robin Bisha is Director of Student Publications and teaches in the communication studies department at Texas Lutheran University. After earning a doctorate in Russian history at Indiana University, she taught at Kalamazoo College and the University of Texas at El Paso. She is co-editor of *Russian Women, 1698–1917* (Indiana University Press, 2002).

Greg Dening is Adjunct Professor at the Centre for Cross-Cultural Research, Australian National University. His latest book, *Beach Crossings: Voyaging across Times, Cultures and Self* is in press.

William Deverell is Professor of History at the University of Southern California and Director of the Huntington Library – USC Institute for California and the West. He is the author or editor of several books examining the history of the American West, including *Railroad Crossing: Californians and the Railroad* and *Whitewashed Adobe: Los Angeles and the Remaking of the Mexican Landscape*.

Janet Golden is Associate Professor of History at Rutgers University Camden. She is the author of the forthcoming *Message in a Bottle: The Making of Fetal Alcohol Syndrome* (Harvard University Press) and of numerous books and articles in the history of medicine.

James Goodman is the author of *Stories of Scottsboro* (Pantheon, 1994) and *Blackout* (North Point Press, 2003). "Blackout" is a working draft of the opening pages of the latter. When he isn't writing (and sometimes when he is), he teaches history and writing at Rutgers University, Newark. He lives in New York City with Jennifer McFeely, Samuel Goodman, and Jackson Goodman.

Maureen Healy is an Assistant Professor of History at Oregon State University. Her book, *Vienna and the Fall of the Habsburg Empire: Total War and Everyday Life in World War I*, is forthcoming from Cambridge University Press.

Marie Theresa Hernández is Assistant Professor in Anthropology and Social Work at the University of Houston. Her work, *Delirio: The Fantastic, The Demonic, and The Reél, The Buried History of Nuevo León* (University of Texas Press, 2001) studies the production of history in northern Mexico.

Sumiko Higashi is Professor Emerita in the Department of History at the State University of New York, Brockport. She is the author of *Cecil B. DeMille and American Culture: The Silent Era*, as well as numerous essays on film history as cultural history, images of women in film, and film as historical representation.

David Igler is an Assisant Professor of History at the University of California, Irvine. He is author of *Industrial Cowboys: Miller & Lux and the Transformation of the Far West, 1850–1920* (UC Press, 2001).

Alun Munslow is Professor of History and Historical Theory at Staffordshire University, UK. One of the founding editors of *Rethinking History: The Journal of Theory and Practice*, he is a nineteenth-century American cultural historian. The bridge between his American interests and the nature of history emerged first in his book *Discourse and Culture: The Creation of America, 1870–1920* (Routledge, 1992). Specifically addressing the nature of history and its practice, his most recent books are *Deconstructing History* (Routledge, 1997), *The Routledge Companion to Historical Studies* (Routledge, 2000) and *The New History* (Pearson, 2003) which is the lead text in the Pearson Series *History: Concepts, Theories and Practice* for which he is the General Editor. He is also the co-editor of *The Nature of History Reader* with Keith Jenkins (Routledge, 2004).

Robert A. Rosenstone, Professor of History at the California Institute of Technology, has published works of history, biography, and criticism, along with more imaginative forms of writing – a family memoir entitled *The Man Who Swam into History* (2002), and a novel, *King of Odessa* (2003). His scholarly books include the prize-winning *Romantic Revolutionary: A Biography of John Reed* (1975); *Crusade of the Left* (1970), an account of the Americans who fought in the Spanish Civil War; *Mirror in the Shrine* (1988), a multi-voiced narrative about American sojourners in nineteenth-century Japan; and *Visions of the Past: The Challenge of Film to Our Idea of History* (1955). Rosenstone created and served as an editor of the film section of the *American Historical Review*, and is a Founding Editor of *Rethinking History: The Journal of Theory and Practice*.

Bryant Simon is an Associate Professor of History at the University of Georgia. Currently he is writing a book about the middle class, public space, and the history of Atlantic City, New Jersey, to be published by Oxford University Press.

Elizabeth Toon received her PhD in the History and Sociology of Science from the University of Pennsylvania, and has taught there and in Science and Technology Studies at Cornell University, New York. She is completing a book, *Selling Prevention: Health Education and Medical Advice-Giving in the Interwar U.S.*, based on research begun for her doctoral thesis. She is a Research Associate at the University of Manchester's Centre for the History of Science, Technology and Medicine.

Jonathan Walker recently finished a British Academy Postdoctoral Fellowship based at Wolfson College, Cambridge, and is currently a Sesqui Postdoctoral Fellow at the University of Sydney, Australia. He just finished a book entitled *Pistols! Treason! Murder!*, on the Venetian spy Gerolamo Vano, principal accuser of Antonio Foscarini in 1622. This includes dialogues, comic strips, four photosequences, and various other kinds of literary experiment and pastiche. The title chapter was published as an article in *Rethinking History* in 2003. A second, short book will deal with Foscarini's London embassy and first trial.

Chris Ward began doctoral research at Essex University in 1979 and spent three years attached to the Department of History of the USSR at Leningrad State University. He has worked at Cambridge University since 1987 and is currently Head of the Slavonic Department. His publications include *Russia's Cotton Workers and the New Economic Policy* (1990); *Perestroika: The Historical Perspective* (1991), edited with C. Merridale; *Stalin's Russia* (1993, 1999), and an edited collection *The Stalinist Dictatorship* (1998).

Judith P. Zinsser, Professor of History, Miami University (Ohio), has written widely on European women's history. Her current project is a biography of the marquise Du Châtelet for Viking Penguin. Zinsser's articles on the marquise have appeared in journals and edited collections in Europe and the United States.

Acknowledgements

All the articles originally appeared in the journal *Rethinking History*. The website of the journal can be found at *http://www.tandf.co.uk*

Marjorie Becker	'When I was a child . . .'	volume 1, no. 3, 1997
Greg Dening	'Writing, rewriting the beach'	volume 2, no. 2, 1998
Maria Theresa Hernández	'Reconditioning history'	volume 3, no. 3, 1999
Sumiko Higashi	'Not a "Kodak moment"'	volume 6, no. 2, 2002
Chris Ward	'Impressions of the Somme'	volume 1, no. 3, 1997
Chris Ward	'Remarks'	volume 5, no. 3, 2001
Jonathan Walker	'Antonio Foscarini'	volume 5, no. 2, 2001
Bryant Simon	'Narrating a southern tragedy'	volume 1, no. 2, 1997
Bryant Simon	'Fact and fiction in the archives'	volume 5, no. 3, 2001
Robin Bisha	'Reconstructing the voice'	volume 2, no. 1, 1998
Judith P. Zinsser	'A prologue for La Dame d'Esprit'	volume 7, no. 1, 2003
James Goodman	'Blackout'	volume 7, no. 2, 2003

Maureen Healy	'Dictator in a dumpster'	volume 3, no. 1, 1999
William Deverell and David Igler	'The abattoir of the prairie'	volume 3, no. 3, 1999
Jesse Berrett	'Liberace: behind the music'	volume 4, no. 1, 2000
Elizabeth Toon and Janet Golden	'Rethinking Charles Atlas'	volume 4, no. 1, 2000

Introduction
Practice and theory

Robert A. Rosenstone

Mr. Godard. Surely you agree that a story must have a beginning, a middle, and an end.

(newspaper reporter)

Yes, of course. But not necessarily in that order.

(Jean-Luc Godard)

Experiments in writing history? An oxymoron, surely? No writers have clung more firmly (desperately, even) to traditional forms than those academic historians whose professed aim is to accurately reconstruct the past. While the discipline has in the past century undergone an enormous expansion in methodologies of research and areas of focus, opening up fields and topics little dreamed of by earlier generations (e.g. quantitative, social, gender, ethnic, cultural, subaltern, postcolonial, feminist, queer, and leisure histories, to name but a few), the means of presenting the findings of historical research has altered little. The monographs and synthetic works that historians produce continue, for the most part, to tell the past as stories narrated in the third person, linear stories with a clear sense of cause and effect, and a beginning, a middle, and an end. Stories based, as Hayden White pointed out some four decades ago, on the model of the nineteenth-century novel.

But the world has changed greatly since the nineteenth century, as, presumably, historians should know. When we attempt to describe the world and tell stories about it these days, either in language, or in photos, or on the motion picture or television screen, we as a culture are no longer so firmly wedded to the notions of literal reality that pervaded the nineteenth century. The impact of the visual media themselves, certainly the chief carriers of messages in our twenty-first-century world, alone assure a certain alteration in our sensibilities. Equally important, the continual revolutions in artistic visions over the past century—the movements or tendencies we label cubism, constructivism, expressionism, surrealism, abstraction, the New Wave, modernism, postmodernism—have helped to alter our ways of seeing, telling, and understanding our realities. Not everyone would agree with the quotation by the great French avant-garde filmmaker which heads this page, but there is nobody who wouldn't understand his broader point, one which would have been incomprehensible a hundred years ago.

Historians are, like everyone else, part of history, much as some of them (us) may wish to appear as judges, standing outside the flow of time. They (we) too are moved by the currents of cultural change, and affected by new forms of sensibility. For the past three decades, the possibility of innovative historical writing, the notion of playing with new forms of narrative, has floated around the edge of the profession. Often it has been discussed in the hallways at history conventions, and in recent years the idea, if not the practice, has even made its way into some of the formal programs. But little innovative historical writing has appeared in print. Like any discipline, History comprises an interlocking structure of incentives and awards—journal articles, book contracts, professorial positions, fellowships, grants—and there have been virtually no outlets or rewards for writing the past in ways that abandon traditional models and adapt to the sensibility of the contemporary moment.

Despite the pressures against doing so, a few brave souls have in recent years begun to pioneer new ways of writing history. Moving beyond the boundaries of nineteenth-century narrative, they have started to explore how to tell the past in prose and genres that reflect the contemporary age. What you hold in your hand is a unique volume, the first devoted to such experiments in historical writing. Here you will find the past speaking in new ways—in the first person of the historian; in the voice of a historical figures; in the language of poetry and fiction, of comic strips and tarot cards; here you will confront a past told in forms such as parody, mystery, pastiche, humor, and the miniature—and all in chapters as thoroughly researched and as well documented as any that appear in the pages of the most sober academic journal. Taken together, the works here suggest how history, written anew, can revivify our sense of the past by making the familiar strange, and the strange familiar.

A basic question in your mind may be: why experiment? Why is it important? What is gained by deviating from the norms of written history? The answer to such a question is not easy to express, but it will be easier after you have read the chapters in this volume. One thing is certain: none of the works in this collection are innovations undertaken for the mere sake of innovation. To read the Afterwords, in which some of our authors reflect on why they have engaged in their experiments, is to see something about the genesis of these innovations, to learn that they all grow out of a desire on the part of historians to express something about our relationship to the past which has hitherto been inexpressible, to include in history things which have long been excluded, to share information or insights or understanding that cannot be carried by traditional historical forms. Certainly none of the authors included in this collection has, like some we may call postmodernists, given up on historical knowing. They simply realize that such knowledge must sometimes be expressed in new ways.

To make this discussion less abstract and more personal (and to indulge in one of the new forms, the self-reflexive), let me describe my own attempts to write innovative history, an experience which leads me to say that there are two reasons for experimenting with historical narrative: the personal and the theoretical. These cannot of course be separated. For me the personal part begins in the mid-1980s, when I was trying to write a book on the experience of American sojourners in nineteenth-century Japan. A book that began, I confess, after my own experience of living and working in that country led me to see America and the West in different ways, through a different value system. After much time spent digging in archives, I decided to focus my story on three representative figures—a missionary, a scientist, and a writer, emblems of early contact between people of the two countries. When I began to write, it was in the same, third-person style that I had used in two previous books. But after producing some two hundred pages, I realized that this traditional form was not working for me. Was not satisfying me. What do I mean? Somehow the writing did not convey what I wanted to say about the past. Did not let me get close enough to my characters. Did not let me see the world through their eyes, smell it through their noses.

This was important because the book was about personal change, shifts in perceptual and belief systems caused by the sights, sounds, smells, experiences, and jarring visual, verbal, and personal encounters that one has in a foreign land. Normal historical writing did not allow me to express the experiences that—as I understood my own theme—changed Westerners with a palpable sense of cultural superiority into early cultural relativists, able to accept as admirable those Japanese beliefs and practices that had initially seemed strange and uncivilized. Putting aside what I had written, I began a search for a new method—a fancy way of saying that I began to play on the page, to try this and try that and try something else in a period of experimentation that lasted for two years. The breakthrough for me came in a scene which involved the missionary riding into a feudal domain, accompanied by an honor guard of samurai, and in my sudden realization that it was impossible to see samurai on horseback except as they have been depicted in Japanese historical films—and so I wrote the scene as if one were seeing it on a motion picture screen.

Ultimately, the style and the form of the book I completed—*Mirror in the Shrine*—included a number of techniques well known to fiction but little used by historians. The work both narrated the past, and, within its own narration, acknowledged something about the conditions of its own composition (the author's personal involvement in the issues because of his own life in Japan) and the limitations of what it could say about the past. Among formal techniques, it utilized the following: the present tense; the self-reflexive; narration in the second person (direct address to the reader and, sometimes, to the historical characters); narration in the first person (not of the author but of his subjects); a character named "the biographer," who occasionally enters the pages to complain about the problems involved in creating this book, which include the limitations of his sources, the nineteenth-century diaries and letters that are far too formal and unrevealing for his psychological taste; and, finally, an occasional shift of time or space within a single sentence, a flash back or forwards or sideways.

Whatever the contributions of *Mirror in the Shrine* (which was, surprise, well reviewed in academic journals), the final work satisfied me in that it said what I wanted to say about the past, expressed the experience of those Americans sojourners in a way that explained (if only to me) why and how Japan had changed their world-views and their careers. I could not have done this without the innovations. For example, the use of the self-reflexive mode, and the direct address to the characters and/or the reader, were all part of a certain kind of honesty in the text, a way of giving a sense that behind the smooth flow of historical narrative is a person who has made a lot of choices—aesthetic, political, and moral—in order to create this work of historical representation.

To turn now to the theoretical: when experimenting with how to write *Mirror in the Shrine*, I worked in a vacuum. There were no models for what I wanted to do and little sympathy from even good friends in the profession, who after reading chapters had difficulty looking me directly in the eye. Only about the time when I was finishing the work did I come across an essay then already twenty years old, Hayden White's "The Burden of History." This essay—perhaps best remembered for its depiction of historians as shifty folks who, if questioned by scientists, claim that history is an art, and if questioned by artists, claim it is a science—argued that History was at best a combination of outdated, nineteenth-century science and art. When historians speak of the "art" of history, White pointed out, "they seem to have in mind a conception of art that would admit little more than the nineteenth-century novel as a paradigm." As "artists" they do not identify with the art of their own time—(and here he means the 1960s) "action painters, kinetic sculptors, existentialist novels, imagist poets, or *nouvelle vague* cinematographers." No, by "art" historians seem to mean the novels of Scott and Thackeray, for they have not yet even absorbed the literary forms of the early part of this century. Historians wholly "eschew the techniques of literary representation which Joyce, Yeats, and Ibsen have contributed to modern culture. There have been no significant attempts at surrealistic, expressionistic, or existentialist historiography."

Forty years after they were written, White's words still stand as a challenge to historical writing. Precious few have yet answered the call to write History that incorporates the techniques or strategies of twentieth-century literature. Among them are the historians are included in this collection. White's words are also part of larger critique of historical writing that has flourished in recent decades, a critique which suggests that my own impulse to innovate was in part structured (as all our impulses are) by a larger cultural imperative. We all know that there has been an enormous amount of theorizing of our relationship to the past by literary critics, philosophers, feminists, and post-colonial theorists. Together such scholars have provided a strong critique of the epistemology, narrative strategies, and truth claims of traditional historical writing.

Let me suggest that one way of meeting this critique is through innovations in the way we write the past. In my book, the self-reflexive, by making the teller part of the tale, works to undercut any notion that history already exists and somehow "tells itself." The use of the present tense not only makes history more immediate, it helps demonstrate that the present is always the site of the past. The direct address to the reader and the sharing with her or him of the problems of sources and composition, shows the written page less as a place where wisdom is handed down from author to reader than as one where author and reader meet to make sense of the past.

In the last two decades there has been a trickle of innovative works by historians. Among them I would include two by authors who also appear in this collection: Greg Dening, *Mr. Bligh's Bad Language*, which not only gives equal voice to Tahitian and European in their South Sea encounter, but makes a case for History as a performative art, and James Goodman, *Stories of Scottsboro*, a book which retells many stories that provide a variety of points of view on that famed 1930s' rape case against a group of African-American youths without ever insisting that a single one of the versions is the Truth. Since 1997, with the inauguration of *Rethinking History: The Journal of Theory and Practice*, these two authors and the others interested in innovation, have had an outlet for their work. For this journal is the first academic publication to openly call for and promote historical writing that transcends the boundaries of nineteenth-century narrative and matches the sensibilities of the contemporary age. Indeed, all the chapters in the book you now hold, save for the Introduction and the reflections by individual authors on their own experiments, originally appeared in *Rethinking History* (though most have been rewritten and updated). We editors see it as a breakthrough work, one meant to give heart to those who are already writing history anew and to encourage others to take the plunge by assuring them (you?) that a critical mass of others exists who will understand and support your experimental efforts.

I must tell you potential innovators, however, that to break with the conventions of a discourse is a giddy and frightening experience. In part, this is because the success or failure of any such experiment cannot be known until the work has been completed – or perhaps, as with avant garde art, not until years later. Here it is helpful to quote Jean-François Lyotard on artists and writers and apply his ideas to historians who innovate—their works cannot be judged by applying familiar rules and categories, for "the artist and writer are working without rules in order to formulate the rules of *what will have been done*"—the rules, that is, by which their works can eventually be judged. To experiment with historical writing is to step into the unknown and to pray a lot to the gods of History. First, we must create new works and only later can we know how they contribute to our understanding of the relationship between the past and the present.

Introduction
Theory and practice

Alun Munslow

Since the 'linguistic turn' of the 1970s doubts about the empirical-analytical method as *the* privileged path to historical knowing have not merely emerged but have now become a major part of the landscape. Put at its most basic, the characteristic feature of our postmodern existence is epistemological scepticism. Hence, it is by now a cliché that history is 'positioned' and doubt about the modernist notion that history can mirror the past is commonplace. Indeed, in all the arts, humanities, social sciences, and even the physical and life sciences, the question has been put, how can we be sure that empiricism and inference really do get us close to 'true meaning'? How does knowing 'something happened' connect with that amorphous and readily misunderstood though culturally valuable 'thing' we call 'the truth'? Asking (and answering) such questions is the essence of epistemological scepticism. In history the question of truth and meaning comes down to how we *represent* our sources and how the form of that representation directly affects what we think those sources 'really' or 'most probably' mean. And, as soon as we talk about 'representation' and 'meaning', then our everyday concept of truth gets much more messy. In other words, the rather naïve idea that the past is re-interpreted only according to new evidence quickly ceases to be either plausible or convincing. Instead we are led to think about the self-conscious and ontological acts of writing/re-writing. We are now faced with the problem of how the historian as author makes the connection between the content of the past (what happened) with the form or shape it is given (as history).

Thus it is that History and the past cannot coincide. While this seems to be an alarming situation, it isn't really, of course. It is because, in the nature of such things, the former (whether we like it or not and a few historians still prefer not to face up to it) is a narrative *about* the latter. In other words, there cannot be a direct correspondence between what happened and the truth of what it means. Or, to put it in a different way, there are no original centres of meaning to be found outside the narrative-linguistic universe we call History. History is, *in and of itself*, a representation of something. It is not the thing itself and it cannot by the magic of empiricism be transported as it actually was onto the page or the film. This being the case, it follows (think about it) that the content of data, *in and of itself*, will not have a certain and discoverable *given* meaning that can be transferred into words. This disjunction between 'the past' and 'history' is the common condition of the relationship between the world (past and present) and words. And, as you will have understood by now, we historians cannot escape language to 'get back' or 'get to' the real past (or present) thing in itself.

It is insufficient to hold that empiricism larded with inference and theory is an adequate way of studying the past and, in passing, answering the question What is history?. And it is certainly an inadequate response to epistemological scepticism to maintain that because historians no longer see themselves in the nineteenth-century image of self-assured, Eurocentric, heterosexual, entrepreneurial, bourgeois males that much complex conceptualization and methodological self-reflexivity exists. That, in some way, we can still do business as usual through the archive and reconstruct the past pretty much as it actually was in terms not just of what happened, but what 'it' means. Being self-conscious about the range of topics covered, the tools of the trade, and even using the latest techniques borrowed from adjacent disciplines, do not address the fundamental issue of how history as a cultural, literary and, of course, a visual artefact engages with the past. To be fair, most historians are not quite as unsophisticated as this description might suggest. Most do realize the medium is important to the message. But still there is, even among the most aware of historians, a deep-seated desire to *reconstruct* the past as it really was – to 'tell the truth about history' in the famous but unhelpful title of a best-selling book on the nature of history – instead of acknowledging that you cannot reveal the truth about a representation, for that, plainly, is what history *actually* is.

The lingering modernism in us all demands that we have to ask, what principles exist behind a sceptical epistemology? In terms of this collection the question should be re-phrased perhaps as, what is the basic theory of experimental history? Perhaps inevitably we need to briefly re-acquaint ourselves with the central ideas/principles of the non-experimental or conventional form of History. For lack of a better description, I shall call this modernist history. As I have implied, it is founded on an epistemological infrastructure that is about justified belief or truth and it has several key features. The first is that there is a knowable reality 'back there' just as there appears to be one in the present. I stress the element of knowability. It is assumed that if we cannot know or learn about what happened in the past, then we would be in a dreadful mess as a society. The analogy is usually made with amnesiac individuals. Hence, not knowing the nature of past reality must mean we are wide open to being deceived and, what is as bad, we cannot make informed ethical judgements. Put plainly, without a knowable past we can become not just epistemological relativists, but worse, lack the ability to tell right from wrong.

This principle of knowable reality works out pretty well for everyday life and for figuring out train timetables and knowing where you are and what you are doing at any particular time and in a certain place. This principle is extended in Western society to defining history as the primary mechanism through which it explains itself to itself. This is dependent upon certain knowledge of 'the past thing in itself' through the traces it has left behind. The route to such knowledge is, of course, the sources/evidential remains of the event, action, object or process that once existed. This is where the correspondence theory of truth kicks in as the basis for what historians call their 'justified belief'. The belief that reference to what happened in the past can be mirrored in the history that the historian writes is turbo-charged by two further beliefs. First, the belief in our ability to gauge the intentions behind human actions (through a detailed knowledge of the archival remains of such agency) and, second, coupled with the logic of inference, we will be able to discover not merely what happened but most likely what it means.

What is thus implied by the scientific model of correspondence is the belief that a detailed knowledge of the content of the past will allow us to discover *the* most likely cause(s), *the* hidden story and, hence, *the* most likely meaning. In other words, knowing what happened must – if you are a good historian who thinks rationally, who knows the sources and who can empathize with the historical actor – thereby produce the 'true' or 'real story of . . .'. Experimentalists challenge this primal modernist principle that equates content with *its* given story form. Because history shares the same epistemological status as all cultural and representational discourses – it is never neutral but always partial (usually ideological) with open meanings – it becomes extremely important that we deconstruct or dissect the mechanisms by which we create it. The central principle of experimental history should now be obvious – it is to hunt out and confront the myth of the given. It is especially important to face what is, in effect, the essential corollary to correspondence that knowing precisely what happened somehow insulates us from 'wrong' interpretations or false inferences. To argue, as is often done by overtly ideologically committed historians (of all political persuasions), that the sources are the only defence of truth, reveals if not their irresponsibility to their readers, an awkward self-deception.

Many well-known watchwords or concepts have been legitimated in our history culture by a long association with these modernist beliefs of given and discoverable and justified belief, truth and meaning. Beyond the primacy of these notions but fiercely and directly connected to them is the concept of the unified, rational and knowing subject. This is the Enlightenment humanist idea of the reasoning historian at the centre of the 'knowing process'. The ideological baggage this has carried with it is the primacy of individualism and the idea of control – not just of nature, economic life, 'mastery over women', superior/inferior races, etc., but knowability in our engagement with the past. The corollaries to this have been challenged since the advent of structuralism and post-structuralism in the work of critics ranging from Claude Lévi-Strauss and Roland Barthes, to Michel Foucault and Jacques Derrida. The first major casualty in this criticism was the deletion of the subject – the idea of the author as the organizer of written/textual meaning. Indeed, the post-structuralist conviction has it that the subject is so disjointed, there is no indispensable nucleus of self (identity) which can be the platform for our modernist launch into knowability. This has had the effect for history of releasing the creativity of the historian. Instead of pursuing the knowability of the past and the grand narrative of givenness (which we can still do if that is our preferred episte-mological choice), we have been launched into a state of engagement with the sublime nature of the past. Learning to live, in other words, with its unknowability in terms of what it means and how, as a result, we can explore its multiple meanings through experiments with form. In other words, explore its own nature as a form of representation.

This has many consequences including the collapse of subject and object – in effect, the confrontation with objectivity. This is often and quite reasonably described as self-reflexivity. In a universe where there are no grand narratives (of truth, givenness, correspondence, and knowability which have conven-tionally been given shapes like Marxism, Liberalism, Nationalism, Empiricism, God . . .), then we need to explore the problematic of the self and our sub-jectivity as well as challenging conventional 'equations' and hierarchies. Examples of the former include equating factualism with actualism, writability with knowability, content with form, the emplotment of stories with true meaning (the true story of Abraham Lincoln . . .), author with authority, and above all, history with the past. Examples of hierarchies include objectivity over subjectivity, history over the philosophy of history, knowing over being, causation over chaos, the prosaic over prose, fact over fiction, documentary text over historical text, truth over relativism, reality over reality-effect, and agency over structure/structure over agency. The grand-daddy of them all is, of course, the empirical-analytical over the narrative-linguistic.

Modernist or conventional history is known by what it represses. The illicit practices that derive from and exist within the realm of experimentalism are, by definition, as various as they seem to be transgressive. Many historians will continue, no doubt, to view experiments in history as misdemeanours and indiscretions – pointless, even inane and feckless – but certainly disobedient lapses from and contraventions of 'good practice'. Some might even see them as dangerous and destructive. At best, they might be given some airtime as being somewhat avant-garde, even innovative and – surely the ultimate damning with faint praise – 'interesting' or 'useful in reminding us that language is important in doing history'.

But they are treacherous. Historical experiments do rethink history. As Hayden White acknowledges, they do not repress the content of their form. They are also carefully constructed, crafted, highly self-aware and reflexive. Experiments in history are not the refuge of poor historians. Ultimately, perhaps, the greatest transgression is the injection of the self into the past. While this carries a heavy cost to those who wish to reconstruct the past as history, it carries with it a great benefit: a willingness to address the cognitive power of narrative while acknowledging the nature of history as a represen-tation. The philosopher Frank Ankersmit argues, exploring the consequences of history being, at best, a text written *about* the past. It is the consequences of this *aboutness* that experimental historians explore and test. Though faced with the experimental challenge to empiricism and inference, even those historians who believe history is a construction (founded on complex theories about the nature of change over time) invariably flinch away from narrative experimentation. The reason offered is usually one of the three that are readily available off the shelf.

First, epistemological scepticism seems not to be a coherent explanation; second, that without hard work in the archive, we will have no facts and so they cannot tell us what they mean; finally, if history is 'made up' by historians, why should we believe any text including postmodern criticism/scepticism? That there remains a lingering desire not to allow nonsense to be made of the idea of the historian as an objective investigative reporter seeking after factual truth may seem plausible, the problem is that once we challenge that belief, we are open to the lure of experiment and we immediately recognize the disjunction between what we write as history and that thing we call past reality. We quickly realize that past events and human actions are different from the narrative written about them. They belong to distinct ontological categories and, in order to connect them, we have to ignore their elemental dissimilarities.

This realization can turn the historian to both repudiation and suspicion. The repudiation is of the postmodern idea that history cannot be a mirror of what once was. The suspicion is of being able to live quite happily without epistemological forms of explanation. The dizzying result is that as a literary (or filmic or hypertext?) form, History is a now unknown territory. The vertigo of experimentalism lies in its intention to defamiliarize the reader, to disrupt the routine perception of the past *as* history with only one road and one destination – to travel hopefully rather than to arrive at *the* story? The specific object of experimental free fall is to force us to understand the past in new and different ways. To do this, the routine thinking and practice of 'proper' epistemological History have to be made strange. And this can only be done by foregrounding the form of history as representation – literary, poetic, dramatic, filmic, and performative. Experimental History thus exists in the fissures between what once was and what it can mean now. The central point is simply this. Since what we think about the past can only be understood *as we write it*, then experiments with narrative become decisive. As dancers choreograph their performance, historians historiograph theirs. History is as much about the 'historian's performance' – the way he or she constructs or stages his or her narrative and invites a responsive understanding from the audience – as it is about the past itself.

Part I

Self-reflexive

Self-reflexivity is, of course, central to experimentalism in history. It is the self-conscious understanding of the authorial and imaginative roles played by both historical actors and the historian. In Chapter 1, 'When I was a child, I danced as a child, but now that I am old, I think about salvation: Concepción González and a past that would not stay put', Marjorie Becker tries to recreate an incandescent moment in the history of Mexico, a moment when ordinary Mexicans spectacularly transformed Mexico's future. As she explores, in the mid-1930s in the midst of President Lázaro Cárdenas's efforts to remake rural Mexico and its people, men and women trained to revere the Virgin Mary entered a church, seized the wooden icons of Jesus, the saints, the Virgin, and torched them in the plaza. Later that evening, a number of men and women re-entered the church and danced before the altar. In a rich mix of commitment and self-reflexivity Becker's chapter explores this moment through a combination of ethno-historical and fictive techniques. The chapter is about specific historical actors' diverse relationships with time, women's bodies, and spiritual life. Empathy is always in and out of fashion at the same time among historians – probably because it is seemingly as dangerous as it is rewarding. Becker's empathy is rewarding because she turns it into self-reflexivity and it is demonstrated as she weaves together important historical issues with actual scenes and imagined dialogue. She creates a composite priest and constructs the Virgin Mary's role in promoting and discouraging the dance as she enters memories and recreates her own ethno-historical relationship with the villagers.

Historical experiments must change with every authorial imaginative act. To address this, we invited authors to reflect, if they so wished (and one or two refused), on their historical inventions. In other words, we invited them to offer further thoughts or commentaries – what we have called an Afterword – on their experiments. How were experiments constructed? Why were they created? What prompted such inventions? Just as their work challenged us, how does it now challenge them? Once history is written, we know it becomes estranged from its author. As experiments in history become, using the literary theorist Linda Hutcheon's term, historiographic metafictions, and our connection with the past is relativized, how do authors react now to their own re-visions? Having entered the realm where history is no longer undertaken as a realist correspondence/mirroring activity, where being playful, inventive and imaginative is now part of the process of knowing, we thought it would be useful to offer the authors an opportunity to revisit their experiment and reflect upon them. What is fascinating and significant in these reflections is the sense of commitment that each author has, not just to their own experiment but also to their responsibility toward the past. For Marjorie Becker, the narrative structure she invented was a means to embody the events to which she refers, but also the emotional possibilities in the past, specifically in the lives of Michoacán women in the 1920s and the 1930s. Her experiment is also a commentary on the narrow conventionality of the historical profession.

Self-reflexivity is also the appreciation that history is a literary-creative act even when the aim might seem to be reconstruction. All reconstructions are, of course, constructions. In Greg Dening's 'Writing, re-writing the beach' the author takes his cue from Herbert Marcuse's thought that 'art fights reification by making the petrified world speak, sing, perhaps dance'. History, as Dening sees it, is returning to the past its own presents – allowing a world now petrified by hindsight to dance, sing, weep, tremble, doubt, and believe. As Dening insists, history is not something we learn, it is something we perform. In taking as his starting point the essential feature of our engagement with the past – that history is not the past – he recognizes and happily accepts that the past is transformed into words or paint or dance or play. He works on the premise that we have not lost 'history' when the word history disappears from our school curricula. But we will have lost history when readers of history lose their ability to be theatre critics, when authors cannot recognize or refuse to display their own presence, when the anti-theatre forces of modernity win out, when the real purpose of presenting the past is not to remember but to forget. Warned about the end of his career before it had begun if he made the choices he wanted to, Greg Dening's Afterword reveals his commitment to 'the other' in the form of a history from the bottom up, to write the history of 'little people'. And, of course, to take professional risks.

Chapter 3, Maria Theresa Hernández's experiment 'Reconditioning history: adapting knowledge from the past into realities of the present' evokes change over time and place. The place is San Isidro Cemetery located in Sugar Land, Texas, on land once owned by Sugar Land Industries that produces Imperial Sugar. Cotton fields and vegetables once surrounded its two-and-half acres. For ninety years a bridge spanned the creek – Oyster Creek – that ran along one side of the cemetery. Mexican labourers who worked for Imperial Sugar buried their dead there and held vigil. In the 1960s the land surrounding was sold for opulent housing. The bridge was condemned and the cemetery found itself surrounded without an entrance. Litigation followed concerning access to the cemetery. In writing this history, Hernández is constructing, through the voices of its actors, the history of a secret inner space to the community that hides an exotic history Sugar Land has attempted to escape from and erase. Deliberately exploring the subject–object relationship and the nature of form, she concludes nothing is fixed and history always creates more questions than it answers. In her Afterword Maria Theresa Hernández reveals how her piece grew out of a series of experimental sketches that addressed creativity, boundaries, poetics, difference and the unexpected. Hernández was, she says, also unafraid to explore her own subjectivity and recognize how history is constantly re-made.

Finally, self-reflexivity takes on a family guise in Sumiko Higashi's 'Not a "Kodak moment"', an attempt to rethink history in personal terms, specifically the Japanese American immigrant experience, by reading family photographs dating back to pre-war Japan. A miniature in size but self-reflexive in intent (clearly our innovative categorization cannot fully contain the nature of experimentalism!), Higashi's piece considers the ways in which personal experience and family history intersect with momentous historical events.

1 When I was a child, I danced as a child, but now that I am old, I think about salvation

Concepción González and a past that would not stay put

Marjorie Becker

When I lived there they told me the Mexican sky had been orange and charred that evening in Ario Santa Monica. Remains of the Virgin had filled the air. The day before the revolutionary men had stripped her image from the church of this northwestern Michoacán village. Later that night the young women trained in a culture of sexual reticence followed their men into the church. Turning to their partners, they made the church into a dance hall.

Did the women dance that night in anger? Did they dance because the priests had made their Virgin into a spiritual schoolmistress who exacted acts of humility, public silence, sexual modesty?

Or did they dance for another reason, a partly formed desire to seize something of the Virgin, and something less common in that time and place, an open expression of female sensuality? And had Michoacán's priests somehow taught them the dance steps?

Many of the dancers' neighbors saw the women differently. Eugenia Arriaga, one of the village's most prominent citizens, harbored a strikingly intimate disdain for the dancers.[1] For her, the dancers had undermined the community's possibilities of redemption.

Though Arriaga deemed that judgment inevitable, I was to be inevitability's instrument. Only one dancer, Concepción González, remained alive by the time I arrived in Ario. I was to stake her out. I was to ensnare her somewhere along Catholicism's lonely road to perdition. And because I was nothing if not sensitive to the concerns of my historical subjects, I almost did.

Ultimately, González herself stopped me. While many villagers were determined to condemn her, she wouldn't have it. Or at least, that was not to be the only rendition of her story. She seemed to be saying something else, perhaps something like, *Why do you have to let them judge me? Is the price so high? Then consider the ways that when I was a child, I danced as a child, but now that I am old, I think about salvation.*

Dance teachers, somehow

The linear approach to historical writing so frequently employed in the twentieth century gives the impression that human experience moves sequentially, act by act, with each experience slightly more significant than the last.[2]

Nonetheless, Michoacán's Catholic priests in the 1920s and 1930s had much reason to wonder whether linear time could express the whole of human experience. What of their hours hearing confessions of last week's promises broken by marital infidelity, trips to the cantina? For that matter, what of the ways that orthodox Catholicism's doctrine of original sin, its ready access to forgiveness, recognizes the ways that ordinary people's behavior goes haywire through time?

Still, much about the times they lived in distressed the priests. The Michoacán countryside smoldered still from the 1926–29 Cristero Rebellion. A church–state civil war, the rebellion probably flared with greater intensity in Michoacán than elsewhere. There peasants, determined to create Jesus's realm on earth, made fratricidal war on their less devout relatives and neighbors. To the priests' alarm, the continuing community rancor suggested the potential for renewed violence.

Moreover, partly because of this religious intensity, Lázaro Cárdenas's Michoacán followers attempted to undermine both the regional prominence of the church and of large landowners. Many priests considered Cárdenas's land redistribution to be outright defiance of God's law regarding the sanctity of private property. And they found the revolutionaries' "cultural Sunday" programs celebrating revolutionary heroes and the region's indigenous history as nothing more than jealous efforts to keep people from attending church (Becker, 1995: 88–90, 112).

Responding to this turmoil, priests subjected the Virgin Mary to a narrative make-over. In the process, they revealed much about their own temporal anxieties. Erasing whatever took place between Mary and her betrothed, between Mary and God, the priests created a woman perpetually new. Stripped of ego, desire, need, her capacity to absorb the pain of others was infinite. It might seem that Mary, like the God of St. Augustine, lived outside of time. However, priests simultaneously made Mary a model of certain types of temporal behavior. Specifically, charitable acts, set to the tick of the celestial clock, would bring on the second coming.[3]

The priests and the dancers place me in a literary quandary. I believe that narrative structures are most sensible and evocative when they reflect the historical actors' engagements with time. Because priests and dancers engaged time differently, no one temporal structure will express their experiences. It therefore seems appropriate to allow Michoacán priests and their preferred form of linear temporal engagement to shape this section. Then I turn to the fact that in the 1930s a handful of Michoacán women effectively challenged that temporal arrangement, a challenge partially responsible for the remaking of the Mexican government.[4] Finally, that challenge leads me to employ an inverse linear construction concluding with the women's youthful dreams rather than with the latter-day destruction of those dreams.

What could it have been like for the Michoacán priests to struggle with a longing for eternal life, with the mysteries of the Virgin, with rancorous parishioners? While the priests' sermons about these issues, and my ethno-historical research, have taught me a great deal about the priests' understanding of Mary, about the relationship the clergy tried to establish between women's behavior and time, the ways the priests wrestled with these issues in the privacy of their minds remains unclear. Finding this reticence unbearable, I have turned to my research intuitions to create a composite priest.

Call him Padre Reyes. Kind-hearted, if slightly cranky, he persistently worried about Cárdenas's efforts to transform the village. We find him now in his study, preparing a sermon about the Virgin. What did his thoughts sound like?

Please listen.

I don't know what to say to them. The revolutionaries promise land. I can almost understand the urge, the way some men believe land is the only thing they want, more than a woman, more than the church. What I can't take is the school inspector, that señorita Josefina. I can't help it. They say she is beautiful and they are right but her looks go to her head. She sees only one thing. Tells the students there's nothing else. Just what they see. As though all of this was nothing but flesh. Only physical.

If she would just come to church. To see what we've done with the image of the holy Virgin. The ways the icon makers let her past drift away. That skin once darkened by the sun. Now she's white, and the church ladies didn't even think of her wearing a peasant dress like the one she must have worn in Nazareth. No. She wears fine silk. And pearls.[5]

Funny about the pearls. People pay a lot for them, but they're really nothing more than sand. Is God somehow saying something about Mary through the pearls? It's true that she was only a peasant woman. They even say that she was Jewish. And her life had been full of nothing but household chores. She never did much besides that. God seemed to feel she didn't need to. That what she did as a humble woman was enough.

How can I explain to them? I don't speak well, never have. I just want to say, let Mary be a model. Be humble the way she was. Accept your social betters. God gave them their place. Be generous. Remember Mary's chastity, and be modest. Be faithful to your husband. Look up to him, let him have his way. Don't make a fuss in public, guard the home instead. But the main thing I want to tell[6] *them this Sunday is that the world is not only physical. Just look at her. She doesn't care about the satin dresses the landowners' wives get from France. The Indians' dark skin doesn't bother her. Her message is different. As she says, "I am a loving and tender mother for whomever asks my help in their pain and suffering."*

Whomever. In this region *whomever* would apply to Indians and mestizos, people of dark skin and light, the rich and the poor, men and women. Mary's reputedly sexless body had been made into a roomy womb, resolving and questioning the priests' demands. Perhaps the women could dance with that.

Winding the timepiece of perdition

Concepción's daughter Estela Villanueva introduced Eugenia Arriaga to me as a member of "one of Ario's first and oldest families." I came to believe her. Michoacanos had long persuaded themselves that the houses of the wealthy, the prominent, should be seen. They were to be part of a rectangular arrangement. Placed side by side on a main square, a plaza, these homes would block the homes of the poor from view. And Eugenia had lived her whole life in a house on the plaza. Besides, the homes of prominent people displayed specific accouterments to distinguish themselves from poor people's one-room houses, and this home possessed windows and lace curtains to stop the glare. On Sundays the family had enjoyed a variety of dishes—*caldo*, *sopes*, chocolate, chicken from their own henyard, making meat habitual in an area where most people expected nothing more than beans and tortillas.[7]

Still, there had been an emptiness to Eugenia's life until the afternoon when the woman spat in her face. Women were not supposed to engage in public activities considered important. They could not vote, hold office, practice law or medicine. They seldom owned or ran haciendas. Then too, the lives of Eugenia's neighbors—the Indians and mestizos who bought dry goods at her father's store—remained obscure to her.

Yet information about those lives lingered nearby. On the margins of the pueblo, back from the showy houses on the plaza. She saw the women in the back of the church. Their worn, faded dresses had been ironed smooth. She knew the injunction to be charitable, "to do what we could for them," and she probably tried.

The Sunday meals might have proved illuminating. Sometimes her relatives came. The men owned estates. Some of them had been to seminar. They would have known things. They would have known about Roberto, the boy who had drowned. People whispered about him for years, and the men at the table probably knew that local liberals believed the man convicted for murder was framed, but, her father was adamant. "We were never to talk at the table."[8]

Other information lurked undiscovered, at the nearby haciendas where most of the men in the area worked. Their wages were meager—just enough for corn and beans for the family and a yearly change of clothing. Occasionally, the men erupted. Rafael Ochoa's father held night meetings. Then the men agreed that the landowner was cheating on their sharecropper contracts, naming Ochoa's father leader. He protested to the owner that, "It's not fair that you cart off our corn, take it away and weigh it in liters. Then you give us our part in liters, all right, but how are we supposed to know how much it originally weighed, and how much we were supposed to get back?"[9]

How could she have known? The overseer himself, dozing nearby, never knew. Who would have taken her to the hacienda? Or perhaps she was to steal off from morning mass or from preparing the midday meal. As though the girl could do it by herself.

The lives of poor women remained even more deeply hidden. Much about their lives was cramped by necessities, particularly the social and financial need to keep a man nearby. Often women abandoned by their men took their claims to court. There a portrait emerged. Ana María Acalán's father waiting by the door at midnight, fighting sleep, desperate for the return of Ruperto Herrera Rodríguez, the man who had impregnated his daughter before leaving.[10] Or María Enríquez, one-time companion of Antonio Mendoza. Assaulted by Mendoza, she was abandoned by sister, girlfriend, and a group of pious women she begged for help. Dismissing her, they later claimed they had taken her for the town crazy woman, Pachita la Loca.[11]

For Eugenia, these things never happened. She spent her time with her own people, with her cousins, the daughters of the sprinkling of wealthy people in the village. It was a quiet, pious life she had come to relish. When they went to church, they took the best seats, close to the image of the Virgin, away from the occasional Indian woman who wandered in to worship. In the evenings they walked in the plaza, arm in arm.

And she spent her afternoons singing with her cousins. "We divided up. Each one of us went to a different street corner. And from our corner, we would each sing a stanza of the hymn, first one of us, then another, then the last two. It gave us such joy."

Very general questions had evoked this image of a seamless past, a time devoted to God. "What did you do together as a family?" I had asked. "Tell me what part the church played in your life." Perhaps because they were coupled with my mannerisms suggesting empathy—the eyebrows that lift at a hint of suffering—these questions led to her memory of a village life devoid of conflict.

But when I asked how the revolution affected that life, her tenor changed. I was to understand that before Margarita Espinosa and the revolutionaries, things were different. "The pueblo was so beautiful, so peaceful. They tried to change things." It was true it was more than just Margarita. The revolutionaries had begun to redistribute land, to outlaw priests. The women's anticlerical leagues, "spying on us, listening to find out if we had sneaked a priest into our homes."

Then they went too far. "One of them—even among bad people there can be good ones—one of the revolutionaries told us that the men were going into the church to steal the icons. So we organized, all the best Catholic families organized. That night our people went in and got them out."

Unwittingly, though, they left a few behind. There was the "precious little Christ, the portrait of Joseph, a sacred heart, and the tiny Santa Monica." That night, the revolutionaries sneaked into the church. They found the abandoned relics and scooped them up. Then they hid them in their homes.

Eugenia woke from her siesta the next afternoon. She peered through the window by the front door. The air was orange, vile. There had been life in the icons, "the precious little Christ." Now they had tried to turn them into charred splinters.

The girl had come by her house. *What was she up to? What could she possibly want here?* True, all kinds of people passed by. The Indian men who had sold the remaining pieces of the property to the agraristas. The blind man, stumbling on his cane. The poor girls, noisy and uncouth. She only knew her friends.

Until that afternoon when Margarita came. "She knocked on my door, and then—can you believe it, señorita? She spat in my face."

Eugenia would not let her leave. She would force her to own up to the breach.

"I said, 'Listen, Margarita, why did you spit at me?'"

"'Because I wanted to very much.'"

Five decades had passed since Margarita had stood before her, but Eugenia refused to let her leave. As she spoke to me, she dropped her voice. *Maybe Margarita thought she could slip away.* It is true that there were things she could not specify—what the girls wore, the names of the songs the band played, how the bare church looked in half light, whether the revolutionaries had replaced the icons with pictures of Zapata and Villa. She hadn't been there, and God knew it. And though it was hard to see God hovering over that room where they had scorned him, at least He would have known what it looked like. *Mercifully, she did not.* But she knew who was there. Most of them were dead or crazy. All but one. Maybe she thought she would slip away. Eugenia wouldn't let her.

"Who were the dancers?" I asked.

"Lila Martínez. Margarita Espinosa. Concepción González. She was absolutely shameless. She was a little piece of trash, not worth a peanut. They all were. The whole pueblo knows it." She wanted them to pay. Eugenia's timepiece ticked toward perdition, and if it had been for her, this story would have ended there.

But now that I'm old

Nobody wanted me to talk to Concepción, except perhaps her daughter Estela. Least of all Concepción herself.

Yet that remained unclear for some time. At first, despite her reticent demeanor and countless protestations that "I don't know anything, señorita," Concepción seemed determined to protect her mother Margarita.[12] Whatever else, we were not to view her as Eugenia Arriaga had imagined her.

Rather, Margarita Espinosa's life had been full of the work of women. "She had no servants. She did everything. Cooking, cleaning, keeping house. It was a hard life."

She insisted that it was sweetened a bit by book learning. "She knew how to read. She had gone to school and she learned to write so beautifully. Here, let me show you her penmanship. Look at her letters. She was educated, señorita."

And there was the church. "She was very Catholic, miss, of course she was. She took us to Mass. She knew what was right and wrong. Of course she did."

It wasn't just Eugenia Arriaga. Other villagers, too, had understood Margarita differently. Estrella de la Puente had spoken to me at length about Margarita. Estrella, like Margarita, was the wife of a revolutionary leader. But Estrella was intent on baptizing her children. Hence her memory of Margarita, the leader of the women's anticlerical leagues. "In the meetings she told us we couldn't baptize our children. They had invented revolutionary baptisms. We were to baptize with honey. I wouldn't do it. I sneaked my children out of town to a priest."[13]

For hours Concepción refused to acknowledge, let alone celebrate, that vision of Margarita. In part this was because Concepción's daughter Estela had insisted on accompanying me. Estela's presence made it difficult for me to act the oral historian. After all, Estela knew me in my persona interviewing devout Catholics. Trained to uncover my subjects' deeper biases and seemingly endorse them, around Catholics I became more Catholic (if considerably quieter) than the Pope. It would be difficult to switch my persona to the version of La Pasionara I used when interviewing the handful of socialists in the area. Yet I would need to. Over the years many villagers had identified Concepción as one of the dancers.

I was caught in a difficult situation. But so was she. For years a threat had hovered just below the surface in Ario. Villagers had probably pursued Concepción for years. Martín Méndez, a former revolutionary, first expressed it to me in 1985. "They danced in the church. Then they claimed they repented, but it did them no good. Before they died their legs shriveled up. Fell off. I'm not one to say it, but they say it was God's will. The legs falling off. The arms. There is no escape."[14]

Concepción was old, and at this point, who is to say that she has not placed her faith in God, in Mary? The torching, the dance, all of that was long ago, and perhaps her neighbors would see beyond a childhood prank, to consider her later efforts to atone as adequate proof of her worth.

And here was her daughter, brash, loud-mouthed, full of good works, with her visits to Eugenia Arriaga. *She probably flattered her. Probably treated her like the first lady of the village.*

And this stranger. *What could she want to talk about? What had she talked to her husband Rafael about? Such a good man, a bit of a socialist, but still Catholic. Then again, behind those lace curtains, she also talked to Eugenia Arriaga.*

She wouldn't have it. To discuss it was to bring it back to life. Walking into the church shorn of icons. Seeing her girlfriends. The boys in the band. They locked the doors and started the music and . . . She was getting old. Her time was coming. She wouldn't have it.

Even when I asked her directly, "I wonder if we can talk about something very delicate. I want to ask you about the women's leagues. Could you tell me something about them?"

Her daughter pushed ahead. "Mother, they say they went into the church and they had a dance!"

Concepción would have nothing to do with it. She just refused. Casting about, she mentioned the "civil festivals. They had parades and speeches, and each one would commemorate a revolutionary, this one Zapata, this one Villa."

Her daughter was relentless. "Mother, there was more than that. They say there was a dance. Everybody says there was a dance in the church. They say they danced with the horses, with the images of the saints."

So there I was. Although I could not bring myself to cheer for the dancers, I also could not let go. "Why do you think they danced?"

"It was not their idea. Young girls are not going to see how they are going to pay. They were very young. They didn't see anything wrong. All they saw was a dance."

Finally, I recovered. "I would think it must have been very exciting to go and see what they had on. To hear the music."

That did it. They had been persecuted for years. In her sweet, quiet voice she admitted it all. "I don't want you to think they were like the girls today. I don't want you to think they wore fancy clothes. They just wore what they had on from working."

She just would not be seen as a slut, no matter what. So I had caught her. After an interview experience in which I had been unable to be courageous enough— or vicious enough?—to evade the safety of the Catholic idiom and insult her daughter, I had managed to do what journalists and oral historians so cherish. I had forced her to acknowledge a fact that she despised and feared. And as an oral historian I was supposed to cherish not the fact (which in fact, I did) but her forced acknowledgment.

When I was a child

Unlike Eugenia, Concepción and the dancers may have known that rich women hid behind the skirts of the Virgin as they systematically ignored the poor. In rural Michoacán of the 1920s and 1930s, poor women spent most of their time together, in villages temporarily stripped of men. They shared chores, shared gossip, controlled information about household activities and about emotional life.[15] It is possible the dancers remembered that a decade before, wealthy women near the church denied María Enríquez solace after she was assaulted.

Still, there had been Mary. A once-poor woman dolled up in shiny crown and pearls. Remembering Mary in her gold and satin, dressed as if a poor woman and her dreams were valuable. Once Concepción may have hoped it meant the desires of the poor could matter.

If there had been much to erode her hopes, there was still something about the Virgin. Mary had been poor, despised, but had come to dominate the most comfortable spaces in the church. Maybe the priest had meant something different but there was something about her lives—Virgin to mother, tattered clothing to silk, that suggested possibilities. And though Mary no longer presided over the church, maybe some of her power lingered there.

Then the man invited her to dance. Claiming to be a revolutionary. To believe in taking the land back from the landowner. In justice. It is true that he said nothing about women's concerns. He never said men would stop cheating, would stop drinking up her food money.

Yet she could move. She could use the floor for something, if only to turn away from the people who despised her brown work dress. She could use this building (maybe there was still some magic, maybe she would be protected), use this building to move out of the faceless, silenced crowd.

Or maybe a thousand other possibilities entered her mind. Since I almost botched the interview, and more importantly, since the very promise of ethnohistorical method reminds us of the impossibility of reading the heart of another, I don't know. But there was something about her determination to use her temporary control of the interview to falsify the dancers' past that saddened and angered me. I wished to stop her from enclosing her real past in some faux hopes about the future.

She wanted to end it otherwise, to complete the transactions long honored by the church, the revolutionaries, most historians, transactions based on bartering women's bodies and possibilities of public speech, their multiple experiences of time, for respectability. I imagine she hoped this trade in women's bodies would result in salvation.

I do not doubt that it is I—and not she—who is eager to question a linear time schema's structural ability to highlight only the return to a world dominated by men, and by orthodox Catholic dictums. I believe she would insist that this story, and its structure, should climax with her renunciation of the dance.

While I am alert to North Americans' deservedly sordid reputation for manhandling the cultures of their neighbors, I do not wish to leave these women in isolation. If I re-enact a North American cultural pattern—seizing on an act, removing it from its context, forcing it to mean something new—it is because I believe that our lives throughout the Americas are more deeply intertwined than we often like to acknowledge. The dominant culture in the contemporary United States differs from what I have called "the culture of purity and redemption" alive in Michoacán for decades. Still, pressures placed on subordinate groups to silence themselves here and there exhibit powerful similarities. There was a courage to Concepción's act, her willingness to relinquish the hope that touching the rosary beads, glancing at the crown, placing candles before the woman in pearl would yield—what? love, comfort, protection from those eyes that refused to see either her or her mother. Complex and original, Concepción's effort to transform her own blasphemous courage into something precious might be of use to us.

Acknowledgements

This is dedicated to Carolyn Gurman, a woman of immense insight and kindness. More than anyone else, she shared my sense that if the Michoacán women's grasp of their neighbors was blurred and incomplete, it was much because in both the spiritual and the sexual arenas they entered, victory was valued so deeply. Displaying his characteristic wit, subtlety and generosity, Dale Wall first encouraged me to write this. I would also like to express heartfelt appreciation for some of the people who have warmly encouraged my continuing efforts to understand the poetry in history. They include Paul Friedrich, Friedrich Katz, Florencia Mallon, Jean Meyer, and Jan Wesley. Robert Rosenstone's own elegant and innovative historical writing has proved inspiring. I would especially like to thank him for prompting me to develop an experimental solution to historians' slavish (if unconscious) commitment to linear forms of representation. And I would like to thank two anonymous reviewers for their perceptive comments about this chapter.

In November 1995 I presented a different essay containing some of the ideas developed here at the University of Chicago Mexican Studies Program directed by Friedrich Katz. Another version of this chapter was presented at "Narrating Histories: A Workshop," held at the California Institute of Technology, Pasadena, April, 1994. I have used some of this material for different purposes in Becker (1995) and in Becker (1994). This article is based on extensive archival and ethnographic research conducted throughout Michoacán and Mexico City during 1988, 1989, and 1990. I would like to acknowledge with gratitude the support of the Fulbright-Hayes Faculty Research Abroad Fellowship Program, the National Endowment for the Humanities, the American Council of Learned Societies, and the University of Southern California Faculty Research and Development Fund.

Notes

1 I believe that history is made by real people possessing real names. Many of the people who appear in this chapter appear by name in my previous publications; that openness was based on a shared agreement: together we would participate in an ethno-historical project that subsequently allowed me to unearth the buried history of the construction of the post-revolutionary Mexican government. I have told that story most extensively in Becker (1995). As that agreement did not extend to the innovative, near-fictive approach to history I have developed in this chapter, I have decided to use pseudonyms for the informants whose stories led to this partially imaginary reconstruction.

2 Yet linear forms of representation have been joined with a bias toward progress. That bias, and a linear understanding of time, privilege the political, diplomatic, and military ways that men have used time. It is hard to ignore the fact that both men and women experience time in multiple ways, or that this fact is practically a commonplace in Latin America. This recognition emerges in the work of novelists such as Julio Cortázar, Carlos Fuentes, Gabriel García Márquez, Jual Rulfo and poets like Octavio Paz. See Cortázar (1984), Fuentes (1964), García Márquez (1983), Rulfo (1953), Paz (1965). Exceptions to this academic reliance on linear time schemas are rare among Latin American historians, though Becker (1997) is one experiment with non-linear formats.

3 The kind of church time depicted by Jacques Le Goff (1980: 29–42) is consistent with clerical use of time in early twentieth-century Michoacán.

4 The women were not, of course, alone. For a reconstruction of the series of alliances developed between Cárdenas and Michoacanos, resulting in the establishment of the post-revolutionary government, see Becker (1995).

5 This verbal portrait is based on iconographic evidence I discovered through participant observation of the churches in Ario, Jarácuaro, Morelia,, Pátzcuaro, and Zamora, Michoacán, in 1984, 1985 and 1990. I have profited from my University of Madrid historical art training.

6 The priest's internal monologue is based in part on "Carta pastoral colectiva de los prelados de la provincia de Michoacán," caja 11, Archivo de la Purísima Corazón (APC), Zamora, Michoacán, and on "Sacremental y disciplina," APC, caja 13.

7 The following depiction is based on a series of interviews with Eugenia Villanueva, Ario de Rayón (formerly Ario Santa Monica), Michoacán, 1990.

8 Information on the celebrated regional court case can be found in "Contra Ladislao Alvarado y socios por calumnia, Zamora," 23 May 1923, Fondo Justicia, Archivo Municipal de Zamora (AMZ), Zamora, Michoacán.

9 Interview with Rafael Ochoa, Ario de Rayón, Michoacán, 1990.

10 AJE, Penales, "Ana María Alcalán en contra de Ruperto Herrera", 6 September 1923, ramo Penales, Archivo Judicial del Estado de Michoacán (AJEM), Morelia, Michoacán.

11 AJE Penales, exp.13–923/28, 13 August 1924, "Instruido en contra de Antonio Mendoza por el delito de rapto," 13 August 1924, Expediente 13–923/28, Ramo Penales, Zamora Juzgado de primera instancia (AJEM).

12 This section is based on my series of interviews with Estela Villanueva and Concepción González, Ario de Rayón, 1990.

13 Series of interviews with Estrella de la Puente, Ario de Rayón, Michoacán, 1990.

14 Interview with Martín Méndez, 1985, Ario de Rayón, Michoacán, 1985.

15 For the price women paid for their temporary control of villages without men, see Becker (1994). For similar historical experiences, see Taylor (1979).

References

Archives

AJEM (Archivo Judicial del Estado de Michoacán), Morelia, Michoacán.
AMZ (Archivo Municipal de Zamora), Zamora, Michoacán.
APC (Archivo de la Purísimo Corazón), Zamora, Michoacán.

Books and articles

Augustine, Saint (1991) *Confessions*, trans. Henry Chadwick, New York: Oxford University Press, pp. 221–45.

Becker, Marjorie (1997) "Time enough for landowners, for peones, even for historians, but what of peasant women?: ghost time and *rapto* in Michoacán, 1924," paper presented at Latin American Studies Association Convention, Guadalajara, Mexico, April, 1997.

Becker, Marjorie (1994) "Torching La Purísima, dancing at the altar: the construction of revolutionary hegemony in Michoacán, 1934–1940," in Gilbert M. Joseph and Daniel Nugent (eds) *Everyday Forms of State Formation: The Negotiation of Rule in Modern Mexico*, Durham, NC: Duke University Press, pp. 247–64.

Becker, Marjorie (1995) *Setting the Virgin on Fire: Lázaro Cárdenas, Michoacán Peasants and the Redemption of the Mexican Revolution*, Berkeley, CA: University of California Press.
Cortázar, Julio (1984) *Rayuela*. Mexico City: Bruguera Mexicana de Ediciones, S.A.
Fuentes, Carlos (1964) *The Death of Artemio Cruz*, trans. Sam Hileman, New York: Farrar, Straus & Giroux.
García Márquez, Gabriel (1983) *Chronicle of a Death Foretold*, trans. Gregory Rabasa, New York: Alfred Knopf.
Le Goff, Jacques (1980) "Merchant's time and church's time in the Middle Ages," in Jacques Le Goff (ed.) *Time, Work and Culture in the Middle Ages*, trans. Arthur Goldhammer, Chicago: University of Chicago Press, pp. 29–42.
Paz, Octavio (1965) *Configurations*, trans. G. Aroul *et al.*, New York: New Directions.
Rulfo, Juan (1953) *El llano en llamas*, Mexico City: Fondo de Cultura Económica.
Taylor, William B. (1979) *Drinking, Homicide and Rebellion in Colonial Mexican Villages*, Stanford, CA: Stanford University Press.

AFTERWORD

Why did I choose this particular narrative structure, a non-linear temporal structure that breaks the rules of conventional historical writing, rules that privilege linear time, a bias toward progress, an inclusion of the literate to the exclusion of those who could neither read nor write? Why did I select a structure in which the hope enacted on a single evening, a hope that was squashed, re-emerged in my text? Why, in fact, do I believe time itself to be a historical actor worthy of embodiment?

This essay is an essay that laments the way history occurred. Its tone can properly be understood as mournful, its approach as both respectful of what occurred, of the people who made that past take place, and yet also open to other possibilities.

Indeed, there is a sense I learned from the great Argentine historian of Mexico, Aldolfo Gilly, a sense suggesting that when the dreams of those whose lives have been little more than poverty, exploitation and near-futile hope have been undermined, those hopes and dreams do not disappear entirely. Rather, they persist as memories. They are, in fact, embodied, as is everything. Despite the composite fictional priest I create in the article (a priest based on so many of the priests I knew in Michoacán), one might claim that human experience *is* physical. (And that would include metaphysical experiences.)

What happened can be related relatively easily in linear terms. To wit: in northwestern Michoacán, a region dominated by a deeply conservative land-owning class, and an arch-conservative Catholic Church, Mexican President Lázaro Cárdenas and his followers attempted to school the poor in revolution.

Yet Cardenista frustration at the depth of clerical influence led enthusiastic revolutionaries in the village of Ario Santa Monica to seize Catholic icons, including an icon of La Purísima, the Virgin Mary at her purest and most chaste. After the theft, the revolutionaries set the virgin on fire in the village square. After the fire, revolutionaries and their wives or girlfriends danced in the church. And on that unusual night, women trained in modesty, humility and silence by the Church itself, enacted a longing for something else. Yet the village refused to honor that longing, and, subsequently, vilified the women.

Such a retelling, however, leaves no structural space either for the longings unleashed by La Purísima herself, or the complex and related counter-longings the dancers may have experienced. The reason it does not, in my view, is because conventional historical writing demands that concrete action follow concrete action. There is precious little room for what might have happened, or even for the possibilities that specific concrete acts unleash. Thus, history has become not only the retelling of the ways the wealthy, the powerful and the literate have appropriated the world. It has also become yet another erasure of the multitude of historical possibilities.

While it seems entirely relevant to say that the thoughts, desires, wishes, fantasies of Michoacán women living in the 1920s and 1930s differ in historically specific ways from those of, say, this analyst, living in the developed West, that does not mean that outsiders, not subject to the specific sorts of silencing the dancing women were, do not have a role to play. It struck me that my role might be that of constructing a narrative in which the attempts to silence, to obliterate the dancers, to render them historically invisible, the efforts that in "real" historical life did take place after the dance, should inaugurate the chapter. That would enable me to allow my readers to explore, as I did, the obstacles the dancing women faced. Then readers could find, as I did, that some of the obstacles were interior, that the last surviving dancer initially refused to claim her own moment of possibility, of transformation for what it may have been. Instead, she accepted the community's condemnation.

Yet I did not. Very little in my life outside of the academy has suggested to me that my emotionality, my tendencies to hope and dream, are improper. Yet almost nothing within the academy has encouraged such behavior. Notwithstanding the oddness of a historical profession seemingly determined to maintain a nineteenth-century posture toward representation and writing, I have been lucky enough to live at a time and in a place, where women dancing in the literal and in the metaphorical sense of women on the move, doing things, saying things, learning things, has been possible. Considering the depth of understanding—and of longing—that the Michoacán women gave me when I lived there, it seemed appropriate in my reconstruction of the dance to break into the dance itself, bearing a crown, a medal, an award for the women audacious enough to step into—if only for a short time—the possibility of a different life.

2   Writing, rewriting the beach

An essay

Greg Dening

Calcutta 1811. *The rich travelled on the shoulders of the poor in Calcutta in 1811. Sir Thomas Stamford Raffles, in his palanquin, bobbed along above the heads of the coolies and beggars in Tank Square. He did not see the short man with a sailor's gait and a scarred, near-toothless face. But Edward Robarts saw him. Seeing Raffles gave Robarts hope. For ten months on this the harshest of his beaches, Robarts had been on the slide. Calcutta was a Company town, an East India Company town. A white man without Company connections, or without a trade that the Company valued, had nothing to sell but his poverty. In an empire city, there was no space between the empowered rich and the disciplined native population who did their work for them. The relentless pressure on the poor white man was downward. A man never went up in the rounds of begging a few rupees from vestrymen's wives and daughters. There was only the trading of one disrespectful gaze for another degrading judgement.*

Just a year before, Robarts had reached the highest rung on his social ladder. But this had been in Penang. He had been butler and cook to Sir Thomas Raffles' sister. There had been soirees and parties aplenty, enough anyway to delude his sense of social status. Death, however, rode the shoulders of rich and poor alike in the East. Raffles and his family fled Penang. Robarts had to find another beach in Calcutta.

Robarts came to Calcutta with what he thought of as his two greatest capitals in life – his 'royal bride' and his story of 'a long and singular career of an enterprizing and unfortuneate [sic] life'. His wife was Enaoata, daughter of 'King' Keatonui of Nukuhiva in the Marquesas. She came to Calcutta with their three children and pregnant with the fourth. Hers was the unfortunate life, we have to think. She had left her native islands with Robarts, first for Tahiti. There she tried to hang herself as she faced Robarts' violence. He brewed rum for the convict colony at Botany Bay and succumbed to it as well. Whenever we meet her on all the beaches of her life, she is in tears. It is hard not to think that with a language none could speak, except her husband, and he haltingly, she was wrapped in a terrible silence. In Calcutta, she could endure only a couple of years in the makeshift compounds behind the godowns of Taretta Bazaar where they lived. Her children survived not much longer.

Robarts always saw himself as 'enterprizing' in the face of harsh circumstances. 'Bumptious' would probably be the word others would have used. If only half the stories of how he rescued people and ships were true, he would have been a hard man to live with. But anyone who has a story that he believes others will want to read probably is to be seen as bumptious. Robarts had already begun to write his story when he went looking for Raffles. He had no trouble discovering him. 'A Great man everyone knows,' he wrote later, 'but a poor man sits in his corner unnoticed.' When he knocked on Raffles' door, it was opened by a Malay servant who recognised Robarts from Penang. He was taken immediately to Sir Thomas.

'Why, Robarts,' Raffles said. 'We've been looking for you.'

At Raffles' side was a bespectacled man with an air of great learning. It was 'that morning star of Literature, the Immortal' Dr John Caspar Leyden – linguist, theologian, poet, medical practitioner, Freemason, professor of Hindustani, Judge of the Twenty-Four Pergunnahs and Commissioner of the Court of Request. Leyden was a collector of stories and languages. He had acquired thirty-four of the latter and thought that through Robarts he might acquire another.

He asked Robarts what he had been doing in Calcutta.

'Looking for employment and writing my Narrative of what I had gone through since I left London.'

'What? You have turned author!'

'Yes, Sir! Anything to raise the wind for an honest morsel.'

'What? Raise the wind!' Leyden laughed at the sailor's metaphor.

'Yes, Sir! I have been lying becalmed these ten months, and if a breeze does not spring up, my unfortuneate Bark will founder on the rocks of adversity.'

'Is your wife from the islands with you? Bring her with you and let me see your narrative, and then I shall be better judge of your abilities.'

So Robarts returned in a few days, with a few pages of his 'Vocabalry of the Marqueasas Language.' Enoata came with him to pronounce the words. The rooms of Leyden's house were filled with Persian scholars transcribing texts. Leyden offered Robarts a desk and forty rupees a month to tell his story. Robarts received only January's first stipend. Leyden had gone with Lord Minto and Raffles on an expedition to annex Java. Searching for manuscripts in Batavia, he caught a fever and died, learned and young.

Robarts' story, written in a neat, small hand, breathlessly without stop, comma or paragraph for 171 pages, is not signed as completed until July 24, 1824. By then he has many, many more vicissitudes to tell of. But in January 1811, sharing a desk with a Persian scholar, he had begun:

In November 1797 I saild from Blackwall on board the Ship Euphrates, bound round Cape Horn in search of sperm whales.........

Gauguin's advice: Melville's example

Voices from the beach can be hard to hear. They can be snatched from the lips by the wind or drowned in the white noise of the waves. There are beaches, too, on which voices are hard to hear because they are lost in a silence that clings like scented tropical air. It is the silence of vast spaces, of grand canyons, of cathedral apses. It is also the cold silence of death.

'Be mysterious' was Paul Gauguin's advice on translating such silences. '*Soyez mystérieuses*', he had carved on the lintel of his *Maison du Plaisir*, his 'House of

Orgasm' at Atuona on the island of Hiva Oa in the Marquesas. It was his last residence in the South Seas.

'Mystery', 'mysterious' are words layered with a thousands of years of meaning. At the heart of these meanings is an understanding that a mystery is the most complicated truth, the deepest silence, clothed in story or play or sacramental sign. Being mysterious means that there is work to be done, not just by the story-teller, not just by the author, not just by the priest, but by the audience, the reader, the faithful. There is no closure to mystery, only another translation, another story.

'I am not a painter who copies nature – today less than before. With me everything happens in my crazy imagination.' Colour, Gauguin was saying in his letters, was the instrument of his imagination. Colour itself was a language, 'a profound, mysterious language, a language of the dream'. The ideas of a painting did not need words. Colour, with much the same vibrations as music, activated the more general meanings in what was being represented. It pulled out the interior force of things.

'I am not a historian who replicates the past', I can say with Gauguin. Forty years ago I discovered that my main historical ambition was to fill a certain sort of silence. It was the silence of those who for one reason or another had no voice, or whose voice was never their own but always someone else's. That is not an extraordinary ambition among those who claim to belong to something they call the humanities. The humanities are the great unsilencing art.

In the humanities, we are forever trying to imagine what the silences mean – those silences that come from the skewing processes of preservation in archives and memory, those silences of the powerless – whether they are powerless for reasons of class, gender or race; those silences of the inexpressible – grief and happiness, love and hatred, catastrophe and exultation; those silences of everyday ordinariness; those silences that in the end belong to the inaccessible person or individual.

The tricks for breaking these silences are infinite in number. But I have always drawn comfort from Paul Valéry's understanding of silence. Silence, he wrote, is the active presence of absent things. Silence isn't empty soundlessness. Silence is always a relationship. Silence always has a presence in something else. Silence is contingent on something we experience in another way.

We catch the contingency of silence in our imagination. Not our fantasies. Our imagination. Imagination is the ability to see those fine-lined and faint webs of significance. Imagination is hearing the silence because we have heard some of the sounds. Imagination is seeing the absent things because we have seen so much else. That is its dream-like quality. It is built on re-arranged experience.

For all my academic life I have taught my students history by fine-tuning their imaginations. I have taught them the past by first requiring them to describe their present. This has not been a presentist gimmick, nor some rejection of the 'relevance' of history. On the contrary, they soon discovered how difficult it is to describe the present. They soon learned that everything they discovered was the subject of reflective discourse by somebody else. The more they claimed the novelty of their experience, the more they had to plumb the plagiarisms of their thinking. They soon learned that cultural living in its bare bones is talk. To describe it we have to catch what Wittgenstein called the fictions of our languaging. As with the present, so with the past. The past has its anthropology as much as its history.

For all these years teaching creative imagination, I had a photograph over my desk. It was of Herman Melville.

I long had a smart-alecky relationship with Melville. I had long known the beach experiences of Edward Robarts. I knew how his experiences and others' experiences had seeped into Melville's account of his beachcombing in the Marquesas in his novel, *Typee*. Their many years experience had enlarged his three weeks experience. It happened as a sort of cultural osmosis as Melville read accounts of Pacific explorers and visitors to the Marquesas who had met Robarts and others there, or who had had access to their manuscripts. 'Wink, wink', I used to say to my photograph of Melville. 'I know from what real experiences you made the fictions of your own.'

But over the years I grew in awe of Melville. His four years in the Pacific, in the Marquesas, Tahiti, Hawai'i and on whaling ships and US naval vessels were the non-fiction of his life that he transformed into the fictions of his writings. In the end I used to say to my friends that I kept Melville's photograph over my desk to keep me humble. What else was he using but his creative imagination? What else was he doing but describing his present so that he might hear the silences of the past? What else was he being but mysterious?

Being mysterious cost Melville, of course. Melville had 'gone native'. 'Going native' was originally a derisive term of the British Raj. Anybody touched by the cultural relativism that was required to 'go native' was letting the empire down. There are many empires for the 'civilised'. Melville seemed shameless to them all – for the things he didn't say and the things he only half said. He allowed other ways, not just 'native' ways, but other 'civilised' ways, to stand in their difference.

The anger at Melville in many matters of homo- and hetero-sexuality, and of alternate moralities, was directed at his equivocal stances. He refused to protest the grotesqueries of his experience. On his beach, he let the natives be who they were. To fundamentalists of all descriptions, the natives should have been changed into something else. But perhaps the greatest scandal of Melville was what Wendy Steiner has called *The Scandal of Pleasure* (1997). He liberated his readers to go where they might. That sort of freedom is a fearful thing.

Valenciennes 1822. *It took a long hard day and a harder night for Joseph Kabris to die on his hospital bed at Valenciennes, September 22–3, 1822. Gangrene poison took him slowly and painfully. There was no family beside him, save in his feverish mind as he mourned for his 'princess' wife and his daughters ten thousand miles away on Nukuhiva.*

There was a stranger from Geneva there, though. He had come looking for Kabris, found him dying and stayed to the end. Not really a stranger. Ferdinand Denis was the publisher of a fourteen-page pamphlet, A True and Accurate Account of the Residence of Joseph Kabris, native of Bordeaux, in the Islands of Mendoca, located in the Pacific Ocean at 10 degrees latitude and 240 degrees longitude.

There was no great self-interestedness in Denis' visit and stay. He admired Kabris and he knew that the true pain in his dying was not the gangrene but the humiliations of his perceived freakishness. And there was another reason for his staying. In the corridors of the hospital lurked more than one purveyor of curiosities. The ghouls had half a hope that they might skin Kabris when he died. Joseph Kabris had his beach written on his skin in his tattoos.

Kabris was 'imprinted with nobility', a certain David Porter had written. Porter had seen Kabris in Moscow at the court of Emperor Alexander I, soon after the Russian explorer, Adam von Krusenstern, had taken Kabris accidentally from the Marquesas Islands in 1804. It was an accident for which Kabris never forgave Krusenstern. He had lived his Marquesan life to its exuberant and bloody fullest. He forever mourned his being snatched away from it.

In those first years of his return to Europe, royal courts – at least those of Russia, France and Prussia – had wanted to see him. Porter thought that Kabris' tattoos were like a 'beautiful damask pattern'. They were 'in forms not inferior to the finest Etruscan borders'. 'To me', he mused, 'there is something very admirable in the idea of a fine male figure without any other covering than these beautiful enamellings.' 'Like a savage god.' He reminded his readers that when the president of the British Royal Academy first saw the Apollo Belvedere in Rome, he had said: 'What a fine Mohawk warrior!'

For Porter there was something achingly beautiful in Kabris' ideal civilised body with its savage markings. Porter could hardly take his eyes off him as Kabris told how he had killed a cannibal 'with the horrid morsel still in his mouth'. Porter just knew that, if this naked hero in a savage uniform had only been allowed to stay, a 'rude civilisation' would have grown among the natives.

Ten years in Russia was enough for Kabris. He spent them teaching the Royal Marines at Cronstadt another savage skill he had learned in the islands, swimming. After the chaos of Napoleon's Grande Armée defeat, he joined the packs of escaping French prisoners and walked back to France.

Back in Bordeaux, he was no longer an 'ideal beauty'. He did a stint in a Cabinet des Illusions exhibiting his 'enamellings' and performing savage dances and wild sacrificial rituals. It only ended in his own disillusion. He wandered the provincial fairs – Le Havre, Rouen, Grenoble, Orléans – making theatre of himself. He shared the stage with a four hundred pound 'fat lady' and a three-headed cow. His moment of despair came in Orléans where posters of Kabris Le Tatoué were pasted side by side with posters of Munito Le Chien Savant. Everything he thought himself to be because of his beach experiences was mocked in that. He came to Valenciennes to die.

Who knows whether he knew in those last moments what the skulkers in the hospital corridors were planning to do? Perhaps he asked Ferdinand Denis as a last charity to protect him. Anyway, Denis oversaw a burial that would destroy the tattoos forever. Corpses weren't scarce in the hospital at Valenciennes. Kabris was buried without a coffin

Figure 2.1 Kabris *Le Tatoué*
Source: Von Langsdorff
(1813: 97)

sandwiched between the bodies of two paupers. However, there may have been some recognition of where he lay. A contemporary Promenade au Cimitière de Valenciennes described a stroll past the graves of a 'goddess of reason', a Jesuit, an English colonel killed at Waterloo, a freemason, a comic artiste – 'et Kabris le Tatoué'.

Denis, looking down on these 'damask patterns' on the skin of the lifeless Kabris, could not have known what they meant or what stories were written into them. Perhaps he recognised the clay pipe imprinted on Kabris' stomach. But he would not have known, anymore than we do, whether this was some native tattooist's joke, or Kabris' signature of his own difference on a native beach. He certainly could not have known that that diagonal line across Kabris' forehead was called pi'e'e, 'running shit', and that patch over his eye, mata epo, 'shitty eyes', that line across his mouth, kutu epo, 'shitty snout'. Those marks were probably his first tattooings. They gave him his 'rubbish names', titles that showed him to be at the beginnings of his initiations and at his most degraded point, the 'shit' of gods and chiefs. That chaos of calabash coils, crab eyes and turtle shells on his skin – the pahu tiki, the 'wrapping in images' – these would have been very different signs, not of degradation but of triumph and honour for the occasions when he pulled himself out of the shit by killing a man, winning a battle, doing some famous deed. Kabris, we have to think, was re-born in a social sense with this new wrapping of his skin. It protected him as an armour. It clothed him with family and kin. It joined him to a mythic understanding of who he was. It gave narrative to his life.

Kabris had another narrative of his life. It was the small pamphlet which he sold at the entrance to the theatre of his exhibitions and his dances. It was full of his conviction that the story told by his tattoos was true. Perhaps Denis picked it up from among the small collection of Kabris' things beside his bed and opened it. Perhaps he didn't. If he had, he would have read:

> *Six months after the unfortunate Quiberon affair I boarded an English vessel leaving for a whaling expedition to the Pacific Ocean.....*

Flying to the Land

We were flying over an immense ocean. That small part of it beneath our northeast flight over the 1500km separating Tahiti from the Marquesas was the northern tip of the Tuamotu Archipelago, known in older sailing days as the Low or Dangerous Archipelago. Its 78 atolls and innumerable hidden reefs fan a two thousand kilometre arc across the eastern approaches to the Central Pacific. Although it was my first time among them, my mind's eye had scanned them many, many times. I had mapped them in all sorts of ways – for the variety of their flora and fauna, for the variety of their cultural forms, for their populations and the relics of their populations, for the canoe voyaging among them.

Forty years ago, my first images of the Pacific came to me through the endless texts that innumerable intruders into this vast ocean had made of their experiences. I have never recovered from the historian's first excited discovery that most of history comes from unpublished sources – from letters, diaries, logs – imprinted as much with tears, sweat, blood and the dirt of time as by ink and pencil. I have always counted it the great privilege of an historian's life to finger these pages, sometimes for the first time after they were made. I have always felt as well that because so much of living is lost in the writing of it down, the historian's obligation is to saturate her- or himself in all there is. So history writing is as much a pilgrimage to all the places where these unique and disparate remnants of the past are to be found as it is a culling from books on library shelves. In the way of things, the history of strangers coming into the Pacific is to be found where they came from – London, Boston, Paris, Rome, Nantucket – rather than the places they came to. But here in a Twin Otter 20,000 feet above the sea, I am making a pilgrimage the other way round. I am flying to the Land.

At that time, December 1974, I would not have called the islands I was flying to, the Land, Te Henua. Nor would I have called the people who lived there, the Natives, Te Enata. I would have called them by the name Spanish outsiders had given them four hundred years earlier, the Marquesas, the Marquesans. But crossing their beach would be my learning experience. I would get the confidence and the courage to call them what they called themselves.

I was apprehensive. The Land and its Natives had changed my life. But I had been to the Land and met its Natives only in libraries and archives. I know that I was stranger to them, and I knew the cost of every stranger's intrusion. The sadness of their story had affected me ever since I began to learn it. But inevitably I came with a sense of trespass. Their terrible story and my knowledge of it have been the capital of my life. The rewards of twenty years study of them to this time had been great. I brought to them in my luggage the pride of my academic life to this time, my first book about them, *The Marquesan Journal of Edward Robarts* (1974). I knew all my shortcuts in that book. I knew all its tricks of camouflage for my ignorance.

Early in my studies of Te Henua, I had read Franz Fanon's *The Wretched of the Earth* (1961). It had shaken me to my core. In a world of victims, he wrote, there are no innocents. No one can write two-sided history who in some way benefits from the power of the victors. No one can mediate between the disempowered living and the voiceless dead. All of us writing in a history so terrible as that of the Pacific – or of the Americas or of Africa for that matter – have had to resolve that dilemma for ourselves. No doubt we all do it differently. For me, giving the dead a voice has been reason enough for my history. I am with Karl Marx, too. The function of my history is not so much to understand the world as to change it. If my history by story and reflection disturbs the moral lethargy of the living to change in their present the consequences of their past, then it fulfils a need. I have not silenced any voice by adding mine.

Hatutu
Eiao

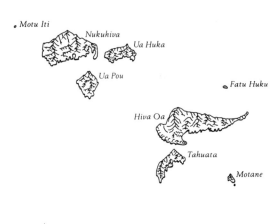
Motu Iti
Nukuhiva
Ua Huka
Ua Pou
Fatu Huku
Hiva Oa
Tahuata
Motane

TE HENUA

Fatuiva

Figure 2.2 Te Henua
Source: Greg Dening

Back in 1974, I had failed rather badly in the photography classes I had taken in preparation for my visit to the Te Henua. I had been too timid to enter the private space of those 'interesting' faces of the poor and old and eccentric my teachers wanted me to invade. Now as the pilots began to tap their compass and reach for their binoculars, I found my timidities were returning.

Still, I had my camera in my hand as we approached the Land, and my face pressed against the cabin porthole. Suddenly, through a gap in the clouds, I realised I was looking down on the one place in all the Land I had wanted to see, Vaitahu on the island of Tahuata. At Vaitahu, the sad history of the Land had begun. Madre de Dios, the Spaniards had christened it with blood in 1595. Less bloodily, but bloodily just the same, James Cook had re-named it Resolution Bay in 1744.

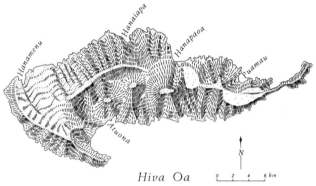

Figure 2.3 Hiva Oa
Source: Greg Dening

Seeing Vaitahu did not mean that I was there. We landed on Hiva Oa, the neighbouring island to Tahuata. The landing-strip looked as long and wide as an aircraft carrier. It was on the top of a ridge behind Atuona.

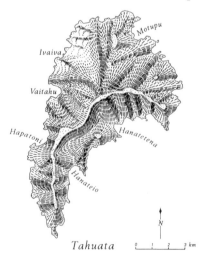

Figure 2.4 Tahuata
Source: Greg Dening

Figure 2.5 Vaitahu from
the air
Source: Greg Dening

On the black sand beach at Atuona, Paul Gauguin had painted 'Riders on the Beach'. Two hooded riders – death on horse-back – lead the other horsemen to an endless horizon. There is nothing 'real' in the painting, no black sand, no dark tumbling rocks, no closed bay. Differences are sponged out in his consuming effort to make mythic and universal this art by the last savage of the last savages. Gauguin doesn't write his beach. He paints it out of his crazy imagination, filled with his own native myths, shaped by all the art history that flows through his fingers.

Figure 2.6 The beach at
Atuona
Source: Greg Dening

Our first ambition was to walk the black sand beach at Atuona. Death had been frequent on that beach. The bay was called Traitors' Bay, from the boat crews that had been cut off there. But death had come more usually for Enata from canoes of their enemies as they came 'fishing' for victims. In times of social crisis or in celebration of some sacred moment in their lives, Enata went fishing (*e ika*) for victims, *heana*. They would go raiding other islands, other valleys. They snatched their victims where they could, off the shore, from their houses. These *heana* were brought back, sometimes alive, sometimes dead, but always in the fashion in which fishermen brought back a catch of their most *tapu* fish. They were strung on poles, with large hooks in their mouths, baskets of bait

Figure 2.7 Traitors' Bay,
Atuona
Source: Greg Dening

attached to their limbs. When the victims had been killed, their corpses were mocked and played with and parts of bodies were ceremonially eaten. Then they were strung up with other sacrifices in the *me'ae*, the sacred spaces of the gods.

Back from the beach – over Gauguin's shoulders as he painted – we walked the dusty roads and up the trails among the silent stone remains. Here and there a *tiki* head had been incorporated into a fence. The massive statues had long gone from this valley. You can see them in the museums of the world staring wide-eyed and meaningless at the bored crowds. I liked the *tiki* in the fences better than all the *tiki* in the exhibition halls. The *tiki* in the fences had a modest dignity. Shadows and flowers gave them a life that spotlights and pedestals took away.

Figure 2.8 Tiki in the fence
Source: Greg Dening

Everywhere in the valley of Atuona are empty stone remains. They were stone platforms on which houses once stood, or stone stages on which people had once danced and feasted, or stone altars in sacred places where sacrifices had been placed. They were scattered among the trees, overgrown and silent, all through the valley. They were relics of populations wiped out in the few short years of their encounter with Euro-American strangers. Diseases for which the people had no immunity killed most; but they died more horribly than that. In a cultural paroxysm in the 1860s, they killed themselves. When they had no explanation of why they were dying in such horrific numbers, they turned to killing one another for the machinations and sorcery they presumed was among them.

The missionaries, early in the nineteenth century, hopeless in their efforts at conversion, had focused on destruction of the *tapu* system which they believed was the key to native heathenism. They promised that the native dying would stop if the evil of the *tapu* was broken. They evolved a series of rituals by which the native gods were challenged to punish broken *tapu*. Men were asked to walk under women's most intimate clothing. Women were asked to walk over the most sacred objects. The effect was not so much change as emptiness and listless hopelessness. Enata were numb for a while, with liquor as much as cultural anomie.

Then in the 1860s, here in the valley of Atuona, there was a terrible revival of an old *tapu* custom, *e ika*, fishing for victims. In the cultural hopelessness of the 1860s, any re-birth of custom would be bastard. The revival of *e ika* was monstrous. Whatever balancing principles there had been to the death and violence of the old ways were now gone. This time, the killings had no ritual. They were not across islands and valleys. They were internecine, familial even, and orgiastic. In a population depleted in fifty years to three thousand from a hundred thousand, they now killed one another by the hundreds.

The death throes of this valley of Atuona were awful. It was and is today a place of extraordinary beauty, the sort of wild beauty that Gauguin ached to find. The peak of Temetiu dominates it. The wide sweeping southern arm of its bay bends out into the straits towards the neighbouring island of Tahuata. Its black sand beach collects the waves coming in on the southeast winds. Its river sparkles over a bed of stones. But its silence clings.

Among the silent stones, Gauguin's imagination does not seem so crazy, and his admonition to 'be mysterious' not so irresponsible. His cowled riders of death have a monkish feel, enough to remind us how much death those who preached eternal life had brought. The wash of his colours reminds us that any re-presentation of the past will have a dream-like quality. The past has its own silences that never will be voiced.

We paid Gauguin honour, of course. We walked up the hill of Hueakihi to the cemetery. His grave is easily seen. Amid white cement tombs open to the sun, his is of reddish rocks and shaded by a frangipani tree. Seventy-five years after his death one of Gauguin's final wishes was granted. The cast of a favourite work, a ceramic sculpture he had called *Oviri* was placed on his grave. *Oviri* was a favourite of Picasso, too, and inspired him. Gauguin had sculpted

Oviri in Brittany on his return to France after his first trip to Tahiti, just before that terrible brawl that left him with a wounded leg for life. Gauguin thought it his finest work of art. He knew it was enigmatic, mysterious. 'Oviri' in Tahitian means 'wild', 'savage'. The woman of the statue is indeed wild, a mixture of incompatible lore. She has the head of a mummified Marquesan skull. She crushes a wolf under her feet, just as those most unwild statues of the Virgin crush a serpent. Gauguin put his customary signature on the statue, 'PGO'. That reads as 'pego'. It is sailors' slang for 'prick'. *Oviri's* wildness creates a disturbing restlessness over the grave. One cannot think that Gauguin's bones rest in peace.

It took us several days to reach Vaitahu, and then only after dramatic rescues from a drifting, powerless boat we had boarded at Atuona. In the end we came to Vaitahu as the Spaniards had come 400 years ago, and James Cook 200 years ago. Like them we could not see the bay, hidden as it was behind the high bluff at its northeast point. But I knew it was there because I could see the effect of the blast of wind that tunnelled down from the mountains. Every ship that anchored there felt that wind, and needed a double anchor on the sandy sloping floor of the bay to stay there. I don't know how many times I have put on a card or a page of paper a note from a log, a journal or a letter about the wind. Just seeing it on the waters outside Vaitahu was a thrill. I was nearly there where ten thousand times I had been in my mind.

Figure 2.9 Rounding Northeast Point into Vaitahu
Source: Greg Dening

We crossed the beach at Vaitahu in total disarray. Our experiences on the water had unsettled us. We needed an aggression for negotiating accommodation and transport that we did not have. Our softness bred distrust. But an old man, Teifitu Umu, took us in hand. He had rheumy eyes and feet swollen with elephantiasis. He is dead now, by a few months, as I write. With a shuffling walk he took us up the path beside the stream that flowed down the valley. From somewhere in my reading I remembered that this stream had become a flooded torrent in 1797 and had carried houses and their inhabitants into the bay.

Teifitu was a widower. Our appreciation of his kindness did not displace our dismay at the conditions of his house. From the moment of our arrival a gaggle of children had adopted us and watched our social gaucheries with great amusement. The adults were more distant, but friendly.

After a sparse supper, Teifitu came to talk. In the growing dark, we sat at his table. I brought out my copy of *Edward Robarts*. I will never forget that evening as we bent over it and I tried to convey in my poor French and poorer Marquesan what its English said. He was clearly excited to talk with somebody with an interest in the island. He wrote his name in my diary, Teifitu Gregoire Umu, and then the line of his genealogy that took him back to Iotete, the *haka'iki* (chief) of Vaitahu, whose story I am about to tell. And to Iotete's father, Tainai, who had welcomed Robarts, Kabris and Crook. And to Tainai's father, Honu, who had welcomed James Cook. He wrote down, too, the names of all the families still on the island. I have these pages still. I hold them precious, not so much for their information, but because they told me how much I didn't know and reminded me of my obligations in regard to silences that were not mine to break.

Things of the past – all those artefacts we call cultural – come into the present as 'cargo' across the beaches of island cultures. Their encapsulated meanings – status in a colour, cosmology in a shape, gender in a texture – are transformed in the new environment of the present into other meanings – of heritage, of evidence, of art, of loot, of souvenirs. The history of things will have to enfold the meanings of the present in which they were made and all the meanings of their successive presents.

It is the same with places. The history in places, especially in places of cross-cultural encounters, will take as much imagination as science to see. Blood and ashes are blown away with the dirt. Shouts and songs die on the wind. Pain and happiness are as evanescent as memory. To catch the lost passions in places, history will have to be a little more artful than being a 'non-fiction'. It will have to have, among other graces, a trust in and a sense of the continuities of living through different times, despite all the transformations and translations that masquerade as discontinuities.

Teifitu walked us round the sights and sites of the valley. Behind the beach of rolling stones in a cleared area, a breadfruit tree stands. Somewhere nearby the Spaniards said Mass and killed those among Enata who jostled during it. Somewhere nearby they set up three stakes for three bodies. Who knows in what theatre or for what purpose, a soldier pierced the side of the body on the central stake with a spear. No word of whether water ran from the wound.

Deep in the valley at the end of a line of trees is a monument to three French soldiers killed in ambuscade by Enata in 1843. Teifitu showed us where and how the deaths occurred. When I asked him where the monument was for Enata dead, he shrugged his shoulders. No, there were no monuments, but there is memory and there will be history.

Make no doubt about that. There will be history. I won't be there to read it. Perhaps not you either nor your children's children. But these dead will be heroes for their resistance. If there is one thing we have learned in the Pacific, it is that if the Fatal Impact of the Euro-Americans killed hundreds of thousands of lives, it did not kill memories. These memories will undoubtedly serve their successive presents. These memories will be debated, revised. No doubt someday someone will start an archaeological dig around these monuments or the French fort. They will collect the musket balls and the sling stones, make their histories, build their museums.

The 'French presence' began on 1 May 1842, the name day of Louis-Philippe, France's uncomfortable monarch. In this improbable place, a backwater in the vast Pacific Ocean, Admiral Abel Dupetit-Thouars established an imperial presence for France with an occupation force of several hundred troops.

The Admiral took possession of Vaitahu with all the appropriate proprieties. He set up a flagpole. He beat the soil with his sword three times. He had the band play *Domine Salvum* for the king and the *Marseillaise* for his changed kingdom. After Solemn High Mass, he had the local chiefs sign the cession of their land. The *Ministre de Marine* insisted that the documents be signed in triplicate. You can see the spidery scrawls and crosses still in the National Archives, Paris.

Taking possession of the Marquesas was easier than knowing what to with them once they were possessed. The whole French caper was largely Dupetit-Thouars's idea. The French public knew nothing of it and were to be enraged when they discovered that they were saddled with the expense and tedium of their useless empire.

As Dupetit-Thouars saw it, there was nowhere else for the French to go in the Pacific. The British had narrowly beaten them to New Zealand. The Russians were developing Alaska and Kamchatka. The Americans were pioneering the Rocky Mountains and were the main influence in Hawai'i. On a map of mercator projection, or in some model in a global strategist's head, the Marquesas were in the centre of the Pacific. They were on the cross-roads between Panama and Sydney, Cape Horn and Shanghai. The British, Dupetit-Thouars said, would need a passport to traverse the Pacific.

But winds and currents and Great Circle navigation don't work like global strategists' models. The Marquesas remained as unstrategic as they ever were. There is an almost pathetic letter from Dupetit-Thouars to his *Ministre de Marine* as he arrived in Te Henua explaining that now he was there there were some questions he would like to ask. There were ten islands in the *îles des Marquises* and dozens of inhabited valleys, he reported. He would probably need about a thousand troops to control them. And, incidentally, what about laws? What systems of justice would there be? Who had power over life and death? Who owned the land? Should there be intermarriage? . . .

Those the French said they owned did not feel owned. In the Land, resistance was savage. At Vaitahu, the French made Iotete 'king'. They gave him a paste-board crown decorated with glass beads and colossal feathers. They dressed him in a red shag coat with enormous gold epaulette in the style of Louis XV. Someone among the officers said he looked like a Bourbon, if one forgot

Figure 2.10 Iotete in
'royal' regalia
Source: Radiguet (1929: 39)

the tattoos. They had given him a flag, too, of red and white squares. It was the French naval signal flag for evening mess. They laughed and laughed at this joke on a cannibal king.

It did not take long for Iotete to realise that whatever greatness had been thrust upon him, he was greatly diminished. The French left two hundred troops in his valley. Only two hundred of his people had survived the 'ecological imperialism' that had come across their beaches in the form of diseases for which they had no immunity. The French soldiers made servants of them all and prostitutes of the women. The soldiers' hygiene was appalling, too. Iotete's people began quickly to die of dysentery. So Iotete took them out of the valley and retired to the mountains.

The sudden silence and loneliness of Vaitahu were disturbing to the French. This was not what empires were made of. They brought in enemies of Iotete and made one of them 'king' and decided to expel Iotete altogether from his island. Their military effort was singularly unsuccessful. Two of the soldiers, including a lieutenant, were killed. Then there was a siege of the soldiers' encampment, but the dysentery was killing the Marquesans more quickly than the muskets. Iotete's people literally melted away with the flux.

So the French left Vaitahu. There are no Solemn High Masses for retreats as there are for possessions. There is no accounting for the costs of vicious absurdity, either. Perhaps it is the banality of their evil that should disturb us, not the scope of it. It is their bad faith in suggesting that it could not be otherwise. It is the immorality of doing to native peoples what their civilisation, their religion and their laws said they could not do to each other.

In this Silent Land, my memory is of sounds – of generators in the morning, of cocks crowing, of children playing, of coconuts falling, of the eternal rolling of pebbles in the waves on the shore. The silence, if I would be true to myself, was really in myself. The beach is always mirror to oneself. On a beach the reflections of self are as if in a crazy mirror, distorted, caricatured. Someone called me recently from Cape Town, South Africa. They had seen words of mine on a banner over the entrance to the South African National Gallery. If they were not written here at Vaitahu, they were certainly learned here:

> *There is now no Native past without the Stranger, no Stranger without the Native. No one can hope to be mediator or interlocutor in that opposition of Native and Stranger, because no one is gazing at it untouched by the power that is in it. Nor can anyone speak just for the one, just for the other. There is no escape from the politics of our knowledge, but that politics is not in the past. That politics is in the present.*

Newport Pagnell 1799. The forty-mile carriage ride up the Great North Road from London to Newport Pagnell was hard and long. There were many stares at his sunburnt, weathered face which was almost as dark as the native boy's sitting beside him. His outdoor look did not fit the indoor appearance of his sombre near-clerical clothing. His talk was pious and godly, but he did not have the posture or voice of a minister of the church. He looked different and out of place.

Different and out of place was how he felt, too. The stares would not have worried him. He was more frightened by the thought of the gaze he would be subject to at Newport Pagnell. He was the Mission Society's first failure, though there were others they did not yet know of. He was the first to come back to England those ten thousand miles from the Pacific mission. His conscience was clear. The fervour of his beliefs had not cooled, though his soul had been raked like no other man's. He had seen scenes too obscene to describe, too terrible to understand. There had not been a minute in all the death around him that he had not thought that he too would die uselessly – mocked and taunted on his beach for his difference.

He knew that the directors would have been disturbed by the only letter they had received from him before he turned up unannounced on the whaling ship Butterworth. 'I desire to blush and be confounded before the Lord forever,' he had written in that letter. 'Temptation has been violent and of such strange sort that I am persuaded it would be the greatest presumption in anyone knowing them to encounter.'

Now that he was approaching Newport Pagnell, he remembered his boldness in that letter. Who was he, nineteen years young, and without any other certainty than that God had called him, to tell these great men that they had got it wrong? The Duff had left him alone on the beach at Tahuata with a bible, some seeds and tools, some paper and ink. The heathens had laughed at his poverty and ignorance. He reminded the directors that he had attached himself wrongly to the opinion of 'some respectable members of your body' against the true founder of the Mission Society, Dr Thomas Haweis. Haweis had thought that there was only one way to convert the heathen, and that was by establishing a community of believers whose shining example of good living would give meaning to their words.

Dr Haweis was right, the young whitesmith-cum-missionary now knew, because language was such a barren thing in itself. 'God', 'sin', 'redemption', 'resurrection', 'eternity' – what use were words when there was no experience of what they meant? What story of salvation was there to tell, when the heathens mocked the weakness of a god who couldn't give his servant food or skills to obtain it. Language and its translation were the key. But there was not true translation without experience of a language's meaning.

So here he was with a native boy who had followed him all those miles. The boy was tattooed with a diagonal line from his left temple to his right cheek. He had been initiated into the band of dancers, ka'io'i, whose moral deprivations were without end. The boy, attracting so much attention, was doomed. He was dying now of cold. How could he have eternal life, bewildered as he was? There would be not much time to extract all that there was in his mind. And he himself had a story no one else could tell. In this place where everybody looked at him with a knowing, cynical look, even his own story was disappearing from his mind. He needed the boy like a mirror to see himself in a different place.

The servants at Newport Pagnell took Crook and Temouteitei through the mansion to a book-lined study. This was to be his. Crook's new beach. He saw the books of the Pacific – Cook, Bligh, Bougainville, Hawkesworth, Forster – almost before he saw the sickly figure of the great Dr Samuel Greethead. He lay on the couch beside them.

'Ah! Mr William Pascoe Crook, I am very glad to see you,' the good doctor said. 'And this is Temouteitei? Kaoha! Welcome.'

Dr Greethead was the Sir Joseph Banks of the Mission Society, a great scavenger of knowledge and collector of stories. He had created a vocabulary and grammar of the Tahitian language out of the memories of the Bounty mutineers when they were dragged back for trial and execution. Out of secret manuscripts describing the mutineers' experiences at Tahiti, out of all the other published literature of the Pacific, out of interviews with captains of whaling and trading ships he had formulated a description of Tahitian society. The missionaries on the Duff had it to learn on their way out and to help them in their strategies of conversion. Now he had the most exciting possibility of his intellectual life. The Pacific had come to him in the person of Temouteitei and of the young, intelligent, questioning Crook.

'Do you know,' Greethead said to Crook, 'I persuaded the Directors that two guineas was not too much to spend to get you here. I know you are disappointed that you missed the Duff on her return voyage. But God works in strange ways. If you were with them, you would be now prisoner of the French. Work with me now on the language of the South Seas. It is in the cause of Christ.'

So they turned to conversations that lasted months over several visits. They culled the books on Greethead's shelves, traced Temouteitei's network of kin, evoking stories from him as they went. Now equipped with a frame of Te Henua's physical, biological and botanical *environment, a dramatis personae of individuals, a list of institutions, a day-by-day narrative of happenings, they wrung Crook's memory for details. That way, they wrote a 280 page 'Account of the Marquesas Islands' and 'An Essay toward a Dictionary and Grammar of the lesser-Australian language, According to the Dialect used in the Marquesas'.*

That part which belongs to Crook's living narrative began:

On the 6th June, 1797, the Duff arrived in Resolution Bay . . .

Taipi

We had not finished with the Land. We flew to Ua Huka and joined an old World War II landing craft for the five-hour voyage to Nukuhiva. We approached Nukuhiva from its southeast corner, and could see its north and south coast stretching away. All was abrupt cliff in the blue haze of the sea.

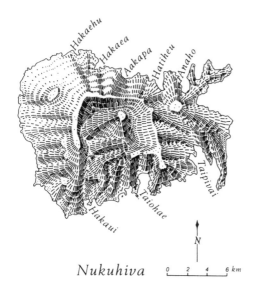

Nukuhiva

N

0 2 4 6 km

Figure 2.11 Nukuhiva
Source: Greg Dening

As we moved along the south coast, I began to recognise bays. Taipivai came first. Taipivai was the valley which Herman Melville experienced as *'Typee'*. He had run with Tobias Greene from the *Acushnet* in July 1842 and made his three weeks beachcombing into a *Narrative of Four Months Residence Among the Natives of a Valley in the Marquesas Islands* (1846).

Typee was a brave book. It roused much anger for its immorality, but more because it challenged commonly held prejudices. Melville saw the beach as a tawdry place where nothing came across in beauty or fullness, where everything was a misanthropic, half-pointless, tattered remnant. He saw Enata in the rags of civilisation and saw the rags as a parable of the larger cultural dump the Land was becoming. To those who saw everything of civilisation as good and everything of savages evil, Melville's perception that the good could be evil and the evil good was uncomfortable. The reading public denounced it as deceiving fiction.

For me, it was a moment of tension to turn into the narrow entrance of Taiohae bay and to be engulfed by the massive caldera ridges all around. We were in some giant's maw, and there in front of us, like an uvula, was the small mound of Fort Collet.

Figure 2.12 Taiohae
Source: Greg Dening

For forces with cannon and artillery, Fort Collet was of strategic importance in the bay. It commanded every part of the valley. Fort Collet was its French name. Lt David Porter USN had called it Fort Madison in 1814. Porter had entered the Pacific in the *Essex* in order to harass British whalers in the War of 1812. Within months he brought a ragged fleet of captured vessels turned into prison ships to Taiohae. He set up a town called Madisonville on the shores of the bay. Three hundred strangers in such a small space inevitably strained resources to the limit. Porter was dragged into the politics of the island to get his supplies. When the Taipi (Melville's 'Typee'), the enemy of the Teii people of Taiohae, refused to cooperate – indeed when the Taipi standing on the ridges above Madisonville 'mooned' Porter's marines and claimed that 'the Americans were the posteriors to the Teii's privates' – Porter chose to see the action as an affront against the American flag.

An unsuccessful punitive raid only made things worse. Porter staged a 'search and destroy' rampage through the whole valley of Taipivai. He was vague on the 'body count', but intimated that it was large. Enata, he decided, had a 'republican spirit'. 'They had requested to be admitted into the great American family whose pure republican polity approaches so near their own.' Porter took it upon himself to admit them to the United States and to assure them that 'our chief will be their chief'. The 'chief', President James Madison, was not so enthusiastic and was reported as saying that he had enough Indians of his own already. So the USA's first excursion into empire was snuffed.

We landed at the jetty near Fort Collet. There was a great crowd on the jetty to welcome, not us, but a third passenger on our landing craft who was coming to inspect the mission schools. He kindly introduced us to the bishop. Recognition is not something I have come to expect, not then, not now. So let me record, not for the boast of it, but for the pleasure of it, that the bishop when he heard my name said: 'Not the Greg Dening.' *Edward Robarts* had come before me.

We ended that remarkable day on the porch of the accommodation provided for us. It looked out over the calm of the bay and through the narrow entrance to open seas stirred by the trades and the south wind. I was surprised that throughout Te Henua sight of the sea was always so blinkered. It meant that a ship or boat or canoe came suddenly into sight. Whatever the purposes of strangers, whether they came 'from beyond the horizon' or more nearly from another island, first sight of them would always hold a moment's apprehension.

At the water's edge before us were the ruins of a stone house platform. I knew immediately that it was Butahaie's, a powerful woman of Robarts' and Crook's days. With her range of *pekio*, or secondary husbands, with the network of the marriages of her children, with her many properties, she was a formidable force at Taiohae and through the whole island. There can be no ethnography of Enata, no story of how they managed rules and reality without Butahaie. She only has a life, though, in the writings of the beaches of Robarts and Crook.

Our nearest neighbours were the dead. 'Royal tombs' nestled in the knoll beside us. We were settled on the lands of 'kings' and 'queens'. When Admiral Dupetit-Thouars left Vaitahu, he came to Taiohae. He came with seventeen hundred sailors and four hundred soldiers. Where David Porter built Madisonville, Dupetit-Thouars built Saumerville. The troubles the French had experienced at Tahuata spurred them on to build their town and fort quickly. They made space, near where we were staying, for a 'palace' for the 'king', Temoana.

Temoana's name meant 'The Immense Sea'. His life had been a pilgrimage across many oceans. He had been to New Zealand and Sydney. He had even visited Napoleon's tomb at St Helena. London had been his shame. In later years drink would make him remember with rage the exhibitions his tattoos made and the curiosity he became. By 1845 with the aid of the French he had built a cottage by the sea. It had a flagstaff and *tricolore* outside. Inside, he began to fill it with stools, bedsteads, spy glasses, fowling pieces and empty champagne bottles. The French bought their land from him for a pittance and paid him off with a pension. They made liquor available to anyone among Enata who wanted it.

Inevitably, some Enata, seeing the destruction of their way of life, distanced themselves from Temoana. One of them was a *haka'iki* who had made his way up from the lower *kikino* classes. Pakoko was his name. The valley of Taiohae was divided. The French found themselves confronted by what seemed to be a cultural revival of Enata ways led by Pakoko. They saw in this signs of resistance to their order. There were jailings and other punishments. Then six soldiers wandered where they were forbidden to go, near a *tohua* or ceremonial dancing and feasting ground. Pakoko's men surrounded them, killed them, and took them off like a catch of 'fish' to the sacrificial altars. The French retaliated with mortar and artillery and burned down all they could reach. They sent an expeditionary force over the passes towards Taipivai looking for Pakoko. The memory of Porter's 'search and destroy' thirty years before was still strong among the Taipi. Pakoko surrendered to save his people's property and lives.

The French commander, Lt Amalric, created a courtmartial with punctilious legal formalities, none of them valid as it turned out. Pakoko was found guilty and condemned to death. He was given a choice of a hanging or a firing squad, and chose to be shot. They marched him to a ditch behind a blockhouse on a knoll against the mountain. Hundreds of his people stood on the ridges around and looked down at his killing. Pakoko refused, the French said, a bandage around his eyes. He stood erect and proud, his long white beard flowing over a chest covered with tattoos, his *haka'iki* fan in his hand. He indicated to his judges – or so they said – that it was proper for him to die. Executioners are always eager for these sorts of submissions.

When they had killed him, his people on the ridges wailed. The women danced naked and tore at their skins until cannon fire drove them away. For years afterwards, Enata when they were drunk would turn to the French and say: 'You have killed Pakoko'.

A strange thing. The French killed Pakoko at 3.00 p.m. on Good Friday.

Just two days before Pakoko's killing there had been another killing. In these days Enata were dying in their hundreds because of dysentry and other mysterious diseases. Having no explanations, Enata turned to their mythic understanding of how it happened and looked to a sorcerer, Oko, as its cause. Lt Amalric, to soften the pain of Pakoko's killing, had Oko taken unceremoniously to a place on the mountains where all the people could be observers. He had him killed with a pistol shot to the head.

Amalric lost his command for this improper death. He even lost the Legion of Honour that he had won for capturing Pakoko.

We made a pilgrimage to the mountains where Pakoko died. We inspected the ruins of the penal settlement for political prisoners that the Land for a time had become. We saw the foundations of a cathedral that was never built. I worked in the archives and small museum of the mission. I confess that the archives were a more comfortable beach for me. I should have known that the dead are easier to talk to than the living.

Re-thinking history

Re-thinking history presents no problem to me. I have re-thought history all my life. Discourse is a changing thing. A sentence in any conversation is shaped by the sentences that have gone before and shapes the sentences that come after. For forty years I have tried to write cross-cultural history. Names for what I do have come and gone. 'Ethnohistory', 'culture-contact', 'zero-point history' – the names come and go as their usage discovers their limitations. I suppose that what has never changed – at least in my own understanding of myself – has been the resolve not to treat either side of a cultural encounter differently. I cannot cope with an anthropology of natives and a history of strangers. I have ambitions to do an anthro-history of them both. I have a passionate belief as well that I am a story-teller. Story is my theatre. Story is my art. I have two ambitions as a story-teller. The one is that my readers enjoy what Susan Sontag and Roland Barthes might have called the erotics of reading, the sensation that what they are reading of mine is what they were themselves about to say. The other ambition is to liberate my readers, to let them go where I have never been. I have never been possessive of either my students or my readers. I fulfil my ambitions by making theatre of my history. My readers will never learn the meaning of my stories by my telling them what those meanings are. My readers must be theatre critics of my stories. They must go out into the theatre foyer and argue what they mean. Out of all the trivialities of my story, out of all the reality effects with which I pepper it, out of its thousands of words, my readers must reduce it to a sentence or two and say what it means. With a little craft, it will be what I had in mind. Theory will never add to the realism of my theatre. Reflection will.

A note on beachcombing texts

Edward Robarts spent seven years in Te Henua. He deserted from the whaler *New Euphrates* at Vaitahu in December 1798. He found in a deserted hut a Bible, some letters and a journal that mystified him. He realised that they had belonged to a pious young man, William Pascoe Crook. But he did not know what had become of him. Actually, Crook was picked up by the same *New Euphrates* at Nukuhiva and taken back to England. He had been landed at Vaitahu by the mission ship *Duff* in July 1797. His missionary companion had refused to stay but Crook agreed to remain alone. Harsh circumstances forced him to move to Nukuhiva. Joseph Kabris deserted from the *London* some time in 1799. He was a fierce rival to Robarts.

Crook's story was publicised in the official history of the voyage of the *Duff* (Wilson 1799), but his 'Account of the Marquesas Islands' and 'Dictionary and Grammar of the Marquesan Language, written with the aid of Dr Samuel Greethead and Temouteitei', has remained in manuscript form in the Mitchell Library, Sydney, NSW. The bicentenary of these events will see its publication in French and English in 1998 (Crook 1998). Robarts journal, the property of the National Library of Scotland, was published in 1974 (Dening 1974). One version of Joseph Kabris' pamphlet is available in translation together with a detailed account of his life in Terrell (1982).

Dening (1980) contextualises these writings of the beach in an anthrohistory of Te Henua. Thomas (1990) applies them towards an anthropology of Enata.

Herbert (1980) provides a literary critique of Euroamerican writings on the beach of Te Henua.

Most of the history we write is a vicarious experience of the past. In writing history, we are really re-writing somebody else's histories. These other histories – as raw as a birth certificate, as latent as a ship's log, as full as an intimate diary – each has its own narrative forms and is subject to our critical reading. To see what these eyes on the beach saw, we need a sense of the cultural filters through which they caught a glimpse of otherness. The value of Crook's, Robarts' and Kabris' writings of the beach lie not so much in their formal descriptions of Te Henua as in their accounts of daily occurrences – conflicts, feasts, births, deaths, wars, voyages. The formal descriptions are subject to templates of all sorts. The narratives of their personal experiences give some slight entry into the way in which cultural living actually occurred.

The eye and its gaze have become an object of analysis in cross-cultural research these past twenty-five years. Not just in cross-cultural research, of course. In gender studies, in art history, in museum studies, wherever the product of the gaze is a representation of some sort, wherever the gaze is more than focused vision and is a social relationship as well, an empowering or disempowering force.

I don't think the eyes have it altogether, however. I think they sometimes see things they did not expect to see. I think we can sometimes see through them to something else. I do not think we live forever in a hall of crazy mirrors.

References

Crook, William Pascoe (1998) *An Account of the Marquesas Islands*, Papeete: Haere Po Tahiti.

Dening, Greg (1974) *The Marquesan Journal of Edward Robarts*, Canberra: ANU Press.

Dening, Greg (1980) *Islands and Beaches: Discourse on a Silent Land, Marquesas 1774–1880*, Melbourne: Melbourne University Press.

Herbert, T. Walter (1980) *Marquesan Encounters: Melville and the Meaning of Civilisation*, Cambridge, MA: Harvard University Press.

Radiguet, Max (1929) *Les Derniers Sauvages*, Paris: Duchartre et Van Buggenhoudt.

Steiner, Wendy (1997) *The Scandal of Pleasure*, Chicago, IL: University of Chicago Press.

Terrell, Jennifer (1982) 'Joseph Kabris and his notes on the Marquesas', *Journal of Pacific History* 17: 101–12.

Thomas, Nicholas (1990) *Marquesan Societies: Inequality and Political Transformations in Eastern Polynesia*, Oxford: Clarendon Press.

Von Langsdorff, G. H. (1813) *Voyages and Travels in Various Parts of the World*, vol. I, London: Henry Colburn.

Wilson, James (1799) *A Missionary Voyage to the Southern Pacific Ocean, 1796–1798*, London: T. Chapman.

AFTERWORD

Fifty years ago I made a discovery that changed my life. I discovered that I wanted to write the history of the 'other side of the beach', of indigenous island peoples with whom I had no cultural bond, of Natives. And on 'this side of the beach', my side as an outsider, as Stranger, I wanted to write the history of people whom the world would esteem as 'little'. I wanted to write history from below. Not of kings and queens. Not of heroes. Not of writers of constitutions, saviours of nations. 'Little people'. Those on whom the forces of the world press most hardly. I wanted to celebrate their humanity, their freedoms, their creativity, the ways they crossed the boundaries around their lives, the ways they crossed their beaches. These peoples on both sides of the beach were to be my Natives, my Strangers.

Fifty years ago, it was not fashionable to have an interest either in the other, native, side of the beach or in the 'little people' on this side. When I told my professor that I needed to give myself the anthropological skills to read into this otherness of the Native and to hear the silences of the Stranger in this sort of history, he said: 'Dening, this is the end of your academic career.' It was impolitic for me, he was saying, to turn my interests to things on which society, culture and university put so little store.

It was impolitic. Sad to say, it is probably still impolitic fifty years on. Happily for me, I did not need to be politic. The course of my life was set. I belonged to a religious order of priests, the Society of Jesus – the Jesuits – who put a supreme value on learning for its own sake. I did not need an academic job or even scholarship support, although I had and was to have both. For twenty years the Jesuits gave me freedom to be engaged utterly and altruistically in learning. That is the true privilege in my life.

Our mentor at the University of Melbourne in the 1950s was a young lecturer just returned from taking his archaeology degree at Cambridge University. John Mulvaney was his name. He became the founder of modern Australian archaeology in the decades to follow. He introduced us to something we called Pacific prehistory. We thought we were inventing Pacific prehistory. It wasn't archaeology. It wasn't history. It spanned that marginal space between the Time Before and the Time After of the encounter of Euroamerican cultures with the first peoples of Australasia and Oceania. We peered into the deep time of non-literate societies through the eyes of men – only men – cultured in gender, science, art, language, religion of something we called 'the Eighteenth Century'. We soon learned that we would have to re-think what we thought of as 'history'. Not that we were estranged from the history we learnt. We were engrossed with R. G. Collingwood and his autobiography. Marc Bloch awaiting execution by the Nazis thrilled us with *The Historian's Craft*. R. H. Tawney's social humanism born of his experiences in the trenches of the First World War stirred our idealism. Max Weber's brilliant insight into religion and capitalism taught us that irony was history's principal trope. Lawrence Stone and H. R. Trevor-Roper swatting at one another over the rise and fall of the gentry drilled us in the adversarial mode.

We were not estranged from our history but we needed to enlarge its scope. We had a scorn for the anthropologists in our field. 'Anthropology with the Coca-Cola bottles left out', we used to call their work. They had an ethnographic present that never was because they were not prepared to do the hard work in archives to see how cultures are changed in the memory of them.

It was an exciting time in Pacific studies. Thor Heyerdahl had completed his Kontiki raft and was turning to the archaeology of Easter Island – Rapanui we would call it now in signal of our re-thinking. A curmudgeon of a scholar, Andrew Sharp, had just written *Ancient Voyagers of the Pacific* denying that the Polynesians had peopled their islands by deliberate voyaging as their myths told them, but by accident. We thought both Heyerdahl and Sharp were wrong. We chased them down with a fierce puritanical intellectualism. Our history became full of lateral pursuits. It became botany, genetics, linguistics, archaeology, mythology, oceanography as we tried to discover other measures of time and change. For me there was a cathartic moment in the great domed Victorian State Public Library as I read Harold Gatty's *The Raft Book*, a pamphlet written for downed airmen in the Second World War in which he described what he had learned from Pacific islanders on how to make a landfall from the reflection of lagoons in clouds, the shadows islands make in the swells, the birds that fly home at evening. It was cathartic for me because I realised that a puritanical methodology in my historical method would not resolve my problems. I needed more trust in the human capacity to reach back into their own past.

3 Reconditioning history

Adapting knowledge from the past into realities of the present

Marie Theresa Hernández

San Isidro Cemetery

> It is on the plane of the daydream and not on that of facts that childhood remains alive and poetically useful within us. Through this permanent childhood, we maintain the poetry of the past. To inhabit oneirically the house we were born in means more than to inhabit it in memory; it means living in this house that is gone, the way we used to dream it.
>
> (Bachelard, 1964: 16)[1]

There is a womb-like feeling evoked by certain spaces. On a Saturday morning in September, 1997, I entered such a space. It felt profoundly nostalgic and intensely familiar. This place I entered often as a child is named San Isidro Cemetery. Approximately 140 years old, it is located 20 miles southwest of downtown Houston.

It had been at least ten years since I had visited San Isidro. The last time I was there, a funeral procession walked across the bridge, since it no longer supported the weight of the automobiles. People parked their cars next to the tennis court across the creek. I remembered, the cemetery was across Oyster Creek. People would cross the creek on an old wooden bridge which had low wooden rails. Then there was a narrow path, just wide enough for one car, which ran between gigantic pecan trees. This led to an arched sign of large wrought iron letters announcing the name of the cemetery. Entering First Colony again in 1997, I was fairly sure the landmarks had remained the same. My father told me some years before that the bridge was gone. Distinctly remembering my regular trips through Sugar Land, I drove through the subdivision certain I would find San Isidro. I found myself at a dead-end road next to the tennis court facing Oyster Creek. As I had remembered, the cemetery was across Oyster Creek. People would cross the creek on an old wooden bridge which had no rails.

Disconcertingly, I saw no sign, no evidence of a cemetery. I stepped out of the car and walked towards the creek. There was a blonde mother with a toddler sitting on the grass. Nearby was an Asian woman in her sixties practicing Tai Chi. I looked across the water and saw more trees, and large homes with decks. I questioned my memory. Had I gone the wrong way, made the wrong turn? Was it a different exit off the freeway?

I then drove to a nearby fire station and asked about the cemetery. The EMT told me there was no cemetery in the neighborhood. He had lived there ten years. He had never seen one. How could he attend persons in the neighborhood who were in crisis and not know this? Did it still exist? Eventually I called my father who insisted the street leading to the cemetery was called Snearles and that I was right around the corner. Later when I was driving down Searles (without the "n") I thought about the EMT and myself not knowing where this space was. To me it seemed to have evaporated. To the EMT, it had never existed. Yet the street without the "n" in the name did lead me to the cemetery. It was in the middle of the subdivision, with a large fence on one side and Oyster Creek on the other.

At the gate of the cemetery is a wrought iron door locked with a combination. A Mexican American man, Mr. Belasco, about 70 years old, is sitting in his van, waiting for someone to come by and open the gate. I call my father again, who says the combination is 2323, 3434 or 4545. None of these numbers work. A few minutes later, an older man and his son arrive. This is Mr. Zamora. He is 86 years old. He looks through his wallet for about 15 minutes and finds a scrap of paper with the number. He works on the lock another five minutes and is able to let us in. The numbers are 2323, the lock needs to have the numbers almost into the next digits to open. Mr. Zamora raises his hand into the air holding the lock. I think to myself: The cemetery is not clearly visible to local people, the combination is only known to a few, and a very few know that the lock has a "trick" to it.

The fence surrounding the cemetery is expensive. It is wooden, about eight feet tall and every 15 feet there is a square brick column. When I first saw it I thought it was the back yard fence to one of the big houses. The entrance we use is new and actually brings us to the back of the cemetery.

The wrought iron gate serves as an entrance point to a space in my memory and that of Mr. Zamora and his son. The place feels enclosed; by the fence, by the creek on the other side, by the very large pecan trees that drape the sky over the cemetery. It feels protected, separated, and hidden, reminiscent of the enclosed space of a home. In my mind, San Isidro creates the image of a body, warm, covered, protective. It is covered with memories and spirits, dreams, realized and unrealized. It is interwoven with my childhood memories and my imagination connected to when I would accompany my father on his frequent trips to the cemetery. The inner spaces of these enclosed areas are secrets, only told to those initiated: Mr. Zamora, the undertaker, those who have been intimately connected to the space for a long time.

Once inside this protective space, I feel as if I have entered a memory. The textures are sensuous and multi-layered. The trees are gigantic, and their green pecans are all over the grounds. There are ancient gravestones and modern ones, and graves covered with artificial flowers, ribbons and toys. The land is bumpy, perhaps suggesting graves that are no longer marked. The rows are somewhat uneven. The gravestones remaining have their own individuality. There is a tall (twenty foot) statue of Christ near the original entrance, which is crowned by a string of letters reading "Cementerio San Isidro." Also near the statue is a metal canopy. The original dates to 1950. Under this canopy, even in 1998, the casket is laid to rest briefly, before it is taken to the open grave. Throughout the cemetery are small shrubs, frequently surrounded by natural or artificial flowers. It is a small space, maybe not more than three acres. Yet inside is contained more than can be described in this essay.

Cy Keary, King Ranch liaison man noted . . . that "we hire about ten percent of the employees and raise the rest."[2]

San Isidro Cemetery, which is the subject of this essay, is located on five acres of land in Sugar Land, Texas, fifteen miles southwest of downtown Houston. Before the city grew around it, San Isidro was located in fields owned by the Imperial Sugar Company, in an area three miles from town. Already, at the beginning of the twentieth century, the tall pecan trees covering the cemetery were bearing fruit. The area was well shaded, green and lush, often over-grown with reed grass. Oyster Creek ran between the cemetery and the company's "Mexican" encampment, *Gran Centro*. The creek brushed the edge of the cemetery. The water was always (and still is) high, even in times of drought.

The cemetery was originally intended for laborers working for Imperial Sugar in the early part of the twentieth century. Since the company originally used some prison labor,[3] there is a section for prisoners that is no longer in use or maintained. There is another section for African Americans that is owned by a local church. The largest section is that of the Mexican laborers whose descendants visit often and tend the graves.

San Isidro was established as part of a concerted effort by the Kempner family (Galveston residents, owners of Imperial Sugar) to improve the Sugar Land community. After purchasing control of the sugar refinery in 1905, the Kempners pursued their existing investments in Sugar Land with the idea of creating a "company culture." Sugar Land Industries controlled where people lived, very clearly delineating the neighborhoods in which different ethnic groups resided, where churches were built, where merchandise was sold (by redeeming coupons, instead of using money) and where people were buried. I. H. Kempner, present Chairman of Imperial Holly (their official name in 1998) says that his family believed if the workers were treated well, provided for, and given respect, they would be more productive. The family's intent was to create an environment where people had the desire and ability to be work efficiently.

Bill Thomas, an African American who was hired as a refinery laborer in 1934, tells me that everything in Sugar Land was about work. No man was allowed to stay there if he did not work. It was the most important ethic of the town's culture. Even the purchase of a car was connected specifically to work. If a person wanted a car, the company bought it in Houston and delivered it to the employee. It was not paid for with money or coupons. It was paid with labor, time. If a man purchased a car and missed a day of work (even if it was for serious illness), the company did not allow the worker to drive the car the day he missed work. There were also heavy sanctions should an employee buy merchandise at a "regular" store; if he was found out he would automatically be fired.[4]

Most workers said the company was understanding and lenient as long as the worker was "loyal," Harold Hyman in his book on the Kempners, writes that Sugar Land was an exception to the corrupt "company town." He was aware of the strong sense of civic responsibility which the Kempner descendants carried into their industrial operations and most likely was aware that other companies provided substandard housing and inadequate food for their employees. Workers were given more than the necessary provisions. Even the caskets for their dead were given by the company. Yet as Hyman writes of the "unsalubrious residents" of "Mexico" town, which was a squatter community near Sugar Land, the reader is left wondering about Hyman's perspective regarding the treatment of "Mexicans." Was the indiscriminate destruction of their "flimsy" homes part of that "civic responsibility?"[5]

Ruth Matthew, an African American who began working for the company as a refinery laborer in 1932, tells me his best friends were Mexican laborers who worked the night shift with him, dumping raw sugar cane into the grinder. Four hundred pound sacks. When Ike Kempner hired Matthew he said: "You are such a little thing, sure you can carry these sacks?" Matthew was only 16 and had not yet grown his full stature, but he needed the work to support his sister. He wanted to return to his home forty miles away, in Eagle Lake, primarily because there had been some violence a few months before Ruth left town. Johnnie Pratt had been shot and killed, then dragged behind a car. Those who killed Johnnie hung his body for four days on a tree just outside of Eagle Lake. Matthew said this was because Johnny was at the wrong place at the wrong time; Pratt was mowing a white man's lawn, the man's wife accused Johnnie of being sexually suggestive to her, just as her husband was returning home.

This type of violence seldom occurred in Sugar Land. The rules were clear inside of the town. They may not have been equitable, but they were consistent. The rules were confusing and dangerous once a person left the Sugar Land property. Mrs. Catarina Arizpe (who was born in Sugar Land) reminds me of a particular incident. She says, "Things were still difficult, but it was that way everywhere, remember what happened to Macario Garcia at the Richmond Drive-In?" Garcia won the Congressional Medal of Honor in World War II. He had recently returned home to Sugar Land and attempted to order food at a restaurant in Richmond (fifteen miles away from Sugar Land). Denied service, he became so angry he destroyed the place. He was arrested, but the media caught hold of the story. Walter Winchell described the town as the "sorriest place in the United States."

Twenty-five years after Garcia destroyed the Richmond Drive-In, two developers bought land from Sugar Land Industries with plans to build the Sugar Creek Subdivision, an exclusive area for residents with six figure incomes.[6]

Just north of Oyster Creek the subdivision encircles San Isidro Cemetery. Realtors told buyers that the cemetery was not "active." Others were told there were only ten to twelve funerals per year. Eunice Collier,[7] whose family purchased a home bordering the cemetery in 1984, had "absolutely no idea" the cemetery was active when the contract to her new home was signed.

Sugar Creek construction bounded San Isidro on two sides by large homes, on a third side by Sugar Creek Blvd. leaving as the fourth boundary Oyster Creek. A wooden bridge connected the cemetery to what had been *Gran Centro* but was now First Colony. The cemetery continued to be used.

I. H. Kempner remembers visiting San Isidro in 1972 with Robert Armstrong, the president of the company. The two and a half acres were already surrounded by new development. *Gran Centro* was gone. Sugar Land Industries had divested itself of most of its additional acreage and real estate. He wondered what the company was doing with a cemetery. (Kempner tells me he thought the part that was "not kept up" was the Mexican part. After we discussed the positioning of that section, he realized he was speaking of the graves of the prisoners, which date before 1912.) After the 1972 visit, he wrote out a Quit Claim Deed, giving the property to the Catholic Diocese of Galveston-Houston. Two years later it was turned over to the new San Isidro Cemetery Association, a coalition of descendants of Mexican employees of Imperial Sugar.[8]

There were no significant problems for over ten years, until the bridge began to deteriorate. The trucks carrying construction materials for the new homes in Sugar Creek had overburdened the bridge. In researching what action to do, the Cemetery Association found it belonged to "no one." The city of Sugar Land did not claim it, the county did not claim it, and neither Sugar Creek nor First Colony claimed it. In 1993, the bridge was condemned by the Army Corps of Engineers. Wanting to avoid a conflict, the San Isidro group contracted with an engineer for an estimate of expenses. A new bridge would cost over $150,000 plus ongoing maintenance. Sugar Creek Homeowners offered San Isidro $25,000, the Kempners offered $5,000. The priest supporting San Isidro encouraged the cemetery group to consider a less expensive option, which was to create an entrance through Sugar Creek Blvd.

The homeowners were strongly against the new gate. Twenty years before, the developers had placed a three-foot "green belt" between the western edge of the cemetery and the boulevard. Creating a "gate" across the green belt would in effect make the Cemetery Association into trespassers. Gary Stanford, spokesman for the homeowners association, said the decision to build a gate opening San Isidro to the center of Sugar Creek felt like a betrayal. Residents always assumed people would enter from the bridge.

In March, 1994, the two groups entered litigation. The San Isidro group filed a restraining order against Sugar Creek, so that the association could build the gate. Terri Rodriguez, a member of the Cemetery Association and secretary of St. Theresa's Church had just been told that the Diocese could not assist the Cemetery Association because of "conflict of interest." The San Isidro group only had one day to find an attorney to represent them. Rodriguez heard about attorney John Burchfield, that his specialty was real estate. She contacted him and when he heard the story he was "so moved" that he wanted to represent San Isidro for free. They never actually went to court. A series of hearings in 1994 led to the use of a mediator, an associate of Sugar Creek resident, attorney John Collier. San Isidro won the right to a gate opening to Sugar Creek Blvd, allowing traffic through the subdivision, into the cemetery. The gate to the boulevard was constructed in 1995. The bridge which had been condemned was eventually removed. It was never rebuilt.

It has been four years since the hearing. Even though San Isidro was successful in obtaining the gate, Burchfield is bitter. He tells me that everyone abandoned the cemetery association; the Kempners, the homeowners, the city, the county. Burchfield was not cooperative, would not see me in person, was rather caustic during our telephone conversation, saying he was really too busy to talk. Yet he spoke for over thirty minutes, seeming eager to give me information, except the location of the transcripts of the hearings, about which he was evasive. In listening to Burchfield and his complaints I wondered what side he was really on. Johnny de la Cruz (the president of the Cemetery Association) had described Burchfield as a great lawyer who was totally committed to San Isidro. Wanting to respect Johnny's opinion of the attorney I decided not to pursue the basis of Burchfield's intentions and attitude.

In March of 1997, the San Isidro group decided to build a restroom on the property. There had recently been a funeral service in which a handicapped person (a relative of the deceased) needed to use a restroom. Because of this, the service was delayed thirty minutes while family members took the person to a nearby gasoline station. Considering future instances of this need, in addition to the long hours association members spend at the cemetery during "clean up days," the group considered the building of a restroom a necessity.

The problems began when the plumbing lines were dug to connect the restroom to the city sewer line. According to Johnny de la Cruz, the person who was digging the line was accosted by a Sugar Creek resident who threatened the worker with a shotgun. Gary Stanford said the problem may have been that de la Cruz did not remind the homeowner of the impending construction. Burchfield said the homeowner's violent reaction was because the lines had to be dug inside her yard, in what is termed "city easement." Shrubs she had planted in her back yard had to be removed. She supposedly was not aware in advance of this pending work and was surprised to find a man in her back yard taking out her shrubs. Burchfield termed the restroom "an outhouse," claiming it was an attempt by the San Isidro people to punish the Sugar Creek home-owners for their reaction to the cemetery's request for a different entrance. He indicated that it was an angry and unreasonable response to previous conflicts. His own angry response during our conversation was in direct contra-diction to his earlier enthusiasm for the cause of San Isidro. The construction was ultimately completed and the plumbing lines were connected through another resident's property without further conflict. The restroom is now used regularly by San Isidro members. It has a composition roof and is a small, neat building inside the space of the cemetery.

Narratives, stories, *cuentos*

> Just where one ventures in the country of the past sometimes depends on where one has ventured before.
>
> (Basso, 1996: 3)

In 1939, Ike Kempner, the owner of Imperial Sugar, told Cosme Galvan that the following morning Kempner would visit the cemetery. Galvan was in charge of San Isidro. He was concerned, the grass was too high. The owner would think Galvan had not been taking care of the cemetery and would want to take the land away. The night before the patron was to arrive, Galvan decided to burn the grass. He forgot that the markers of the graves were all wooden crosses, including the cross marking the grave of his own son, Isaac who had died the same year.[9]

Since then, San Isidro has gone through various stages. Before 1950, there was no one to formally prepare the dead. The company store provided wooden caskets. The families themselves would bring their dead to San Isidro and lay them under the canopy near the entrance. They would ice down the caskets and have their wakes, outside, in the space of San Isidro. They made new markers for those graves they could remember, concrete ones that would not burn. Eleven years after Galvan burned the cemetery a funeral home began to prepare the dead and give them formal burials.

A few years later I began to visit the place, as a small child accompanying the funeral director, my father, José F. Hernández, on funerals, listening to his stories as he drove the hearse along Highway 90 to Sugar Land.

> At the cemetery the experience of alterity is not tamed by figuration—by the appearance, even threatening, of a face.
>
> (Pandolfo, 1997: 238, 239)

People took pictures of the dead who are buried at San Isidro. They sealed other photographs inside ceramic cases on the headstones. They look at death as a quotidian thing. Funerals were also parties. Wakes were fun, places to talk and see old friends and relatives. People were not afraid of the existence of death.

As they are at ease they also hold on. Decades later, when the future of San Isidro is in question, the same people I saw at the wakes are desperate to protect the space of their dead. It is as if there is no separation between the dead and the living. The dead belong to the lives of those *Mexicanos* remaining in and near Sugar Land. The spaces of the dead hold the memory and foundation of their lives. They hold the memory of Kempner coming to see a burnt-out cemetery, of people dying of sunstroke in the fields, of people drowning in Oyster Creek, of crossing the wooden bridge decade after decade.

When the face of death is placed behind the boundaries of life, the space of San Isidro becomes a home of sorts. It has water, a place to prepare food, a place to sit, shade to stay out of the hot sun and a restroom for personal relief. The people of San Isidro have progressed through the test of legality. The land is theirs. They have now made it their own. Their image of a sacred space, which protects their dead, their memories, and their selves becomes their home in the imaginary, where they can sit in a chair, look across Oyster Creek, and imagine the old barracks of *Gran Centro*, the workmen and the children. They can again hear the voices, the singing in the evenings, after the men brought the mules and the plows back from the fields.

The issue of "the old home" is more than significant. In a country where most of their people had to move constantly to follow *la cosecha* (the harvest), the people of San Isidro made the cemetery and the community into a home that was fixed, permanent. The geography of their lives has been between their homes in Sugar Land and the cemetery. This fixed point of culture has provided a marker for their history. While their outer lives continue to change and alter with modernity, they have a concrete base that remains behind, providing all the necessities, providing the confidence and security of a history that remains alive.[10]

The flow of water in Oyster Creek passes by San Isidro Cemetery, the large homes of Sugar Creek Subdivision, and the First Colony suburban development. Years ago, the creek separated the fields of *Gran Centro* from the cemetery with a wooden bridge connecting the two. The creek seems to circle and entwine the town and the people. It divides neighborhoods, separates groups of people, distinguishes social classes. As it continuously passes through the space of Sugar Land and the entrance of San Isidro, it brings the constant change of modernity. It erases marks of the past and creates marks in the present. It washes away losses and tragedy, cleansing the space for the new work of technology and capitalism. There are no longer fields, there is no more *Gran Centro*. There is now the First Colony mall and thousands of new homes. The cemetery remains, yet only because of the stubborn insistence of those who could not forget.

It may be that in certain aspects they are polarized in relation to the new citizens who have formed their households on the land of *Gran Centro*. At a superficial level, the new people have attempted to form a group that is homogenous, with similar landscapes and narratives. Their desire for middle-class status and capitalistic comfort, their need for privacy and safety has become the agenda of their public community. The private is so exceedingly private that it has been nearly erased. Their stories, houses, and automobiles look the same. The similarities create a blank space of narrative, leaving the observer to assume all is well and all is the same. The imaginary cohesiveness of their suburban lives, focused on their spatialized community with its semblance of perfect order, may be misleading. In the similar homes, similar cars, and similar suburban activities, each individual has conceded a bit of his/her identity for the purpose of belonging to this orderly world.

The stubby, uncomfortable remnant of that otherwise erased history is the cemetery that Imperial Sugar allocated a century before. For those who have chosen to become part of the master-planned suburban community, San Isidro creates an impediment to forgetting. It is space in contradiction to modernity. It is a visible reminder of slavery and the convict labor that was used to work the fields. It is a striking place of memory, encompassed by a community which has chosen to forget.

The conflict may emanate from issues of racism and concerns of contamination (by the *other*). Although those opposed to the gate for San Isidro constantly deny a racial motive for the discord. In July, 1998, the homeowners association denied San Isidro's request for a sign to be put over the gate facing Sugar Creek Blvd. The sign would have been identical to the original (which still stood at the former entrance). It is a curious image, a cemetery that is hidden behind a ten-foot fence. Tightly held but not announced.

This wish to hold closely and secretly may be where the boundary between the opposing groups actually blurs. Hiding the cemetery may indicate shame for its existence within Sugar Creek, yet it also acts as a protection. Perhaps Sugar Creek wants to keep the cemetery inside itself. The escalation of conflict may indicate a paradox. It is conceivable that Sugar Creek desperately wants the cemetery, for its history and narrative may fill in the memories left empty by their master-planned suburban development.

> *Mira como ando mujer, por tu querer*
> *Borracho y apasionado nomas por tu amor*
> *Mira como ando mi bien, muy dado a la borrachera y la perdición*

> Look at how I am woman, because of your loving me
> Drunken and impassioned because of your love
> Look how I am, so given to drunkenness and destruction
> ("*Tu Solo Tu*," written by Felipe Valdez Leal)[11]

Just after my father arrived in Ft. Bend County he was hired by the local District Court to translate in a murder case. The defendant could not speak English. A man named Hylario Semershy had killed another man, Aniceto Sanchez. It happened on the land of Imperial Sugar, in *Gran Centro*, just outside one of the barracks.

My father's version of the story tells of a man who could sing. Hylario Semershy could play the guitar and had a good voice. In April, 1949, Semershy often sang "*Tu Solo Tu*." It was a popular song, telling of a lost love and a despondent lover. Although Semershy's name was Czech, he was Mexican. He sang in Spanish.

Hylario worked the fields of Imperial Sugar, as did Aniceto Sanchez. They used plows pulled by mules. They had no tractors at the time. People say the mules were big and fat, so strong, fed well by Imperial Sugar.

Hylario would return to the barracks before Aniceto. Their families lived in close proximity. Since it was still cool, someone built bonfires outside the barracks. There Hylario would sit and sing *"Tu Solo Tu."*

Aniceto Sanchez believed that Hylario was singing to Mrs. Sanchez. My father does not know how long Aniceto worried about this possibility, he only tells me that one night, upon returning from the field, Aniceto hears Hylario sing *"Tu Solo Tu."* Sanchez can't stand it anymore. He goes into his room and gets his shotgun. He kills Hylario Semershy.

The trial brought a number of people together. Sanchez obtained legal representation, probably the best available for someone in his position. His attorney was James De Anda. The two assistant attorneys were Arnulfo Azios and John J. Herrera. In later years, De Anda was appointed a federal judge, Azios a District Judge and Herrera became known and respected civil rights activist.

My father remembers sitting with Aniceto's attorneys in the same Richmond Drive-In which ousted Macario Garcia five years earlier. While having lunch they discussed the case, and wondered if indeed Mrs. Sanchez was involved with Semershy. Herrera jokingly responded by saying that she was too ugly, and anyway, how could she be attractive after having ten children? They decided to bring the ten children to court, hoping the judge's decision would be affected by the children's presence.

The final argument was that Sanchez believed his home and family had been threatened by Semershy. Sanchez had admitted to the murder from the time he was initially arrested. The question was regarding his position of having his "homelife threatened."

My father told me that Sanchez received a probated sentence. Yet the narrative now changes.

Recently I searched through court records. I found the murder occurred at midnight. There was talk of Semershy being found under the bed in Sanchez's room. Was Mrs. Sanchez involved after all? My father says that De Anda, Azios and Herrera probably made that up while searching for a motive of self-defense.

The records also indicate that Sanchez indeed served time in prison. Forty-six years later, when my students find the grave of Hylario Semershy at San Isidro Cemetery, Johnny de la Cruz tells us that Sanchez is still alive, living near Sugar Land.

There is testimony about "how a person can always tell when someone is Mexican," how people "speak Mexican," how De Anda sought a mistrial on the premise that Sanchez had an all-white jury. The history of discrimination towards Mexicans in Texas was documented in the request for appeal.

> The . . . appellant [Aniceto Sanchez], a Mexican, . . . lived on a large plantation . . . On the night of the tragedy, shortly after twelve o'clock, the deceased . . . came to the residence of the appellant . . . He [Hylario Semershy] was singing a song in Mexican which . . . is entitled "You, Only You" and is said to be a Mexican love song. Apparently this incensed

appellant who, without any words, went into his house, got his gun, came out and shot, killing the deceased . . . About this there is no controversy.[12]

The day after Christmas, 1997 is when I find the documents. Touching them, reading about the murder at midnight and the song, *"Tu Solo Tu"* created an uncanny feeling. I remembered how two months earlier, when I took my students to San Isidro, one of them found Semershy's grave. The letters engraved in the headstone had recently been painted with gold. Someone took care of Semershy's space. Was it his children? Was it his widow? Does Mrs. Sanchez (if she is still alive) ever think of that night in which he sang that love song and her husband thought it was for her?

Is there something else? This narrative resonates with something much deeper than a love song and a momentarily crazed farm laborer. I wonder, could someone standing at the edge of San Isidro Cemetery see where Semershy sang *"Tu Solo Tu"*? Was he singing for a woman or was he singing for himself? Had he entered desperation for having been seduced into living in southeast Texas? Did he have a choice? Did he know that only fifty miles away his life would have been worth even less?

How aware was Semershy of the "model community" developed by the Kempners and their partner Eldridge? People say that life at *Gran Centro* was much harder than at the refinery. Was Semershy singing of drunkenness and desperation a sign of his own despondency? Or was he only finding a logical means to assuage the pressure he faced regarding his work, the adequate maintenance of his family and his position as a person "in between," with a Czech name and a Mexican identity?

Those who remember, tell me there was little violence in Sugar Land. The murder of Hylario Semershy was an anomaly. Perhaps his was more of a sacrifice. In his singing, which soothed and comforted his anxiety, he may have betrayed a forbidden desire. The elimination of the singer restored order to *Gran Centro*. People learned not to sing to other men's wives. It was dangerous.

The memory of *"Tu Solo Tu"* and Hylario Semershy is located in the space of San Isidro. The sadness of *Gran Centro* has transposed itself into the confines of the cemetery. Because *Gran Centro* no longer exists, the traces of its memory need to locate themselves in some familiar place. It has been forty-nine years since Aniceto Sanchez killed Hylario Semershy. Time has diminished the intensity of this particular narrative. Yet the significance of its repository and the response of the surroundings at times retrieve the spirit of Hylario Semershy and the song he was singing when he died.

> the ghost haunting them could be haunted too.
>
> (Gordon, 1997: 175)

Lemons are used to heal and resolve conflicted situations in the folklore of Mexican Texas. They are used whole, rubbed on the "patient's" forehead; they are cut in half, placed in a bowl of water and covered with salt; they are

immersed intact in a large goblet of water; they are left in the glove compart-
ment of an automobile to reduce the risk of accident. People who make use
of the lemon's properties are not necessarily *curanderas* or *brujas* (witches). They
may be using the lemon simply as a folk remedy.

There is another way to use a lemon. I learned about this from Eunice Collier.
She lives in Sugar Creek. Her back yard borders San Isidro. Recently as she was
walking through the cemetery she found a lemon on a grave. It had been peeled,
having been re-constructed with pins to look whole. It looked fresh, most
probably had been peeled earlier that day. She dismantled the re-constructed
lemon and found a handwritten note inside. The woman writing the note was
asking for assistance in ridding her relationship of a ghost, which had been
appearing in her bedroom at night when the author of the note was sleeping
with her husband. The ghost was the same person in the grave. Eunice was
both fearful and enticed by her discovery. Wanting to avoid a conversation on
Mexicans and witchcraft, I did not ask Eunice how she interpreted her discovery
of the lemon and the note.

Eunice did say she was surprised to see the lemon, but realized that it was
one more aspect of the situation. After all, she says, "San Isidro *is* a cemetery."
Finding a peeled lemon on a grave is certainly exotic. Living next to a cemetery
is exotic. There is a hint of enjoyment in her relationship to San Isidro. In
her description of connection to San Isidro I get the sense that she feels a type
of ownership. She "likes" having the cemetery next door. She tells me of a small
child who is buried in San Isidro. His parents live in a foreign country and
are not able to visit the grave. She is affected by people coming and going to
the cemetery and has come to have some understanding for what it stands for.
Yet she appears ambivalent.

It was Mrs. Collier who repeatedly called the police department when she
saw adolescents in San Isidro after dark, having seen them engaging in sex and
using drugs on the cemetery grounds. A college student named Johnnel Paquin
tells me that he frequented San Isidro with his other friends, while in junior
high. He stopped going to the cemetery when a friend of his was shot at by
a homeowner. Johnnel's family are Filipino immigrants who settled in First
Colony over a decade ago. They would not have approved of Johnnel's clandes-
tine visits to San Isidro, yet he tells me that it was a rite of passage for most
of the adolescents in First Colony. Vivian Wu, a college student whose parents
live near the cemetery, recently told me that she remembers the conflict over
the bridge. She said it was the homeowners who did not want the Mexicans
driving their funeral processions through Sugar Creek. Most striking is
Sylvia Van Zegert, who also lived there several years and never knew San Isidro
existed.

Perhaps it was the aura of "ghostliness" that attracted the young people who
knew about the cemetery. Crossing the wooden bridge was similar to time
travel. In that tight space everything changed. There were no rules of behavior,
no controls. If a person from a funeral home came to leave equipment for an
upcoming funeral, the teenagers would help unload the truck.[13] There were no

confrontrations, except for those with Mrs. Collier whose daily vigilance of the cemetery irritated the local police. There was a lackadaisical attitude towards the adolescents using San Isidro for drugs and sex. The "problem" was only noted by Mrs. Collier. With some attempt of moderate objectivity, I wonder if the community actually wanted the young people to use the cemetery for their pleasures. There were no other complaints regarding their activities.

In her detailed descriptions of finding the adolescents having sex, I wondered about Mrs. Collier being a voyeur. Not only for the sex and drugs but for the other intensely emotional events that occur in San Isidro. Her ambivalence ranges from outrage over the new restroom to tearfulness over a child that is buried in the cemetery. Mrs. Collier shows herself as territorial, almost seeming as if she wants San Isidro to exist, but only for herself. Near the end of our conversation she reminds me of how often she wanders through the cemetery grounds.

Conclusion

The history of Sugar Land is based on the myth of a wild Texas. The places surrounding San Isidro and the people surrounding the Mexican Americans have an imaginary that faintly remembers the wildness of before. This dim memory is transposed to the fences, guards, solid borders and the space of the cemetery itself. What is no longer existent in the re-invented town of Sugar Land has been displaced into the shade of San Isidro. The strict order of the company town firmly encased a space to hold death, memories and losses. Within the space of death, the memories of identity remain with the uneven lines of graves and the pecan trees of unknown age. There inside lies the history of oppression and death, of overworked field hands and a war hero's unwanted return. San Isidro may also contain the rejected ethnic identity cleansed by suburbia, left to be held by those *Mexicanos* who refused to let go. It is likely that those who forgot their memories in order to live in such a suburban space, may also be tinged with envy towards Johnny de la Cruz and the others who withstood the gaze of the company town, yet moved with time and change.

Many who visit the cemetery describe an experience of being in a space that takes them back in time, and provides them with a visceral feeling of the past surrounded by the future. The Mexican American university students I have taken to San Isidro tell me the presence of San Isidro is similar to the vestiges of Mexican culture they feel within themselves. These traces are pressured and pushed by what is new.

San Isidro is similar to the re-constructed lemon peel. It contains narrative, stories of hauntings and a past which those in Sugar Creek may choose (or desire) to forget. As the lemon contains a communication with a ghost, so does San Isidro. Its presence, stubbornly resisting pressure to become stagnant or disappear, provides a space in which the living correspond with the dead. The San Isidro Association has made it a home, providing for all necessities, water, restroom, grill, benches. Although many Mexicanos in Texas were (in the last century) not able to protect their space from the aggressive encroachment of Anglo society, San Isidro has protected itself well.

The fences surrounding the cemetery are tall and impregnable. That is, all except one. It is a home with a wrought iron fence. While the metal stakes of the fence create a boundary between the land of San Isidro and the land of that home in Sugar Creek, the gaps in-between create a permeability. These gaps permit a visual interconnection. There is movement between the two spaces. Perhaps a type of inter-subjectivity is created as the Sugar Creek homeowners look between the black rods of their fence onto the uneven rows of graves, the occasional mourner or my father leading a funeral procession. Those on the "other" side may look back. The boundary that creates "the other" is transformed.

This permeable section of the boundary may allow some of the lost ghosts of Sugar Creek and First Colony to return. While the blanching process of suburbia may disavow their presence, the continuing stream of people and images may assist in relocating those memories that may have become confused. Those who are able to enter the boundary, either physically or visually, have the privilege of using the comforts of "the home space" to guide their memories back into place. Both sides benefit from San Isidro's presence.

> The text is born of a relation between departure and a debt.
>
> (de Certeau, 1988: 218)

As I complete this essay, I realize there are several convening images/imaginations that form this text. There is the image/imagination of Johnny de la Cruz, Mr. Zamora and the other members of the San Isidro Cemetery Association. There is my own past history, the little girl accompanying her father to this surreal space of death, my present as an anthropologist, writer, photographer, full of my own nostalgia for what may have been or what might happen now that the cemetery has been engulfed into the womb of the suburban landscape. There is also the image/imagination of the suburban homeowners living next to San Isidro, the image of the blonde woman with the small child on the other side of the creek. Does she see anything beyond the shrubs and small trees in front of her? Is she aware that there is another memory hidden behind the tall wooden fence with the brick pillars? Does the Asian woman practicing Tai Chi realize that there is also history across the creek, just as some of her own history remained across the ocean?

In my mind and memory, the perceptions of the past and present regarding San Isidro are strikingly vivid and transcendent. Is there a purpose in writing the stories of San Isidro? Will concretizing my imaginings into written form alter the story? I am not sure, because this history inside of my mind felt as intense and real before I wrote this essay. Only now it has traveled from that dreamlike space to these words and sentences which reify and concretize the images, if only for a moment.

Perhaps this writing erupts from a barely avoided misfortune. The jagged experience of almost losing the "ancestral land" leaves the obligation for the writer to narrate the story in a form that creates permanence.[14] Other ruptures— the dismantling of the "company town," the loss of tradition, and the intrusion of modernity—push and feed the story. The child who for fifteen years attended most of the funerals held at San Isidro has no father or mother buried there.

I could not be buried in San Isidro. Only the employees (or their spouses and descendants) of Imperial Sugar are allowed membership in the association and burial in the cemetery. Not having membership but having experienced the changing images as the cemetery passes through the end of this century has left enough of an obligation inside of myself to push the words together to form this text.

Acknowledgements

I am deeply indebted to my father, José F. Hernández, for his endless storytelling about south-east Texas and to George E. Marcus, for his incomparable advice and support as I wrote this chapter.

Notes

1 For an interesting view of history, memory and space, see *The Poetics of Space: The Classic Look at How We Experience Intimate Places*, Bachelard (1964).
2 David Montejano, in his book, *Anglos and Mexicans in Texas* (1987), quotes C. Keary (1953) "The King Ranch, 100 Years of Ranching", *Corpus Christi Caller-Times*.
3 In 1998, the Texas Department of Corrections has four prison units in the Sugar Land area. They are the Central, Jester Unit, Harlem I and Harlem II. Until 1914, TDC contracted the labor of the prisoners to Texas ranches.
4 Alfredo de la Cruz (Johnny's father), who worked for Sugar Land Industries forty years, reported in an October, 1997, interview that he ran the risk of being fired when he would drive to Richmond with his wife to buy clothes at a privately owned dry good store.
5 Harold Hyman wrote an idealistic description of the life and work of the Kempners. Although listing numerous examples of the inequities within the "company culture" of Imperial Sugar, he was supportive of the operation established by the Kempner family. Placing Hyman's writing in historical context, it portrays the Jim Crow perspective towards people of color common in the American south before the time of the civil rights movement. In *Oleander Odyssey*, Hyman writes of when the new foreman, Ulrich, who demolished "the noisome shanties of 'Mexico.'" This was done without "known complaints by the unsalubrious residents" (1990: 325).
6 The was initially populated by middle-class whites, although in the past ten years the Asian community has grown significantly (1997 population: 16.7 per cent Asian, 9.8 per cent Hispanic, 68.4 per cent White, 4.9 per cent Black). Yearly household income in 1997: median—$76,500, average—$106,000. College Degrees—30 per cent.

7 Eunice Collier is a pseudonym for a Sugar Creek resident. She is the wife of attorney John Collier.

8 There are several accounts telling that the deed had been lost and at some point found in the vault of the Catholic Diocese. Terri Rodriguez, Cemetery Association member and secretary of St. Theresa Church in Sugarland, says the deed was never lost. In fact she has a copy in her files which dates it to July 9, 1974, when the Diocese signed it over to the Cemetery Association.

9 There are various accounts of when the fire occurred. Initially I was told it was 1920. After further inquiry I found that Cosme Galvan's wife, Guadalupe, who is still living, has some recollection of the event. The Galvan's baby, Isaac, died the same year as the fire, but Mrs. Galvan was not sure of the exact date. She thought it might be 1939. She recalled that the baby's grave was lost after the crosses were burned, yet remembers that he was buried near the south boundary of the cemetery. After searching the death records of Ft. Bend County, I found that Isaac Galvan died on January 2, 1939, at the age of two months. Cause of death was pneumonia.

10 Gaston Bachelard writes in *The Poetics of Space* that there is a calm and confidence in the "old home." Transience takes away this comfort. This issue may be particularly important to the Mexicanos of the lack of home they had constantly encountered. For those that had immigrated from Mexico there was the loss of country, for those that were migrant laborers there was an ongoing "loss of home." The "defense" of San Isidro is a direct counter to these losses.

11 *"Tu Solo Tu"* written by Felipe Valdez Leal, has been sung in Mexico and the southwestern United States since the middle of the twentieth century. A famous recording in the 1950s was by Cuco Sanchez. It was re-recorded by Selena in 1994. In 1998 the version by Selena is still played frequently on "Tejano" radio stations that cater to Mexican American listeners.

12 Cited from Judge Beauchamp's response to Aniceto Sanchez' appeal.

13 My father tells me that while the bridge still existed whenever he entered the cemetery to leave equipment, the teenagers present would quietly help him unload. He wondered if the intent of their "helpfulness" was to get him out of their "space."

14 It is the loss of land that propels the appearance of the text. De Certeau writes that Jewish scripture became a replacement for the destruction of the Temple and loss of the land. The debt is that the writer is expected to maintain allegiance, the narrative confirms his/her loyalty.

References

Bachelard, Gaston (1964) *The Poetics of Space: The Classic Look at How We Experience Intimate Places*, trans. Maria Jolas, Boston: Beacon Press.

Basso, Keith (1996) *Wisdom Sits in Places: Landscape and Language Among the Western Apache*, Albuquerque, NM: University of New Mexico Press.

de Certeau, Michel (1988) *The Writing of History*, trans. T. Conley, New York: Columbia University Press.

Gordon, Avery (1997) *Ghostly Matters: Haunting and the Sociological Imagination*, Minneapolis: University of Minnesota Press.

Hyman, Harold. M. (1990) *Oleander Odyssey: The Kempners of Galveston, Texas, 1854–1980's*. College Station, TX: Texas A&M University Press.

Montejano, David (1987) *Anglos and Mexicans in the Making of Texas, 1836–1986.*
    Austin, TX: University of Texas Press.
Pandolfo, Stefania (1997) *Impasse of the Angels: Scenes from a Morrocan Space of Memory,*
    Chicago: University of Chicago Press.

Documents

Ft. Bend County, Texas, District Court. 23rd Judicial District. State of Texas vs.
    Aniceto Sanchez, Cause # 7103. 1951.
Fort Bend County Clerk. Death Records. January, 1939.
Fort Bend County Deed Records. Volume 627, Page 694, 1974.
Fort Bend County Chamber of Commerce/Claritas Inc. (1997) Demographic
    Comparison Report of Fort Bend County, 8 July.

AFTERWORD

The variability and innovation of "Reconditioning History" mirror its creation. The original work consisted of five shorter essays concerning the cemetery, written between fall 1996 and spring 1998, during my tenure as a graduate student in anthropology at Rice University.

The first essay was written as part of a proposal for a seminar taught by Professor George Marcus. It was only five pages long. We had been asked to write a proposal as creatively as possible. Being a photographer, the idea of visual images seemed interesting. I thought of images I still carried with me from having grown up in south-east Texas. Some of this came from reading Maurice Halbwach's work on memory. There were two images in my mind that seemed to never go away. That of a "family" dance hall that was said to be originally a "quasi" site of prostitution, the other was of an old cemetery. What made me think they could be interesting was that they seemed to just be on the boundary of everyday American life. These were Latino families, some recently immigrated, others American citizens for several generations. The dance hall and the cemetery were locales where people lived their lives. While not overloaded with tragedy as many narratives are when concerning people of color, the difficult experience of working for the "big boss" was not lost to the narrative, yet became integrated with other experiences of celebration and loss. My memory being stimulated by the writing, I decided to actually visit the cemetery again, for the first time in six years. By that time the proposal had been written and submitted to Marcus.

The next fall I commuted to the University of Texas to study with Professor Kathleen Stewart because I wanted to learn about her approach to poetics. Her suggestions to read Michel de Certeau, Gaston Bachelard and Susan Stewart pushed further at the images in my mind of the cemetery and the small Mexican community in Sugar Land, Texas. In one of the essays for her class I wrote a visual recollection of the cemetery, from that particular visit I had made that year and from my visits as a child. I began the essay with basically a step-by-step description of how I had searched for the cemetery in 1997, and the visual markings once I was inside the space.

The last three essays were written the following semester in an independent study with Dr. Marcus. He had me write a different paper every week. I would turn in a paper to him after reading three ethnographies he had assigned. Most of the reading concerned ethnography and folklore—work by Richard Price, Renato Rosaldo, Jean Favre Saada, Barbara Tedlock, Anna Tsing, among others. Using the ethnographies as a basis, I began to recount stories concerning the cemetery. Some were about the space itself, others were about people whose lives were connected with the community and Imperial Sugar. I joined the three together to present at a social history conference in Chicago. This was how they were first submitted to the journal.

After a discussion with editor Robert Rosenstone regarding publication of the essay, I, the author was convinced it needed something different, with a different type of movement, so to speak. Sections from the first and second essays were added, as others were deleted, creating the piece that was published in the fall 1999 issue of *Re-Thinking History*.

Intentions

The primary objective of the chapter was to present a historical narrative describing the cemetery and the Mexican community in Sugar Land. I wanted to see what "stories" people told about the cemetery. Archives and local newspapers were considered later in the process. Anthropological/historical texts on Mexican Americans lacked two aspects of study that I believed were significant. One was the "everyday," how people lived and how they remembered they lived. The second was the uneven, ambivalent nature of the relationships with their "bosses." I would not be presenting "a history" in the traditional sense. It was more a "history of narratives." I must credit Richard Price for his work in *The Convict and the Colonel* for this example (1998). His text, a self-reflexive style combining ethnography and history studied the trajectory of narratives in early twentieth-century Martinique.

The plan was to integrate varying aspects of the community that helped tell the story, using allegory as a vehicle. My frustrating search for the cemetery, told early in the chapter, was a physical representation of how the place had been hidden away, and how few people knew about it. Later in the chapter, the story of Hilario Semershy's murder presents everyday life when it confronts the second of violence. He was singing a popular Mexican ballad when a jealous husband shot him. The murder trial and resulting records gave salience to the limited power of the Mexicano laborer working for Imperial Sugar. The irony of desperation and limited freedom juxtaposed themselves against the story of a man set free after committing a murder. The place that so totally controlled its workers simultaneously condoned murder. The chapter speaks of total control, even regarding purchases. Yet, retired workers told me there was an "arrangement" between the company and the county court. If a good worker committed murder, he would be exonerated. There was a precedent to this. The company manager murdered five people before he came to work for Imperial Sugar in 1917 (Armstrong, 1991). The records of his trials disappeared from the county courthouse. The "lost" records were kept in the company's vaults (Ware, 1994). The juxtaposition of being murdered while singing a love song, with the murderer clearly admitting his culpability, yet later set free, lends a surreal quality to the story. The rules of everyday life, at least in this instance, were inverted.

An integral aspect of my argument is the unpredictability regarding (what we see as) the structure of society. What is assumed is not often what really "is." The powerful may also be weak. The disenfranchised also have power. Narratives are usually constructed to show accomplishments, acts of oppression, or noteworthy tragedy. Many of the narratives I found while working on this project, were repeated because they were "different"—their endings were unexpected. The ending of the chapter is also unexpected. It contains no actual conclusion, except that life was difficult, and people "made do." In certain instances, power could be turned upside down as in the case of the land dispute regarding the cemetery. Even so, it was an uneven victory, eliminating the possibility of pure redemption, which is a frequent conclusion in texts that are about oppression.

Re-membering

In the chapter, the writer's own memories of the people and the land go through four decades of transformation. The developmental view in the writer changes —as it travels from the eyes of a child, to an adolescent, to a nostalgic adult, to the (hopefully) critical eye of the ethnographer/historian. The story of San Isidro is re-assembled from multiple times, spaces, and voices.

Returning to San Isidro as an adult and speaking with the people associated with the cemetery was like going back and forth in time. Many of the people remembered me, more as a child than an adult. They also told me they remembered when my father buried their family members. My position as insider/ outsider gave them permission to tell me their stories. It was safer to tell me than other association members. The long-term effects of the resulting text were not a concern to them, yet the immediate reaction of their neighbors hearing "gossip about themselves" could cause serious problems. Occasionally there were secrets passed back and forth as people conversed with me about the cemetery and Sugar Land. What needed to be hidden were the instances that "things were just not right." Charges of dishonesty or violence against co-workers or friends were rarely mentioned, and even so with great reticence. In contrast, stories of manipulation and mistreatment by company supervisors or local police were discussed routinely.

The connection through time and relationships between those I spoke with was poignant at times. Someone would tell me about picking cotton when he was eleven and having to miss the first two months of the school year. This man and I were the same age, lived a few miles apart, both of Mexican descent. The company owned his house—his father was a sharecropper. The "town" near his home also belonged to the company. There were no real stores—it was a controlled, regimented place. I lived a "free town." I did not have to pick cotton, nor miss weeks and weeks of school. As I heard his stories of picking cotton I wondered to myself, why are these differences so striking? How did I become so privileged while he was forced to miss so much school? The nagging question that haunted the writing was, why were Mexicanos always portrayed as sharecroppers and ignorant? Was this redundant representation a factor in pushing so many Mexicano men into sharecropping and their children into the cotton fields?

The chapter on San Isidro addresses both a loss and a debt. The loss of the community and the near loss of the cemetery are not the only "dispossessions." The departure was the loss inherent in the people of San Isidro being what could otherwise be termed "indentured servants" with a language, cultural practices and a designated social status that kept them "outside." The departure is joined by an author who was never really "inside" the San Isidro group and by virtue of entering the academy has now taken a stance with multiple meanings of departure.

The debt is considerable. Authors writing about the lives of Mexican Americans are keenly aware of the need to pay homage to their fathers (Foley, 1997; Limon, 1994; Montejano, 1987). My debt as an author is perhaps further complicated because my father benefited economically from the business (funeral) services he provided to the people of San Isidro. Their losses created his wealth. Perhaps in response to this economic relationship I was taught as a child that: "One should do one's duties towards the dead"[1] and demonstrate "a gesture of respect and of farewell" (de Certeau, 1988: 321). These instructions were given as I was also told that I could never go to the cotton fields, even if I wanted to. There is a loss in being told you cannot experience what the others have seen. The nucleus of San Isidro's story lies between the loss of place and subjectivity and the obligation to remember.

Larger and smaller things

At the time I wrote the cemetery chapter my focus was the history of Mexican Americans in south-east Texas and my own interrelation with that history. I took note of the accelerated growth of the suburban community around Sugar Land. It appeared that the larger symbolism of this transformation was associated with local corporate growth. After the chapter was published, expanding the project, I slowly treaded through historical sources and currently circulating narratives that were either spoken by individuals or were published in local newspapers. Fort Bend County, with its history of slavery, reconstruction, Jim Crow, and prison labor seemed the perfect site for a long-term historical project. Yet, there was even more. As it turns out, one of the most significant US Supreme Court cases on voting rights emanated out of Ft. Bend County—*Terry vs. Adams*, 1954. This case was resolved the same year as *Brown vs. Board of Education*. There is a relationship and symmetry between the two cases (Tushnet and Lezin, 1991)—as there is between the cemetery and *Terry vs. Adams*. The cemetery provides a clue to a larger story regarding the history of human rights in Ft. Bend County. In 1954, the cemetery grass was overgrown, the Mexican workers still lived in villages nearby. In 2003 the cemetery remains vibrant, hidden behind a new backdrop of history. There is now another player on the scene. Congressman Tom DeLay, a conservative who represents the Sugar Land area is the House Majority Leader of the US Congress. He is considered one of the three most powerful Republicans in Congress. While DeLay runs Washington, San Isidro cemetery hides behind a tall wooden fence in Sugar Land holding stories of power, oppression, murder and violence. It will take a long time to understand the interplay between these remarkable events, places, and people. History continues to be re-conditioned.

Note

1   De Certeau cites Sigmund Freud, *The Birth of the Psychoanalytical Movement*, New York: Basic Books, 1954: 171, in *The Writing of History* (1988).

References

Armstrong, R. M. (1991) *Sugar Land, Texas and the Imperial Sugar Company*, Houston, TX: D. Armstrong, Co., Inc.

Certeau, M. de. (1988) *The Writing of History*, trans. Tom Conley, New York: Columbia University Press.

Firestone, D. "DeLay Is to Carry Dissenting Message On a Mideast Tour", *New York Times*, 25 July 2003.

Foley, N. (1997) *The White Scourge: Mexicans, Blacks, and Poor Whites in Texas Cotton Culture*, Berkeley, CA: University of California Press.

Limon, J. (1994) *Dancing with the Devil: Mexican American Poetics in South Texas*, Madison, WI: University of Wisconsin Press.

Montejano, D. (1987) *Anglos and Mexicans in the Making of Texas, 1836–1986*, Austin, TX: University of Texas Press.

Price, R. (1998) *The Convict and the Colonel*, Boston: Beacon Press.

Tushnet, M. and Lezin, K. (1991) "What Really Happened in Brown vs. Board of Education", *Columbia Law Review*, 91, 1867.

Ware, D. L. (1994) "Creating a company town: William T. Eldridge, Isaac H. Kempner and Sugar Land, Texas (1906–1947)", Masters thesis, University of Houston, Texas.

4 Not a "Kodak moment"
Picturing Asian Americans

Sumiko Higashi

On research trips I photographed glossies of silent stars in old scrapbooks and shot still frames of feature film wound on Steenbecks. Seldom did I capture family and friends during sunny "Kodak moments." When my husband, Bob, flew out to join me in LA one summer, he was the one who photographed my parents in their colorful backyard. Stalks of orange and purple bird-of-paradise looked plastic to the eye. Plants of every species covered the ground and clambered up fences to filter the southern California light. Cacti with needled and succulent branches pierced the cloudless sky. A panoply of trees yielded apples, oranges, lemons, grapefruit, peaches, apricots, figs, persimmons, and avocados. Behind burglar bars, my mother disciplined nature indoors in serene floral arrangements—a touch of *zen* in a district we dubbed Fort Crenshaw after the Rodney King verdict. At the Kokusai, a nearby movie theater that used to show Japanese melodramas and *samurai* swashbucklers, pentecostal singing resonated. Japanese American merchants had been closing their shops and leaving the neighborhood as blacks moved in. Several blocks away, Martin Luther King, Jr., stared from a billboard that proclaimed, "The Promised Land is found in Financial Independence." Beneath his gaze, Latino vendors sold floral bouquets and bags of oranges to drivers waiting on the Santa Monica freeway ramp.

I framed the snapshot of my parents, which would have disappeared in the clutter of slides, index cards, manila folders, note pads, and mementos on my desk. But when I glance up from my computer screen, I see them looking so miserable that the atmosphere exudes their pain. Standing erect in the glaring California sunshine, my frowning 6-foot father looks angry and bitter. A foot shorter, my mother composes herself for the camera, but her face is etched with lines betraying depression. I know why they became that way, but little about how their tragic stories began. I have no record of "Kodak moments" because there is no past to link to the present—just vague recollections of a family trapped in history's nightmare.

Several years after Bob photographed my parents, my brother, Terry, and I moved them from their garden in Fort Crenshaw to a condominium in downtown Little Tokyo. My father, who had excelled in *kendo* and judo as a student in Hiroshima, was afflicted with white matter disease and wheel-chair bound.

Among the things we packed and unpacked were old photo albums revealing so many relatives that my mother could scarcely remember them all. I possess only two of the photographs that connect my parents to their youth in pre-war Japan. The sepia-toned portrait of my mother, in soft focus, had dropped out of a book that I wrote about Cecil B. DeMille's silent films. Apparently, my father had filed between the pages of my study his memory of the lovely young fiancée he met before sailing from Yokohama. I stared at the photograph for a long time before my mother suggested that I keep it. She wanted me to have a memento of a distant time and place, to remember how beautiful she was. I could not help but think how her exquisite beauty would fade not so much with time as with hardship. I felt guilty stealing from my father a reminder of a past rendered even more opaque by struggle in a hostile country and cataclysmic historical events. But the nineteen-year-old girl, whose eyes avoid the spectator, was too intriguing. She has her hair styled with ornaments in a coiffure signifying her unmarried status, and wears a geometrically printed silk *kimono* bound with an *obi*. Standing beside a picturesque garden fenced with bamboo, she seems unaware of the world or even herself (see Figure 4.1). She is innocent and youthful enough to harbor hopes despite her sadness. That is why I kept the picture.

Figure 4.1 Satsuko Higashi posing for a formal portrait taken shortly after her engagement

But the lovely young girl who posed for that portrait was not destined for a narrative with a happy ending. Daughter of a local politician, she had been educated in a private school, taught to arrange flowers in the *ikenobu* style, and reared to become a proper wife and mother. Although her brother, Masato, disapproved of the *shamisen*, a stringed instrument that, unlike the *okoto*, was associated with *geishas*, she continued her lessons. She was part of a close-knit family and community that looked to her father, president of the town council, for guidance. She was, however, the eldest of four sisters, and weddings were costly. According to custom, the bride's trousseau included not only *tansus* filled with silk *kimonos*, brocaded *obis*, and *getas* (footwear), but polished mirrors, jewelry, musical instruments, parasols, and other personal possessions. A selection of futons and *zabutons* (floor cushions) for both daily use and special occasions, as well as housewares was essential. All goods were lavishly displayed for neighbors to see before the marriage ceremony. Acting like a selfless heroine in an Ozu film, my mother spared her parents the expense of such a wedding by agreeing to marry my father in the US. During trips to Hiroshima, where they saw *katsudo shashin* (movies) and sat in a coffee shop, he asked if she would emigrate after he established himself. A young man born in California, raised in Japan, and returning to a country that in 1924 prohibited further Japanese immigration, he sought a bride who, like himself, could claim American citizenship. A portrait taken on the day before she sailed, two years later, shows her in the center of the frame, next to her dejected mother and surrounded by her loving family. Contrast that image with an earlier photo taken after her engagement that shows her seated at the edge of her new family and looking sadly resigned. She was being a dutiful daughter but would never again be so cherished. She still remembers, with sorrow, how she stood on the ship's deck and waved to her mother, who became a tiny speck standing still long after others had left the Yokohama shoreline.

The studio portrait of my father as a child—a photo that my mother gave me—remains an enigma. Posing in front of a backdrop with a house and foliage, he has a hat in one hand, polished driftwood in the other, and a stuffed animal at his feet. A mere child, he seems weighed down with artifacts. Standing next to him is his eldest sister-in-law—unprepossessing, depressed, and at least a decade older. She occupies the center of the frame and is more softly lit, but she lowers her eyes and clutches an imitation alligator bag—the only Western touch in the picture. Seated next to her, on the left, is my father's mother—a regal matron in formal dress and coiffure who looks detached. She would become ill and die before too many years elapsed. Although this cheerless photograph is framed in stiff cardboard and stamped with the studio's rising sun logo, a deep crease bisects the body of the child who grew up to be my father. (The damaged picture came into his possession after his sister-in-law's death.) Already sad and resentful, he poses with two women whose relationship to him is vague (see Figure 4.2). But his father doted on him and sent him to a private school in Hiroshima. Unusually tall, he boarded with a family in the city or commuted by train, a route that included a two-hour walk. Since a duplicate of the creased

Figure 4.2 Setsuo Higashi photographed with his mother, soon deceased, and eldest sister-in-law

photo in my parents' album is undamaged, it invites less interpretation. Certainly, a more arresting image in those pages is the portrait of my father as a handsome young student seated next to his judo instructor after winning a prestigious first prize. Carefully placed on his lap and held by his strong, graceful hands are documents attesting to his prowess (see Figure 4.3).

Since multiculturalism was not yet in vogue, I learned very little about my parents' past and instead studied Greek, Roman, European, and US history at UCLA. A one-semester course in Japanese history that fulfilled the only departmental requirement for non-Western study represented adequate knowledge about the so-called Third World. Growing up in postwar America, a televised land of the Nelsons, Ricardos, and *Father Knows Best*, I wanted to fit in, not revise curricula. Stripped of their future by the war, my parents invested in their children's education. When I was a teenager, my mother bought me books, an encyclopedia, and a subscription to *American Girl*. My father drove me to the neighborhood public library and let me choose the movies we saw together. Yet becoming American meant that my parents' prewar existence was erased from memory. And spending my college teaching years in the Northeast, where most whites encounter Asians and Asian Americans in exotic restaurants, has obscured the past even more. Apart from some New York neighborhoods,

Figure 4.3 Setsuo Higashi seated next to his judo instructor after winning first prize in a contest

there are no significant enclaves labeled Chinatown, Koreatown, or Little Tokyo, let alone Little Saigon or Thai Town, that remind me of Asian cultures. So I scrutinize my parents' old photos for signs. Signs of what they might have been or could have been. Signs of continuity with their childhood in Japan despite painful and cruel ruptures. Signs of their ability to withstand repatriation in a country where they were marked as alien, hated and cursed, imprisoned in concentration camps, exploited as cheap labor, treated with condescension. Signs of their tenaciousness in sustaining a concentration camp mentality behind burglar-barred windows. And signs of paranoia in Japanese-American communities—an inverse reflection of "yellow peril" paranoia still saturating white America.

To this day my mother is not fluent in English, but she often leaves the confines of Little Tokyo and bargains with Chinatown and Fashion District merchants in downtown shops. My father, who recently died in a nursing home, accumulated dictionaries, thesauri, and textbooks so that he was more fluent during the years spent in this country. And yet neither of them had made definitive plans to remain in America, their birthplace, when they were repatriated as *kibei* (Japanese Americans brought up in Japan) before the Second World War. So why, asked my mother's youngest sister, Kikumi, did my father leave behind a large house surrounded by farm land? I can only speculate. All his life, he was immensely curious, loved to travel, and had a sense of adventure. And he had an opportunity to amass some capital by inheriting a small family business run by his older brother, Moriso, in downtown Long Beach. But war intervened. The West Coast had a history of unremitting hostility toward Asian immigrants. A short time after the attack on Pearl Harbor, the FBI arrested Moriso at his market and searched his home. Caught by the events of war, my mother was glancing at the pages of *Life* magazine in a concentration camp in Colorado when she saw startling photographs of the nuclear fallout in Hiroshima. She recognized the train route that led from the bombed metropolis to her suburban town. She learned later that my father's elder brother, Tsutomu, and sister-in-law, Harumi—both badly burned during the blast—were brought to her parents' house. Blood-stained *futons* had to be discarded when they were moved again because they wished to die in their own home. Doctors were unable to treat her cousins, Kimiko and Nobuko, scalded when they rushed outdoors after the explosion, so that they too died. Another cousin, Michiko, was disfigured and labeled *hibakusha*, an atomic bomb victim. Conditions after the war remained grim and food was scarce so that my mother's sisters wrote imploring her not to come home. She spent several years thereafter standing in post office lines to send her family heavy boxes containing flour, sugar, lard, coffee, canned goods, and sweets. She had already stood in interminable mess hall lines in a concentration camp fenced with barbed wire and patrolled by armed guards in the middle of a desert.

Contrary to the Horatio Alger myth, immigrants marked as the racialized "Other" often become downwardly mobile in the *Land of Liberty*, the title of a DeMille film screened at the New York World's Fair in 1939. So many unwelcome foreigners have had to reinvent themselves to survive in distant lands. When my husband went to Grenoble on a research trip, he discussed his valvular heart surgery with a Vietnamese waiter who had been a physician. A South Vietnamese officer in one of my graduate courses supported his family by working in a graveyard assembly line. Such stories are legion. My own parents' fateful journey through history has left me with a legacy of ambivalence. As a California expatriate living in Connecticut—a Yankee state with fault lines revealing more class and ethnic, less racial difference—I doubt that I will ever feel at home in the US. Despite changes in the complexion of its politics, California remains a state with a history of race relations that reads like Mississippi's. Asian Americans are today an invisible "model minority" in the discourse on race that privileges a black–white dyad, with references to a Latino underclass. Academe, supposedly liberal, is hardly a haven because its balkanized and hierarchical structure dictates a problematic reception for so-called "people of color." What defines home in my lexicon is thus a sense of aesthetics that is instinctively rooted in Japanese culture as a source of Western modernism. On my trips back to LA, I am always struck by the form, texture, and color of my mother's *ikebana* arrangements. I save photos of them. As a way of filling in the lacunae of missing grandparents, aunts, uncles, and cousins, my mother has always sent photographs that her relatives mailed from Japan.

Occasionally interspersed between their mostly unsmiling faces are snapshots of her floral arrangements. She is especially proud of her displays in local exhibits. Although her photos of delicate petals unfolding in a drama of leaves rolled like haircurlers, stark branches, and cut bamboo are badly lit and framed, I keep them in my album. Reading family photographs can be dismal but for these sunbursts in ceramic vases.

Acknowledgements

I thank John Kuo Wei Tchen for soliciting and critiquing this piece for an unpublished project, Judith Kitchen for perceptive comments, and Robert J. Smith for helpful editorial suggestions. As usual, Robert Rosenstone has been a wise and able critic, especially in providing me with ample time to rethink my family history.

Part II
New voices

Experimental history self-consciously uses different voices, sometimes multiple. As always the historian has at some point to grapple with the problems of finding/giving a form to explain what went on in the past. This is at the heart of the issue of history's 'aboutness'. This process is especially difficult and complex in the face of the sublime, usually ambiguous and always tentative nature of the past. Cognizant of what he calls 'the context of the postmodernist sensibility', Chris Ward's 'Impressions of the Somme: an experiment' uses, as he says, one of the major battles of the First World War to investigate the difficulties of representation in history – content explicated through its form? Ward's experiment works within the context of the following problems: the historian's motivation and intentions; the constitution and instrumentality of evidence; the relationship of that evidence to experience; and the attribution of meaning, whether by historians, commentators, writers or participants. In this experiment Ward is attempting to avoid the 'cause–event–consequence' continuum of much academic history and, as he says, adopts instead a variety of techniques and voices – poetry, prose, listings, imaginary conversations, raw quotations, and distortions of chronology. These are designed by him not only to focus your – the reader's attention – on the event itself, but also to overtly exhibit the ways in which the historian's motivation shapes historical explanation and writing. In his Afterword, he explains his motivations as being a combination of boredom with conventionally framed forms of historical representation and his argument that history is a literary and imaginative rather than an author-less positivist activity. He maintains that the past can only be explored more fully by occasionally abandoning the formal discourse of history in order to re-capture the event. As he says, the profession encourages the search for new content while discouraging innovations in form.

The second piece in this Part is Jon Walker's, 'Antonio Foscarini in the City of Crossed Destinies' which is, as he says, about ambassadors and spies in seventeenth-century Venice and London. The article, he suggests, was the consequence of his endeavour to find a form appropriate to a story plagued with riddles, contradictions and uncertainties, in which his attempts to interpret the evidence shadowed earlier attempts by seventeenth-century commentators (voices). As Walker argues, this is a story in which the conventions of 'empirical' history (represented, of course, by the notes) were, so he thought, inadequate to answer the questions raised by incomplete/fragmentary sources. The form he chose is, he says, an allegory (a parable, metaphor?) for/of the content. In other words, the way the story is told is a commentary on what the story is about. By presenting the relationship between form and content (or past and present) as allegorical or metaphorical, he claims, can simultaneously assert both our distance from the past *and* our ability to speak meaningfully about it. Like Ward, in his Afterword, Walker notes the historical profession's being wary about experiments in form. Walker says that his experiment is a pastiche, functioning as a comic strip in which the Tarot cards provide the mechanism for story-telling. His piece is an allegory on how history is constructed, arguing, contra Hayden White, that stories do exist in the actions of people in the past – putting emplotted meanings into their lives. Walker recognizes the epistemological exclusionism that exists between his narrative and empirical reality, but intends that his experiment provide a metaphorical equivalence though playing with form.

First and foremost, so Bryant Simon maintains, his 'Narrating a southern tragedy: historical facts and historical fictions' is an experiment in historical narrative. The voices here, in addition to that of the author, are discourses – of race, class and sex – as well as sources. These are the voices of fiction and facts. In the spring of 1912 in a small South Carolina town, two African-American men were accused of 'raping' a white man. Given the context of time and place it is, perhaps, inevitable that they were lynched. But the only thing certain in this case – filled with homo-erotic overtones – was the two dead bodies. Simon attempts to explore the confines of evidence and the uncertainties of historical reconstruction. The form he selects is sectional. In the first section – entitled Historical Facts – newspaper accounts, a letter, and data from the government census are presented. Then, in the second section – labelled Historical Fictions – Simon exploits fictional devices to explore what might have happened on that dreadful night in 1912. Shifting perspectives and voices, this part of the chapter consists of four different versions of the same story. Each separate story overlaps, but also contradicts, the other separate stories. Together, however, Simon argues they suggest *what is possible* in terms of race, class, and sex in this particular time and place. In a larger sense, this chapter should be read as part of a conversation – among scholars and you, the reader – about the state of the historical narrative, about what can and should be called history, and how to reconcile the contradictions and uncertainties that we stumble on in the archives. In his Afterword Simon claims his experiment began in the archives but that he had to move beyond them, given the paucity of data available. In producing a fiction Simon was forced to pose questions historians rarely do. How do historians actually talk about the past? What kind of audience was he writing for? In the end, the form resulted from his decision to borrow from *Rashomon*, John Dos Passos and Norman Mailer. He ends up overtly addressing a central issue in experimental history – the relationship of fact and fiction.

In what she calls a pseudo-autobiography, 'Reconstructing the voice of a noblewoman of the time of Peter the Great: Daria Mikhailovna Menshikova: An Exercise in (Pseudo-)Autobiographical Writing', Robin Bisha explores the world of the speaking subject, Daria Mikhailovna Menshikova who is first encountered as she is writing the story of her life while being escorted toward internal exile in Eastern Siberia. In the effort, as Bisha says to reconstruct (irony here or not?), the inner world of the early eighteenth-century noblewoman Bisha is exploring issues only hinted at in the thin records of women's lives in this period. Bisha suggests that several issues are significant to the study of women's history. These include the problems encountered by women in Petrine Russia and the extension of her voice from the domestic to the public sphere. Bisha's experiment clearly signals how the fictive can live comfortably with the factual. As she says, the (re)creation of Menshikova's voice is based on extensive research in published and archival materials on the history of early eighteenth-century Russia.

That the historical genre of biography is a favoured experimental history form is evidenced by Judith Zinsser's 'A prologue for La Dame d'Esprit: the biography of the marquise Du Châtelet'. In this Zinsser suggests her subject – Gabrielle Emilie le Tonnelier de Bréteuil, the marquise Du Châtelet (1706–49) – offers many challenges to her biographer. The extant lives and scholarly articles are partial. Each tends to highlight only one aspect of her protean life: her accomplishments as a *philosophe* or her escapades as a courtier and as Voltaire's companion of fifteen years. This experimental prologue is part of a larger project: a biography that is intended to convey not only the multi-faceted nature of Du Châtelet's life, but also the various ways in which it has been constructed by other historians and now reconstructed by Zinsser. This prologue introduces the marquise, the biographer, and the approach. It presents three different beginnings for the biography to demonstrate the malleability of the past, the interweaving of past and present, and the dilemmas common to all story-tellers. In her Afterword, Zinsser explains how her engagement with the marquise Du Châtelet grew out of feminist commitment and how such obligation led her to challenge the realist myths in empirical-analytical verities. Zinsser appeals to the notion of revisioning with, as she says, a sense of mission. But Zinsser's reflection is an apt one with which to close our Afterwords. She squarely faces the ultimate dilemma that experimentalism exposes. If experimenters want to 'to know' more fully and deeply about their subject, not only must they confront their own self-conscious constructionism, they have to define objectivity and truth differently. Or, if you like, rethink history in both its theory and practice.

James Goodman's experiment is an eerily prescient piece published just before the mid-August 2003 power outage in north-eastern USA and Canada but written about the earlier event in 1977. The piece is a draft of the opening pages of his book about this called *Blackout*. Unlike the more recent event, the one that took place a quarter of a century or more ago was accompanied by looting and arson in four boroughs of NYC, costing hundreds of millions of dollars. What caused all this Goodman asks? Unemployment, poverty, despair?

Who was to blame? The book and hence his piece here, Goodman describes as 'creative non-fiction and history'. Its rich and evocative flavour is, as you will read, constituted by its imaginative use of the multi-voice, choppy descriptions, and considered and more leisurely realist fiction. It is a vibrant and challenging way to ask and answer its questions about what happened and why.

5 Impressions of the Somme
An experiment

Chris Ward

> But all grows dim – the rolling wagon-streams
>   To Amiens between the aspen trees,
> The stables, billets, men and horses seem
>   But murmurs of forgotten fantasies.
> (Geoffrey Dearmer, 'Envoi – (The Somme 1916)')

Making a start

> The history of the British Army on the Western front is also the history of the writing of that story.
> (Tim Travers 1987)

At first I thought it would be relatively easy to write an article on the British and the Somme. It would go something like this:

1 Causes – a survey of the war up to 1916 with asides on the culture of the British army and its place in Edwardian society.
2 The battle piece – the military, political, social and economic situation in 1916, the planning and execution of the battle, successes and failures.
3 Consequences – short- and long-term, social, economic and political; remarks on the interaction of the Somme with post-war culture and military science.

What would be happening? – a formal presentation: an exercise in which I separate myself from the text, objectify the process of writing and present an artefact to my readers. But this wouldn't be the end of the story. For the presentation to work, everyone would have to agree to engage in the willing suspension of disbelief. In the first place, readers would have to accept the proposition that even though causes, processes and consequences are refracted through my personality, they nevertheless exist independently of me, not just of the interpretation I choose to give them. Second, I would have to pretend to depersonalize myself, to abstract myself from the text and to scientize my motives. Finally, we would all have to agree that events are in some sense coherent, can be replicated on the page, and do actually have discoverable causes and consequences. To put it differently I could use two of the three headings listed above – a 'cause' or 'subject' (the situation before 1916) and a 'process' or 'main verb' (the Somme battle) – as apparently depersonalized justifications for the article, and then travel towards a familiar destination: a 'consequence' or 'object' (the situation after 1916).

But the more I thought about it, the more difficult it became. I realized that I'm no longer sure what comprises history or how it would be presented. I'm no longer convinced that events exhibit types of coherence, cause and consequence which can easily be rendered into the presentational forms and prose styles commonly used by historians.

So this is going to be about the Somme, but also about the difficulties of representation, of what constitutes evidence, of the relationship of evidence to experience, and of the ascription of meaning, whether by historians or participants. The chapter arises from my dissatisfaction with what I've written previously, as an historian of modern Russia. It is an experiment, an attempt to find a different way of getting at the problem of dealing with the past. It is not offered as a solution to the epistemological difficulties which confront historians, it is not even the sketch of a solution; it is only the beginning of a personal response to a particular event. I would have called it 'an experiment in literary investigation' if that portentous sub-title hadn't already been deployed elsewhere, at great length and to considerable effect.[1]

Choice of topic

What is an historian of the Soviet Union doing here? An observation by Hugh Seton-Watson (a 'standard' historian of late Imperial Russia) helps to explain why I'm writing about early twentieth-century Britain rather than mid-twentieth-century Russia:

> It is difficult to write the history of a foreign country. The foreigner has not grown up in its physical and mental climate, and he cannot understand them, still less feel them, in the same way as its own people do. He can spend long periods in a foreign land, learn its language, work and live among its citizens, to some extent think as they do, and be accepted as a friend. This is not the same thing as being one of the people of the country, but it is still something.
>
> (Seton-Watson 1967: viii)

In the context of modern sensibilities Seton-Watson's 'something' – an outsider's knowledge of another country, in my case, Russia – has become deeply problematic. This is because the cultural signifiers of Russia's past belong to natives in a manner in which they can never belong to foreigners, no matter how hard they try. Doubtless by extension one should argue that the same applies to other foreign cultures too, and of course the rebuttal could always be made that since all cultures and the entire past are equally foreign – including the past of one's own culture and country – the difficulty is removed, and we can study anything we like with equal facility.

That's surely so, but only up to a point. If nowadays we are less inclined to believe that history has structures or destinations, and if we have become more interested in exploring how events were experienced, handled and represented by participants, then increasingly it's our response to the semiotics of the past – its cultural, social and linguistic signs and resonances – that's at issue. This is why for some historians some pasts become more foreign, more distant and problematic, than for others. I'll leap ahead for a moment and give two examples, both drawn from the British experience on the Western Front in 1914–18, of how I think this operates (where > equals 'suggests'):

1   The Battle of the Somme (1916), commonly 'the Somme':[2] Somme > sombre = dismal, shadowy, dark, dark-hued, threatening > thundery; thunder > storm > sky > threatening skies > shells raining down on helpless, exposed, cowering soldiers; darkness > blindness, death, ignorance, unknowing, muddle > soldiers blindly stumbling in confusion + mud[dle].

2   The 3rd Battle of Ypres (1917), commonly 'Passchendaele':[3] passchen/ > passion (extreme emotion, terror) + the Passion of Christ > sacrifice and suffering + soldiers as lambs to the slaughter; /daele > dale = valley > Valley of the Shadow of Death (23rd Psalm); Passchendaele sounds soft, watery = muddy > soldiers mired in mud > hopelessness > the Slough of Despond (Bunyan's *Pilgrim's Progress*).

This exercise in free association reveals colour, tone, and the layers of meaning immanent in the sound and shape of words. There is little doubt that these or similar associations consciously or unconsciously sculptured perceptions and memory of the Somme and Passchendaele.[4] And they travel through time. They are available to native-speaking historians immediately (one is tempted to say naturally), through long familiarity, but they can be apprehended by foreigners, if at all, only with difficulty.

These are reasons for not writing an article on Russian history – an awareness of my inability to engage with Russian culture beyond a certain threshold of experience. But if they explain why this is an article on British history, they don't explain why I've chosen to write about the Western Front in 1914–18, specifically about the Somme.

To start with, I have to make a detour, because in part this had to do with what has been happening in Great Britain over the last twenty or thirty years.

The situation in Ireland, the rise of Scottish nationalism, and to a lesser extent Welsh nationalism, immigration from East Africa and the Indian sub-continent, the general drift towards regionalism and disintegration in other European states and, most importantly, the vexed question of the relationship of the British state, British institutions and British political parties to the European Union – all these have rendered the 'United Kingdom of Great Britain and Northern Ireland' and the notion of 'Britishness' highly contentious. As the Union comes under strain and Britishness is challenged, so questions of identity arise. For the Celtic fringe and for ethnic minorities non-British identities can be co-opted, manufactured or mythologized relatively easily: there is enough cultural and historical detritus to hand to build a house to live in. Not so for the English. Since for so many centuries England has been imperial (the United Kingdom is, after all, at once the heartland and the last bastion of Empire), it is hard to separate Englishness from Britishness. Englishness is amorphous, difficult to factor out from the imperial equation, a weak force which requires a strong nexus for its continued existence.

In consequence, we now witness ever more desperate attempts to pump life into the failing body of Britishness by those anxious to preserve privilege and the status quo. One way is to revivify symbols and rituals which celebrate Britishness, and if there is one moment every year when the English political elite displays itself to the Union, mythologizes the Union, and attempts to co-opt the emotions of a significant part of the population in support of the Union, that moment occurs in front of the Cenotaph on 11 November. Here the purpose of remembering war is to bind, and since the 1980s the ties that bind have become more overt, more aggressively displayed and celebrated, than was the case in, say, the 1960s and 1970s. In modern Britain, Geoffrey Dearmer's 'forgotten fantasies' serve clear political, social and cultural purposes.

Revitalizing and foregrounding rituals previously located firmly in the background of British culture sensitize the reflective mind, and since academics concerned with the humanities tend to lead what Socrates called 'the examined life', the Great War starts to present itself to the imagination, to loom out of the fog of that half-explored landscape of one's own culture. That war's susurration, for decades internalized and dismissed, yet heard almost everywhere in England, like the sound of distant traffic, becomes distinct, louder, more insistent. You begin to notice the monuments on every side: in railway stations, in town centres and villages, by parish halls or in churches (the brass plaque near the altar recording the death of the local landowner's son), in the old universities, even in department stores.

Additionally, there is the sudden awareness of the attrition of time. Almost all the men and women who experienced the First World War have disappeared forever. To the middle-aged English like me who remember these people everywhere, all around – my grandparents' generation and their sepia-toned world – memory is becoming history in the sense in which it never quite was before. That which was near, commonplace and familiar is rapidly mutating into something remote, strange and unfamiliar.

So much for the First World War. But why the Somme?

The Somme, some general problems, and gavel history

The simple answer is that one has to start somewhere. A more elaborate explanation is that the Somme was the first really major battle fought by the British in the First World War. It looms large not only in the context of the war, but also in myth and memorialization. It is also to this day a deeply contentious affair, even a divisive one,[5] and from the survey reading I have done so far, it is apparent that there is no agreement among historians on the strategy, tactics or politics of the campaign.

Interesting as these problems are, they are not the prime focus of my concerns at present. For the Somme is not just a problem in military or political history. It was, and still is, a cultural and social event. To Edwardians it appeared as a vast tragedy, and it provoked an unprecedented outpouring of memoir, recapitulation and self-examination, and desperate attempts to translate the experience into familiar and manageable cultural categories, and in some cases to transcend those categories. (If 'the examined life' is a property of intellectuals today, how much more so was this true of the middle-class intelligentsia in early twentieth-century Britain?) This huge reservoir of writing – letters, accounts, novels, poetry, diaries, memoirs – is a magnificent resource, but, as far as I can judge at the moment, it is one which has been poorly handled by historians. Their response to it might be characterized as follows:

1   Reject as subjective artifice.
2   Accept as subjective artifice which has to be cross-checked in order to establish the truth about the Somme.
3   Accept as the truth about the Somme.
4   Excavate for examples to illustrate points about military, political or social history.

Of course, two and four are permissible, one is foolish and three is impermissible – to think otherwise is to stop being an historian. Moreover (current fashions notwithstanding), 'truth' still has meaning in history. When we scrutinize sources we are like a judge rapping a gavel in a courtroom so that plausibilities can be established on the basis of the evidence. Gavel history at least saves us from basic errors in chronology or attribution, but it may also tell us more about what we are concerned with now than about the past. If the Somme is imagined as a cultural and social event, then memoir and fiction possess qualities other than those we value when we wield gavels, necessary though that may be.

The Somme, experience, and the absence of events

'History belonged to an age of rationalism,' wrote Modris Eksteins:

> to the eighteenth and particularly to the nineteenth century . . . Our century has, by contrast, been an antihistorical age, in part because

historians have failed to adapt to the sentiments of their century . . . It is noteworthy that among the mountains of writing built up on the subject of the Great War, a good many of the more satisfying attempts to deal with its meaning have come from the pens of poets, novelists, and even literary critics, and that professional historians have produced, by and large, specialized and limited accounts, most of which pale in evocative and explanatory power before those of *littérateurs*. Historians have failed to find explanations to [*sic*] the war that correspond to the horrendous realities, to the actual experience of the war.

(Eksteins 1990: 291)

This is a wild overstatement. Ours has not been an anti-historical age, there's more history written than even before and, in Europe at least, while modern capitalism may disport itself in an eternal present, Catholicism does not. Moreover, for most of the century, historicist ideologies have dominated the continent.

But there are valid points here in relationship to the First World War. As Eksteins intimates, academic history was born of the Enlightenment and of Victorian positivism. It is predicated upon the assumption that the individual stands in a rational and comprehensible relationship to the outside world, a relationship which can be translated into language and via language transmitted to others. It is therefore founded upon the affirmation of a particular faith – the optimistic notion that there are observers who can apprehend and understand others (no longer existing) and can relate other experiences (of which they have no experience and which are no longer current), all of which can be understood by interlocutors.

Moreover, Enlightenment certainties beckon practitioners towards the imitation of a mechanistic model of science long since abandoned by physicists. Crude mechanism invites one to adopt a common-sense forensic approach – cause, event, consequence – and in this tripartite model so often the central element gets squeezed out. Why? Pushed, poked, prodded, kneaded and banged about by gavels in the quest for cause and consequence, events slide away, disappear, become absent. And there is another reason: only with the greatest difficulty can experience – the quintessence of events – be fitted into the forensic model. One sees this most clearly in biography. When examining a single life it is not only that, time and again, the tripartite model fails to convince (Why did someone do something, feel something, fall in love with someone? On what basis does one sort and prioritize the amorphous mass of phenomena which constitute a life? How does one draw boundaries between the personal and the social? How does one constitute a personality at all?), it is also that the model tells us precious little about experience.

It seems to me that in order to gain on events one must be willing to relinquish common-sense forensics – Newtonian mechanics, if you like – and embrace what might be called a quantum approach. Poets and novelists do this when they explore experience. They sacrifice form to content. They utilize allusion and imagination to make a point. They take risks with or abandon chronology. They live with contradiction. They revel in the inexplicable and ineffable. Frequently, indeed, they present experience without comment. Perhaps this is why novelists and poets often write better biographies than historians. And this is why (Eksteins in surely right) so often literary readings of the Great War speak louder than historical accounts. And it is also why the literary detritus of the Somme – poetry, novels, memoirs, letters, diaries, etc. – is so useful. It is not just another source; it is *the* crucial resource which takes us beyond the mechanical. Edwardians and Victorians, of course, sensed all this. Nearly twenty-five years before the Somme Robert Louis Stevenson recalled how as schoolboys he and his friends would wander around twilit golf links near a Scottish fishing village with lanterns concealed under their cloaks. To passers-by, each was a 'mere pillar of darkness', but initiates knew that light was shining. Stevenson used this memory as a metaphor for life and history:

> The observer (poor soul, with his documents!) is all abroad. For to look at the man is but to court deception . . . To one who has not the secret of the lanterns, the scene upon the links is meaningless. And hence the haunting and truly spectral unreality of realistic books . . . in each, life falls dead like dough . . . for no man lives in the external truth, among salts and acids, but in the warm, phantasmagoric chamber of his brain, with the painted windows and the storied walls.
>
> (Stevenson 1892: 225–7)

To clarify what I'm getting at I'll have to proceed crabwise, to ambush the same problem from another direction.

The moral and the mechanical: sense and sensibility

In Fredric Manning's novel of the Somme, Bourne, the chief protagonist, speculates on the reasons for his reluctance to accept a commission:

> When one was in the ranks, one lived in the world of men, full of flexible movement and human interest: when one became an officer, one became part of an inflexible and inhuman machine; and though he thought the war as a moral effort was magnificent, he felt that as a mechanical operation it left a great deal to be desired.
>
> (Manning 1929: 166)

It is the *moral* aspect of the Somme in which I'm interested – 'full of flexible movement and human interest' – rather than the mechanical. I do not, of course, wish to restrict my history merely to 'tales from the ranks', nor do I mean to discount the importance of Bourne's other category, since the *mechanical* – the system of rules, regulations and orders, as well as landscape, technology, weather, home-front politics, the culture of the Edwardian army, etc. – defined the field in which the moral manifested itself. But there is another reason for concentrating on what Bourne calls the moral which, by now, should be apparent. The moral focuses our attention on the moment and on experience. It is less concerned with past and future or with cause and consequence and more concerned with events themselves. It does not pose problems in order to solve them. It directs our imagination towards the question *what was it like to be there?*, not *how did it come to happen?* or *what were the consequences?*

How can one approach the moral? Writers attempt to transmit experience to readers, but no amount of attention to the scientific method or the rules of evidence will lead historians to drink at this particular trough. Jon Silkin, introducing a selection of First World War poetry, draws on an observation of Samuel Johnson's about eighteenth-century rationalism (Enlightenment certainties) to amplify the point:

> Human beings are not composed of mind, or cerebration, or even intelligence . . . Since we are all composite, the most successful breach in the human mind is made in a composite fashion. Samuel Johnson recognized this when he advised that the business of poets was to reach through to the reader's *senses*. This de-emphasizing of intelligence, at a time when it might be supposed it was the prime attribute, supposed so on account of the ethos as well as the particular critic, suggests how strongly the intelligence, when it is working fully, recognizes the limitations of its mode.
>
> (Silkin 1981: 18)

I wish to read Johnson's 'de-emphasizing of intelligence' as the partial abandonment of the rules of evidence and the scientific method, this to be replaced by an interest in sensation, by an attempt to use what comes to hand or suggests itself as the most efficacious way of involving reader and writer with the experience of the past. To put it another way, when we are concerned with things 'full of flexible movement and human interest', intelligence, in recognizing 'the limitations of its mode', requires not only the support of art and artifice, it also invites its overt transfiguration into art and artifice.

Impressions of the Somme

I chose 'impressions' as part of the chapter title in order to bring out four aspects of my attempt to think and write about the Somme:

1   impressions as preliminary sketches (this chapter);
2   the impress events made on the minds of participants (the impressions they took away with them and transformed into accounts);
3   the impression these accounts make on the historian's mind;
4   impressionism as a prose style (by analogy with Impressionist painting).

The first aspect needs no further comment. The second and third link back to what I've discussed above: to contemporary sensibilities and to the interrelationship of events, accounts and historians. The fourth relates to capturing moments, also discussed above but requiring a brief explanation.

Viewed close up an Impressionist picture reveals little. It is only when one stands back that the image presents itself. In their search for the transient moment the Impressionists broke the rules of academic painting – broad brush strokes, daubs, exaggerated colour and lack of detail conspire to produce the whole. As with such images, so with the past: sometimes one can respond only with 'astonishment' or 'silence'.[6] It is with this in mind that I composed the sketches which follow. Where I have refrained from analysis, elaboration or interpretation it is precisely because the most appropriate comment seems to be astonishment and silence.

But first, as for any exhibition, a short narrative guide is necessary.

Structure of the British Expeditionary Force (BEF)

Army (c.200,000 men, officer commanding (OC) – general):   No more than an *ad hoc* administrative unit, an army comprised any number of subordinate units allocated by General Headquarters to a particular general for the duration of a particular campaign. Battalions, regiments, brigades, etc. could be shifted from one army to another without any awareness on the part of the troops and without any of these units necessarily physically moving from one place to another. For the duration of the 1916 campaign most soldiers in the Somme came under the auspices of General Rawlinson's Fourth Army, but to them this fact would have no particular cultural or social meaning.

Corps (c.50,000 men, OC – lieutenant-general); Division (c.12,000 men, OC – major-general); Brigade (c.4,000 men, OC – brigadier/brigadier-general):   As for armies, but these attachments usually implied the geographical proximity of the component units.

Regiment (c.2,000 men, OC – colonel):   The first of the permanent structures of the BEF. Soldiers enlisted in regiments and regiments were usually territorially based with a 'home' headquarters in Britain. Nevertheless, an entire regiment rarely came together, and many soldiers would have visited their regimental headquarters only when they enlisted.

Battalion (c.800–1,000 men, OC – major/lieutenant-colonel):   Whether as an officer, NCO or private, the real focus of the soldier's life on the Somme. The battalion was a self-contained unit comprising (in the case of the infantry) ordinary fighting men plus specialists (sappers, bombers, signalmen, machine- and Lewis-gunners, wireless operators, cooks, padre, etc.). The battalion moved *en bloc*. Men sent for other duties were detailed within the battalion, and if they attended specialist courses in 'the rear' or went on leave, they returned to their battalion. 'Battalion loyalty' was therefore often very strong, particularly, one might hazard, among New Army soldiers (see below). Much of the memoir literature of the Great War focuses on the battalion experience. Only if they were badly wounded and absent from France for a long time, or if battalions were severely depleted, might soldiers be assigned to a new regiment, and thus to a new battalion.[7] The flood of New Army volunteers caused the number of battalions per regiment to expand far beyond the peacetime norm of two to three. Every region of the British Isles supplied battalions. Initially, only the Newfoundland battalion was raised outside the UK.

Company (c.250 men, OC – captain); Platoon (c.60 men, OC – lieutenant/second-lieutenant); Section (c.15 men, commander – lance-corporal):   As for battalions, but while the battalion usually left 10 per cent of its personnel behind before going into action (thus providing a nucleus around which the unit could be rebuilt), companies, etc. were often annihilated in the space of a few minutes.

Regular Army battalions: Comprised officers and men who had enlisted before 1914; units of the small, professional army used mainly for colonial policing.

Territorial Army battalions: Comprised volunteers from a particular British locality who had some military training before 1914; units of part-time soldiers now on active duty.

New Army battalions: Comprised the mass of untrained civilians who volunteered after August 1914, swamping the regular army and prompting the rapid growth of regiments (e.g., 15th battalion, Durham Light Infantry). But this was not an amorphous mass. The complex regional and social latticework of late-Victorian and Edwardian Britain inflected recruitment. Men joined up not only by locale but also on the basis of identity – by sports team or social club, as friends, as members of an ethnic group, by trade, or by street, town or village (e.g., 12th battalion, East Yorkshires [Hull Sportsmen]; 23rd battalion, Northumberland Fusiliers [4th Tyneside Scottish]; 15th battalion, Highland Light Infantry [Glasgow Tramways]). Many Ulster battalions were formed simply by incorporating into the BEF armed units of the illegal Ulster Volunteer Force, a paramilitary organization founded just before the war to resist the Liberal government's Irish policy. Most New Army battalions had a thin leavening of regular army NCOs, but few had professionally trained officers.

Early in 1916 the BEF was 60 per cent New Army. A good part of the remainder comprised territorial units.

A narrative

Front:	*c.*12 miles
Duration of battle:	1 July–mid-November 1916
Number of shells fired:	*c.*30,000,000 (British and German)
Intensity of shelling:	shellburst every five paces over the entire area

British troops committed:

first day:	*c.*110,000
by mid-November:	virtually the entire BEF had passed through the Somme

Ground gained:

by 2 July:	*c.*2.75 square miles
by mid-September:	*c.*6.00 square miles

British casualties:

first day:	*c.*58,000 (including *c.*20,000 dead)
first two weeks:	*c.*300,000
by mid-November:	*c.*600,000

In the 139 days after 1 July British casualties averaged about 2,500 per day. For the same period the total, Allied and German, probably reached 1.3 million.

The stage was set when in 1915 the BEF extended its share of the Allied line southwards, from the Ypres salient in Belgium to the Albert–Amiens sector in north-western France.

At 07.30 on 1 July 1916, after a massive and prolonged preliminary bombardment concentrated on the German front-line trench system, the British Fourth Army, assisted by elements of the French Sixth Army wedged into a triangle just north of the Somme marshland, launched its infantry attack. The objective of the artillery plan was to cut the wire in front of the German trenches and entomb or annihilate the defending soldiers. In addition, just before 07.30, huge mines were exploded under known German redoubts and fortified villages.

The rest of the plan was based on the assumption that all resistance had been crushed. As the artillery fell silent, the task of the first wave of British infantry was to leave their trenches – line abreast on a 12-mile front – to cross No Man's Land and to occupy what was left of the enemy front-line trenches, there to kill or capture any remaining Germans. Afterwards, by mid-morning, when the artillery had 'lifted' to concentrate fire on the German second- and third-line trench system, a second British wave ('the reserve') would pass through the first. Assisted by cavalry, their job was to break through the by now disorganized Germans, thus restoring mobility to the Western Front and allowing the Allies to drive the enemy out of France and Belgium. The entire effort 'hinged' not only on a successful preliminary artillery bombardment but also on Gommecourt, where a diversionary attack by the British Third Army was to lure the Germans northwards, away from the main thrust.

The plan went wrong from the start. The Gommecourt diversion fooled no one. South of Gommecourt much of the wire remained uncut because the wrong kind of shells had been used. Though the German front line was pulverized, few shells penetrated to the deep dugouts which housed the defenders. Moreover, about 20 per cent of British ordinance failed to explode. On top of that, the artillery had neglected to 'suppress' the German guns ('poor counter-battery work'). When the bombardment stopped, therefore (a signal that the infantry was on the move), the battle turned into 'a race to the parapet': if the Germans got out of their dugouts and into their trenches before the British arrived, the attack would fail. Since the British had been instructed to walk slowly (to keep 'good order') and since German artillery immediately began to shell No Man's Land, thus decimating and slowing the attackers, there was enough time for the defenders to reach their parapets, man their machine guns and kill or maim the tens of thousands of troops walking directly towards them. The British were further disadvantaged by unseasonable rain (which shelling churned into mud), by 60 lb rucksacks (containing supplies and equipment for the next few days), and by having to walk uphill: the German trenches were on the lower south-western slopes of a modest north–south undulation known as Pozièrs Ridge. Most of the 58,000 British casualties came in the first hour.

The battle continued into November. As the British struggled to achieve their first- and second-day objectives (the battle plan anticipated 'breakthrough' by 2 July), German resistance 'stiffened' and ever more Allied troops, drawn from a rapidly expanded BEF swollen with New Army volunteers, were rotated through the maelstrom, including Dominion and Imperial units. From the British perspective, one or two actions were relatively successful; the night attack in front of Montauban in mid-July, for example, or the final assault which ended the agony around the pulverized village of Thiepval. But, on the whole, British attacks seem to have been poorly conceived, planned, co-ordinated and executed.

The affair finally ground to a halt in mid-November about halfway between Albert and Bapaume in front of the Butte of Warlencourt, a conical mound of white chalk which marks the burial place of a Celtic chieftain:

> That ghastly hill, never free from the smoke of bursting shells, became fabulous. It shone white in the night and seemed to leer at you like an ogre in a fairy tale. It loomed up unexpectedly, peering into trenches where you thought yourself safe: it haunted your dreams. Twenty-four hours in the trenches before the Butte finished a man off.
>
> (Carrington 1972: 117)

Thereafter, the front went 'cushy'. In 1917 the British switched their attention northwards to the Ypres salient, where another breakthrough plan ended in failure. Only in Spring 1918 did the Somme become 'hot' once more. A massive surprise attack by the Germans swept the British out of the region, ending nearly three years of continuous residence. A few months later the British in turn drove the Germans backwards, rushing over the old killing grounds in a matter of days. But for decades afterwards in popular memory, 1916 was the Somme and 1 July 1916. Before it all happened the troops called it 'the big push'; afterwards 'the great fuck-up'. The appropriate volume of Sir James Edmonds' official history is called simply *Military Operations: France and Belgium 1916*. Only later did it become 'The Battle of the Somme'.

The kingdom of the Somme

> It had been possible to consider the army as a class or profession, but the war had made it a world.
>
> (Fredric Manning 1929)

Viewed as a subject for social or cultural history, the Somme was more than a battleground, a siege, a prolonged exercise in attrition, or a locale occupied by an invading army. Since the BEF was not disputing the land behind the front line, the Somme was also a region settled by British troops from late 1915 to Summer 1918, when the Ludendorff Offensive swept away all the gains of the previous two years. Characterized thus, the Somme might be compared to a temporary kingdom, or perhaps to a principality within the wider Flanders–Artois–Picardy 'Kingdom of the BEF'. It occupied a clearly defined territory, centred on Albert, but stretching westwards at least as far as Amiens and north-wards to about halfway between Albert and Arras. Frontiers existed, some bordering on hostile powers, some on friendly ones. The kingdom possessed countryside, towns, villages, and a native population with which the settlers interacted. Here there were distinctive means of communications: post and telegraph systems, telephones, runners, maps, signals, lamps, sirens, streets, pathways, tracks, airstrips, railways and roads. And, of course, trenches: com-munication, reserve, front-line, assembly and support trenches; trenches to be avoided, trenches to stay in, trenches to get out of or to pass through; trenches to extend, or to fill, widen, narrow or excavate; dangerous trenches, comfortable trenches, domesticated trenches (trelliswork for climbing roses); crooked trenches, straight trenches, wet or dry trenches. The Somme had its own rulers and class system, its own laws (official and unofficial), its own customs, its own languages and dialects. The settlers evolved their own culture – painting, drawing, music, prose, poetry, song – and their own aesthetic sense.[8] The Somme had its own peculiar flora and fauna (rats, poppies, lice, shattered trees); its own colours (the rich sherry-hue of mustard gas dissolved in muddy water, bloodied khaki and field grey); its own geography, topography, atmosphere and smells (cordite, meadow flowers, rotting corpses); its own architecture (gun emplacements, observation points and pill-boxes, wrecked villages and farm-steads, 'bolt-' and 'cubby-holes' cut into trench sides and chalk escarpments). The Somme had an economy – imports, exports, means of exchange, system of finance and credit, division of labour, specializations. It had diseases and cures, its own patterns of mortality and ways of dying, its own mythology, rumours, beliefs, hopes, joys, sorrows and terrors, and its own sounds too (the moan of shells, whinnying mules, the rumble of cannon lying miles back, the staccato of machine guns firing just overhead and the plop of gas canisters, and the screams of the wounded). Here were places of work and places to rest. Here people dressed distinctively, consumed distinctive foods and beverages, looked at distinctive things, viewed landscape as a military problem, a resource for art, or as a field where heroism, or futility, or suffering or irony were acted out. Here men learned new trades and skills, formed new attachments, lost old ones. The Somme had its own temporal rhythms – daily, weekly, monthly, and by season . . .

Trench and other names; a settler impact: Scottish Trench, Cornish Alley, Deadman's Ditch, Machine Gun Alley, Beer Alley, Pint Alley, Hops Alley, Ale Alley, Wedge Wood, Oakhanger Wood, High Wood, Hop Trench, Cliff Trench, Angle Wood, Savemake Wood, Caterpillar Valley, Caterpillar Wood, Trones Wood, Crucifix Corner, Beadle's Trench, Wood Trench, Bailiff Wood, Leipzig Redoubt, Nab Wood, White City, Pendant Copse, Kaiser's Oak, Hawthorn Ridge, Basin Wood, Station Road, Transport Road, Railway Road, Waterlot Farm, Abbey Road, Mucky Farm, Munster Alley, Mash Valley, Sausage Valley, Sugar-loaf Salient, Centre Way, The Chalk Pit, Casualty Corner, Carnoy Valley, Dinkum Alley, Gordon Dump, Black Watch Alley, First Aid Trench, K Trench, Pinney's Avenue, Blighty Valley, Minden Post, Danzig Alley, Avoca Valley, The Park, Breslau Trench, Montauban Alley, Lousy Wood, Chimpanzee Trench, Happy Valley, New Welcome Street, Whiskey Street, Cross Street, Casement Trench, The Citadel, Sickle Trench, Tara Hill, Usna Hill, The Dell, Skyline Trench, Frankfurt Trench, The Triangle, The Pope's Nose, Stuff Redoubt, Schwaben Redoubt, Zollern Redoubt, Flers Trench, The Grid Lines, Regina Trench, Y Ravine, Munich Trench, The Quadrilateral, Switch Line, Orchard Trench, Straight Trench, Death Way, Death Valley . . .

The provenance of names: Some were formed simply by anglicizing French words (Mucky Farm = Mouquet Farm). The Triangle and various other redoubts were German strongpoints a few hundred yards in front of the British line. Kaiser's Oak was a German observation point. Tara and Usna Hills had Irish connections; these gentle undulations just off the Albert-Bapaume road marked the start of the ill-fated Tyneside Irish rush on 1 July. The Pope's Nose was a sharp protrusion in the German line – to be punched in by Ulster Protestant battalions entrenched just opposite. Minden Trench came from north-western England via eighteenth-century Germany.[9] Death Valley lulled the unwary who lingered there into a false sense of security: though out of sight of the Germans throughout 1916 it was subjected to sudden, lethal bombardments. Gordon Dump and Black Watch Alley were named after regiments, Dinkum Alley had something to do with the Australians . . .

One begins to sense, very powerfully, the presence of a *world*.

Fear[10]

[And after tea it was a summer evening, simply heavenly if it wasn't for the midges and it was odd not having Fatigues[11] or anything much of course you couldn't get far & you couldn't get a wet[12] anyhow and the whole up and down of the valley like a proletarian holiday. But the engines positioned for the assault and the paraphernalia of the gunners and all that belongs to the preparation toward a general action and corrugated tin shelters hastily contrived arbours and a place of tabernacles and of no long continuing nor abidingness, yet not by no means haphazard nor prejudicial to good-order. Well you couldn't get far afield because of the stand-by but blokes came across from 'A' and the other companies to see their friends and people talked a good bit about what the Show[13] was going to be like and were all agog but no one seemed to know anything much as to anything and you got the same served up again garnished with a different twist and emphasis maybe and some would say such and such and others would say the matter stood quite otherwise and there would be a division among them and lily-livered blokes looked awfully unhappy, people you would never expect it of and the same the other way the oddest type seemed itching for a set-to quite genuine it would appear but after all who can read or search out the secret places you get a real eye-opener now and then and any subsequent revealing seldom conforms and you misconstrue his apparent noble bearing and grope about in continual misapprehension or can it by any manner of means be that everyone is interiorly in as great misery and unstably set as you are and is the essential unity of mankind chiefly monstrated in this faint-heartiness and breeze-right-up aptitude] or maybe *wind-up* attitude or perhaps a blighty one[14] but to catch one you'd be lucky & a shot in the foot that's a court-martial mate still there's rum & water before you go over the plonk dutch courage from the sergeants.[15]

[Extreme *wind up*, prolonged beyond the nerves' endurance, sometimes ended in madness. The following adjectives signify "mad" in some degree or other. *Batchy* is mad, or merely silly; etymology extremely doubtful. *Batty* almost certainly (*batchy* just possibly) comes from *bats in the belfry*, and the rhyming *scatty* is related to the Derbyshire *scattle* (easily frightened) and the obsolete Yorkshire *scatterling* (a heedless person); both *batty* and *scatty* mean quite mad. *Crackers*, as in "he's crackers" or "he's gone crackers," links up with *cracked*, a little mad or quite mad. *Dingo*, slightly insane, derives from the French slang *dingot*, eccentric, mad. *Dippy* and *loopy*, properly *looby*, are highly expressive; *looby* is very old indeed, appearing in Langland's *Piers Plowman*, 1377, when it denoted lazy, though later it came to signify stupid, the final transition to silly, a little mad, being an easy one. *Dippy* is temporarily insane or only stupid or even momentarily slow-witted: perhaps from *dipsomaniac*. From India we have *doolally*, mad, from Deolali, famous in the Regular Army and a variation was *doolally tap*, where *tap*, Hindustani for fever, may have been influenced by *tapped*, also used for "mad," one whose brains have been "tapped." India gives us the little used *piache*, mad, very rarely heard outside of Regulars with Indian service; on the analogy of *stone mad, stone piache* was employed for a change. Like *piache, poggle* or *puggle* arose in India, and was an old army word. Egypt presents us with *maghnoon*, properly a dolt, but meaning slightly mad. *In Ponkey Land* was congenitally silly or weak-witted, and only rarely did it find itself used for madness. *Touched* was originally touched with the sun (as also, in fact, was doolally), or perhaps *touched in one's mind* or *brain* or *wits*, where touched is "tainted," "spoilt." *Winick* or *stone winick* (*to be* or *to go*) denoted extreme foolishness, or slight or temporary insanity: Winick in Lancashire has a lunatic asylum. So have other towns.]

Humour[16]

[ARE YOU A VICTIM TO

OPTIMISM?
YOU DON'T KNOW?

THEN ASK YOURSELF THE FOLLOWING QUESTIONS

1 – Do you suffer from cheerfulness?
2 – Do you wake up in the morning feeling that all is going well for the Allies?
3 – Do you sometimes think that the War will end within the next twelve months?
4 – Do you believe good news in preference to bad?
5 – Do you consider our Leaders are competent to conduct the War to a successful issue?

IF YOUR ANSWER IS "YES" TO ANY ONE OF THESE QUESTIONS

THEN YOU ARE IN THE CLUTCHES OF THAT DREAD DISEASE

WE CAN CURE YOU
TWO DAYS SPENT AT OUR ESTABLISHMENT
WILL EFFECTUALLY ERADICATE ALL TRACES OF
IT FROM YOUR SYSTEM

. . . we have attached to our staff at an enormous salary Mr. Teech Bomas[17] the well-known war correspondent. His thrilling articles will be read with great interest by everyone, especially as he sees incidents overlooked by all others . . .

A MESSAGE FROM MR. TEECH BOMAS

BY OUR SPECIAL CORRESPONDENT MR. TEECH BOMAS

MR TEECH BOMAS SPEAKS[18]

No Man's Land, 20/7/16

I WRITE FROM the middle of the battlefield. There are a lot of bullets but I don't mind that. Also the air is thick with shells. That also I don't mind. Let me tell you about it while I can think clearly. Before the battle commenced I took up a favourable position in No Man's Land, the little larks were larking and the morning was fine . . . Let me tell you about the gallant dash of the Umpshires: Into the pick of the Prussian Guard they dashed. The few of the Guard who remained cried "Kamerad" and surrendered. That rush was epic. I then walked over the German lines to have a look at them. There were a lot more bullets but what would you expect?

Now I thrill with ecstasy. Here they come, the wood is ours. Strange associations, here we see the submarine co-operating with the cavalry and shells falling thickly. Then – the peasants – I witnessed the thrilling scenes of the last peasants leaving their happy farms in No Man's Land, harnessing their mongrel dogs into their little carts and driving off when the battle got a bit hot. It was epic. Taking a place is one thing but putting it back is another. Profound but true, and so the wood was won. A correspondent must always see to write. This may appear unnecessary to the cognoscenti, but it is so. To-morrow I will tell you more. I return now to the battle.

H. TEECH BOMAS]

Class, subordination, deference, regionalism, battalion loyalty, the fragmentation of the front, the assertion of self-worth and the irony of memory

(In 1916 the 168th Brigade comprised the Kensington and 1st London Scottish battalions, the Royal Fusiliers and the Rangers):

'On 25 April 1916 there was a Brigade route march. We started off full of spirit on a fifteen mile march, but it was a sweltering hot day and the sun pouring down on our steel helmets soon began to have its effect. Soon fellows began to drop like flies, and the Officers allowed their packs to be carried on their chargers. The Brigadier spotted this, and gave orders that the packs were to be given back to their owners. We struggled on with ambulances following us up. Some of the marchers fell out with sunstroke, and I noticed many with blood oozing from their boots, and in a state of utter exhaustion. We were very nearly "all out," but made up our minds that at any rate the [1st London] Scottish were not going to give the Brigadier the satisfaction of seeing that he had marched us to a standstill. When we saw him, therefore, at the crossroads (on his horse!) watching us as we passed we pushed out our chests and tried to look as if we were enjoying it. When at last I got back to my billet I simply sank down on the ground, and for a time had not sufficient strength to rise, nor even to remove my equipment. When eventually I was able to stand up, my feet still felt as though they were being pressed onto a bed of needles. The Scottish had the fewest number to fall out in the whole Brigade. We learned later that three fellows in the rest of the Brigade had died from exhaustion, as a result of a *practice* march.' (Stuart Dolden 1980: 63–4)

'We eventually left Watford for Saffron Walden, marching long distances for three days, stopping at Ware and Hertford in barns or billets for the nights. There was much competition between the four battalions of the Brigade, for march discipline, etc., our [Kensington] battalion being the winners, to the chagrin of the London Scottish who prided themselves on their marching ability; we had the smallest number falling out. No doubt the London Scottish were hampered in the hot weather by the weight of their kilts. The Scots were very cunning, hiding their casualties behind hedges and haystacks.' (Tucker 1978: 17)

[The Somme, July 1916] 'Some of the "Scottish" stragglers were sprawled around us in a state of utter exhaustion. We made all the tea we could, and then put the stoppers on the cans and stood them along the wall so that as the troops came in, they could help themselves. This was all we could do as, of course, it was impossible to get the tea up to the trenches . . .

'The battalion had gone into action [near Gommecourt] 856 strong, but after having taken four lines of German trenches, had to retire to our own front line through lack of reinforcements. Casualties were very high and amounted to over 600, leaving only about 230 of the battalion left . . .

'The Brigade assembled in a field outside the village, and the Army Corps commander and the Divisional General thanked the Brigade for the work done on 1 July. We then learned that the objective had been reached, for we had merely been a containing force and not the main attack. The object was to cause a concentration of masses of the enemy and their artillery, and to hold them, in order to relieve the pressure on the troops making the main attack further south on the Somme. We certainly attracted hordes of the enemy . . .

'Next night a sergeant and a party of us were sent out as an advance bombing post in "No Man's Land" . . . A brigade was out digging on our right, and after midnight the Germans evidently discovered them, for a terrific fusillade started . . . There was a "Scottish" patrol out in front of us, of which we had not been warned. They came upon a party of Germans, and had to retire to the trench with two casualties. We saw them pass us on their way back to the trench and so we were left out there . . .

'At dawn on 14 July, we could see a bombing raid being carried out on the right by the 4th Royal Gloucesters. It was a very wonderful sight to see the bombs bursting all along the line. But a sight best witnessed from a distance. Shortly after the raid, the British started a bombardment, and smoke was sent over from a trench in front of us . . . That night I again went to the advance bombing post. About midnight a "Scottish" patrol that had been put in front, retired on us suddenly, with the news that they had encountered two German patrols numbering about twenty, and this set us on the alert. Our own patrol retired to the trench behind, and left three of us out there in "No Man's Land" on our own to hold up and Germans that might come along.' (Stuart Dolden 1980: 72, 74–6)

A trench conversation

> Historians are forever chasing shadows, painfully aware of their inability ever to reconstruct a dead world in its completeness . . . We are doomed to be forever hailing someone who has just gone round the corner and out of earshot.
>
> (Simon Schama 1991)

They can hear it in Kent and Sussex and East Anglia. It rolls and rolls from the east. A shiver of leaves and it's gone, but there, when the breeze stops – there again; in Kensington Gardens and in Green Park. Caught in a shaft of sunlight, a pen nib trembles in the empty Cabinet room. Out here, across the Channel, you couldn't have imagined it if you'd tried. It's beyond noise. It's a thrumming through the earth and through your body and in your throat. It's the violence of sound that's not sound. It's a physical assault. It's coming from inside your head; bleeding, blocking your nose, bursting your eardrums outwards. Stunned, unfeeling, you look north across meadowland. Straight ahead, a lark rises madly from the shaking grass. Beak open, it's gone. On your right, completely obscured by a wall of smoke – black, blue-black, white, yellow – the German trenches, stretching into the distance as far as you can see. Erupting continuously, fountains of earth thrown high into the air block out the morning sun. On your left the white chalk scar of a British front-line trench topped with a straggling line of red poppy blooms, harbingers for doomed youth.[19] Now and then the weaving tip of a bayonet's visible. As the mines go up under Hawthorn Ridge and La Boisselle the land heaves, rocking you sideways. Something zings dangerously like a manic flying discus . . . a helmet, cooked blood streaming on the rim thuds shimmering at your feet and half buries itself in the ground. You suddenly realize you're in No Man's Land, caught between two empires. Afraid at last you run and slide down into the trench that isn't being shelled.

Here! What's this then? What's goin' on?

Who are you?

Private John Ball. 2nd battalion Kensington Pals and late of the Great Eastern Railway, Liverpool Street Station. Who's askin', anyway?

I beg your pardon. I've dropped in to see how things are going. I'm the historian. What d'you think of it so far?

Bit of a cock-up if you ask me. Not much better than Neuve Chapelle.[20] You've 'eard about that one? Yes? Well, 'nuff said then. Still, they've been pounding the Boche for days (which, by the way, has given me a bleedin' 'eadache). What? Well, over there's Mash Valley an' just next to it Sausage Valley. And that's the Tara and Usna Hills; Tynside Scots and Irish down there . . . Got any baccy? Thanks, mate. Anyways, where was I? . . . Oh, the guns: so maybe this time . . .

I thought we were talking about my article.

Yes, well, that too . . . comes to the same thing, don't it? After all, you're just makin' this up as you go along . . .

I wouldn't say that, I—

. . . Yes you are. Oh, I know you've got your sources and your footnotes an' all that stuff. 'Rules of Evidence' an' 'The Scientific Method' an' whatnot. But you've got to use your imagination; like a story-teller, right? You've got to try and think what we was like an' what we did and didn't think or believe or feel, an' all this too, all around us: landscape an' trench life and shelling and whatever. So that makes you a kind of fact and fiction writer – Science Fiction writer, right? Like Mr Wells. Ha, Ha!

That's one way of looking at it, I suppose, But you see up here we've all rather lost confidence in what we're doing, the science thing, I mean . . .

And before you asks where we are again, 'I think we're in a rat's alley, where the dead men lost their bones'.[21] Well, course I knows it ain't bin written yet, but it will be, won't it? So what's the difference? You could have put it at the front of the article – sort of epigraph, right? Like ol' Dearmer there – an' no-one would've batted an eyelid. Anyways, why are you so interested in all this? Bit odd, isn't it?

I don't know really. I tried to explain at the beginning. The churches. The little monuments in villages and railway stations. Sometimes even in department stores. The lists of names. Somehow, at the turn of the century, you're all around me. Does that make sense?

Not really, mate. But you knows best, I'm sure. Anyroad, I suppose you've come down here to try to imagine the experience, as it were?

Something like that.

And then you thought maybe you could compare this with other kinds of sources and get what you'd probably call 'a more rounded picture', right?

Well, actually, I thought I'd abandon all that and concentrate on individuals. You see, you're all so different, and your reactions are all so different, that I thought the best way to go about things would be to look at your biographies (if I could find them) and try to understand it all that way.

Won't wash, mate. No. Won't do at all, I'm afraid. You see, this is only me *now*, in'it? An' I won't be the same tomorrow, so I won't be talkin' or thinkin' about all this the same way neither. An' if you was to meet me as an old man, up there, in the future where you come from, it'd be even worse, see, because it'd all be overlaid with other things. Not that you will, of course . . . An' on top of that there's thousands and thousands of us, right? So that's thousands of biographies, all changing day by day. Not on, is it? Best leave it to the poets and novelists, chum.

This is all very discouraging. History being a series of timeless moments, you mean? And the traveller who, when he arrives at the farther shore, is not the same person who left the nearer shore?

Now *you're* quoting.

I know. It's an occupational hazard. We're always seeing things in terms of other things. Metaphors and so on.

Ah, well then, if you're getting literary you'll be wanting to talk to the officer here. He's another composite. You've made him up too.

What?

Private Ball is right. We won't be the same. Dead or alive, we'll be gone. Here, take a look at this memoir: 'The excitement and heroics of my childhood imagination have subsided and left me with the realities and disillusionment of war, the fears, horrors, filth and stench. Now that I have recorded my memories perhaps the ghosts will rest . . . the sense of realism has mysteriously disappeared, events becoming almost dreamlike. The wound scars are there to convince me, but even these are becoming faint with the passing of time.' Or how about some poetry? 'Their war was fought these twenty years ago / And now assumes the nature-look of time, / As when the morning traveller turns and views / His wild night-stumbling carved into a hill.' Or if you prefer prose fiction, what about Charles Morgan, who went through it all too?: 'in each instant of their lives men die to that instant. It is not time that passes away from them, but they who recede from the constancy, from the immutability of time, so that when afterwards they look back on themselves it is not themselves they see, not even – as it is customary to say – themselves as they formerly were, but strange ghosts made in their image, with whom they have no communication.'[22] Not bad, see what I mean? – nothing much to add to that, is there? And Ball is right about the composites too – you've imagined us both (or rather, you've imagined me and borrowed him from David Jones).[23] And after all, you've only got him working on the Great Eastern at Liverpool Street so you could drag in *Our Mutual Friend* and 'come up and be dead!' from the East End fifty years ago.[24] Like climbing out of the trenches to die, a nice little parallel to make the point. Am I getting somewhere? I see I am. Shall I show you how you are going to do it? . . .

I'd really rather you didn't . . .

. . . here goes – something like this:

It was Dickens who associated death with climbing, with struggling upwards. In *Our Mutual Friend* (published 1864) the crippled child Jenny Wren, perched on top of the counting house at St Mary Axe, calls down to the scurrying denizens of the trench-like alleys and the drowned bodies wallowing in the filthy Thames, 'Come up and be dead! Come up and be dead!' And London is 'a heap of vapour' with 'circling eddies of fog', a hopeless, rainy, leaden place with 'an air of death'. Did John Ball ever read *Our Mutual Friend?* It is quite likely. After all, as Fussell notes, these were the years of popular education and self-improvement, when any private might have a copy of Quiller-Couch's *Oxford Book of English Verse* in his haversack (Fussell 1975: 157). Did Ball see the irony in front of La Boisselle – 'a heap of vapour', 'circling eddies of fog', 'an air of death', drowned bodies wallowing in the mud and No Man's Land above the trench line always beckoning, 'Come up and be dead!'?

Then you were going to make all those other connections. Like the little soliloquy on 'this western-front business' in book 1, part 13 of Scott Fitzgerald's *Tender is the Night* . . .

You're ruining everything!

Bound to happen. Once you let us loose like this you can't expect us to obey your rules anymore now, can you? But let me continue . . . Tender is the Night comes from Keats' 'Ode to a Nightingale' (to be found, naturally, in Quiller-Couch), and this leads on to birdsong – or rather *Birdsong*, of course, by Sebastian Faulks[25] – and then we're only a short hop, so to speak, from 'Lark Ascending' (Vaughan Williams) and all that pre-1914 nostalgic melancholy, and '. . . larks still bravely singing fly / Scarce heard among the guns below', and before you know where you are we're 'In Flanders fields the poppies blow / Between the crosses row on row / That mark our place'[26] – but this is Picardy, of course, where roses bloom.[27] There's really no end to it once you start this kind of business. Need I go on? Yes? Well, this is only 1 July 1916, so it's going to drag on for most of the rest of the year, and happen again with the Ludendorff Offensive two years later and again with the Foch Offensive . . . By the way, here's a bit of Somme folklore for you: Vera Brittain nursing at Etaples in Summer 1918 just as the Germans rolled over the old battlegrounds – what do you make of this?:

['"'Ave you come down from Albert way?" inquired a sergeant of a corporal in the next bed, who, like himself, wore a 1914 ribbon.

"Yus," was the reply, "I have. There's some mighty queer things happenin' on the Somme just now, ain't there, mate?"

"That there be," said the sergeant. "I can tell yer of one rum thing that 'appened to me, meself."

"Git on then, chum, let's here it."

"Well, when the old regiment first came out in '16, we had a Captain with us – O.C. of our company, 'e was – a mighty fine chap. One day at the beginning of the Somme battle some of the boys got into a tight place – a bit foolish-like, maybe, some of them was – and 'e comes along and pulls 'em out of it. One or two of 'em had got the wind up a bit, and 'e tells 'em not to loose 'eart if they gets into difficulties, for 'e sorter knows, 'e says, when the boys 'as need of 'im, and wherever 'e is, 'e says, 'e'll do 'is best to be there. Well, 'e was killed, 'elpin' the boys as usual, at the end of the fightin' on the Somme, and we mourned for

'im like a brother, as you might say . . . 'E were a tall fine chap, no mistakin'
'im, there wasn't. Well, the other day, just before the Boches got into Albert,
we was in a bit of a fix, and I was doin' all I knew to get us out. Suddenly I turns
round, and there I sees 'im with 'is bright eyes and 'is old smile, bringin' up
the rear.

"Well, Willis, it's been a narrow shave this time," 'e says. "But I think we
pulled it off."

"An' forgettin' 'ow it was, I makes as if to answer 'im, and all of a sudden 'e
ain't there at all. Struck me all of a heap for a bit, like. What do you make of it,
mate?"

"It's more nor I can tell," answered the corporal. "'Cos another very queer
thing happened to some of our chaps in our company. In the old days on the
Somme we had a tophole[28] party of stretcher-bearers, and one day a coal-box[29]
comes and wipes out the lot. But last week some of our chaps seen 'em again,
carrying the wounded down the communication trench. And I met a chum in
the train who swears he was carried out by two of 'em."

A Lancashire boy from an opposite bed leaned forward eagerly.

"I can tell yer sommat that'll beat that," he said. "T'other day when we was
gettin' clear of Péronne, I found a chap beside me lookin' very white and
done-up, like, as if 'e could scarcely walk; fair clemmed,[30] 'e seemed to me. I
found I'd got one or two of them 'ard biscuits in me pocket, an' I pulls one out
and hands it to 'im. ''Ave a biscuit, mate,' sez I."

"'Thank you, chum,' 'e sez, 'I don't mind if I do.'"

"And 'e takes the biscuit and gives it a bite. As 'e puts out 'is 'and for it I sees
'e's got one o' them swanky identity-disks on 'is wrist, and I reads 'is number
as plain as anythink. Then 'e gets mixed up wi' t'others and I don't see 'im no
more. And it's not till I gets back to billets that I remembers.

"'Lawks,' I sez to meself, 'if that ain't the chap I 'elped Jim to bury more'n a
week agone, my name ain't Bill Bennett.'

"An' sure enough, mates, I remember takin' the silver identity-disk off 'is
wrist, an' readin' the number on it plain as plain. An' it were the number of the
man I gave the biscuit."

There was an awed silence in the ward, and I turned from the dressing I was
doing to ask rather breathlessly:

"Do you really mean that in the middle of the battle you met those men
whom you'd thought were dead?"

The sergeant's reply was insistent.

"Aye, sister, they're dead right enough. They're our mates as was knocked out
on the Somme in '16. And it's our belief they're fightin' with us still."]

(Brittain 1933: 414–16)

*Some of it's a bit suspect, surely? Constructions like 'and we mourned for 'im like a
brother', 'with 'is bright eyes and 'is old smile', or 'and it's our belief they're fightin' with
us still' remind me of what Kipling does: middle-class diction knocked about to make it
sound proletarian. But I don't doubt the general veracity of Vera Brittain's report. There's*

no reason I can think of for her to invent this incident, and there's plenty of evidence to suggest that people under great stress or utterly exhausted see others around them who – objectively, you might say – aren't there at all. I've read similar Great War stories: soldiers convinced that cavalry rode alongside them as they fought, for instance. And there's the famous account in Scott's diaries (1912, isn't it?) when the last two survivors firmly believed that a third, indistinct but real, stumbled with them in the Antarctic blizzards. So for these soldiers, yes – their mates really did rise from their graves and come to their aid as they retreated across the old battlefields . . . It's a puzzle, isn't it? It's neither true nor untrue . . .

. . . And maybe soldiers need superstition for comfort, especially in a war like this one where death's a matter of chance. But let's get back to our game of historical and cultural connections, because it doesn't stop there, with the 1918 retreats and offensives. Oh no. Just down the road there's Agincourt, and Crécy's not far away, and nor's Waterloo. Then the Germans and British will be fighting here again in 1940, and in 1944, but before all that they'll put up the big Lutyens' Memorial to the Missing[31] and tidy up the graveyards with the inscriptions that (since you mentioned him) Kipling thought up for the Imperial War Graves Commission – 'Their Name Liveth Forever More' and 'An Unknown British Soldier / Known Unto God', which brings us straight to 'Recessional' and his presentiment of the end of Empire (which this will accelerate)[32] – 'Far-called, our navies melt away', and 'All our pomp of yesterday / Is one with Nineveh and Tyre'. And on top of that, of course, you and thousands like you are going to drive over this place, in a hired car from La Boisselle to Pozières in, what shall we say – five minutes? Which distance took us months and tens of thousands of lives . . .

This is unbearable. It feels like my head's about to burst.

Not, perhaps, in the best of taste, old chap, given where we are and what's happening, but let's continue. Now, of course, there're the poppies and the Haig Appeal – 'Poppy Day' – to be considered, and the other manifestations: the two minutes' silence and all our memorials with the cross turning into a sword, 'victory in death' and 'the supreme sacrifice' and so on. And we shouldn't forget all the other ramifications – diplomatic, economic, social, political, cultural and artistic – should we? Anyway, time to stop. I don't know who's imagining who anymore. Am I imagining you or are you imagining me? Well, as I said, best not let us get a hold of the narrative or who knows where we'll end up. Before you know it we'll be writing *Foucault's Pendulum*.[33]

Anything but that. But to be honest we ought to write in an odd way, oughtn't we? After all, what most people experience most of the time isn't a set of coherent phenomena but a kind of tolerable and tolerated low-key randomness; things which are instantly translated, moment by annihilating moment, into fleeting and undisciplined squads of emotion. And while all that's going on what they think about (when they think consciously at all) isn't the present, but the present involved with the past and the future, or flashes of the past, impressions of the present and speculations about the future all jumbled together. If we historians try to sort it out, if we try to organize it, if we make it linear and plod along a sentence – cause, event, consequence – we're falsifying, we're telling lies, because experience just isn't like that. Especially, perhaps, when there's stress or novel stimuli, or when things are dangerous or happening quickly. Then time gets muddled – a moment can be an age and an afternoon a moment . . . a couple of seconds might be remembered for the rest of your life and a year forgotten completely – all while seemingly inconsequential things pop into your head all the time. And for all that you need to adopt a quantum approach. Or course, historians have always disrupted time. They go backwards and then forwards again on a different tack; pause, speculate and start again, or dwell endlessly on a moment out of time (though they're not very inventive or flexible in comparison with poets and novelists). Which is exactly what I'm doing here. I've stopped time at 07.30 on 1 July 1916. I've stopped the war, the Somme – everything, between the end of the barrage and the beginning of the assault, so we can hear ourselves think . . . Hey! What are you doing?

We're getting ready to die, of course. Since you mentioned it's 07.30 hours neither you nor I can stay here forever. The sergeant there's forming up the men, walking behind the ranks and making sure all the bayonets are securely fixed. They're gulping down the last of the rum and water, and (if I can control my trembling) I'm just checking my watch and moving up to the fire step; and just about now, in fact, as the barrage lifts and a silence descends, after so many days more stunning and shocking even than the continuous gun fire, I'll blow my whistle and . . . we're off!

Wait! I cried. *There's so much I want to ask you! How do I write about the dying? How do I imagine it? How do I deal with any of this?* But they'd already gone. Scrabbling up the wet, chalky sides of the trench they picked their way over the wire and stumbled off into the smoke, towards the machine guns and the thunder of the counter-barrage.

Ten days on and it's the night attack in front of the Bois de Mametz, a mile or so south of La Boisselle and sometime after 04.15 hours. Shelled 'in full summer foliage and on undulating chalk downland' Private Ball, hampered by his rifle, blunders about in the wood's blood-soaked margins.[34] And

> [it came as if a rigid beam of great weight
> flailed about his calves, caught from behind by ballista-baulk
> let fly or aft-beam slewed to clout gunnel-walker
> below below below.
>> When golden vanities make about,
>>> you've got no legs to stand on.
>> He thought it disproportionate in its violence considering
> the fragility of us.
> The warm fluid percolates between his toes and his left boot
> fills, as when you tread in a puddle – he crawled away in the
> opposite direction.

It's difficult with the weight of the rifle.
Leave it – under the oak.
Leave it for a salvage bloke . . .

Slung so, it swings its full weight. With you going blindly on
all paws, it slews its whole length, to hang at your bowed neck
like the Mariner's white oblation . . .[35]

You're clumsy in your feebleness, you implicate your tin-hat
rim with the slack of it.
    Let it lie for the dews to rust it, or ought you to decently
cover the working parts.
    Its dark barrel, where you leave it under the oak, reflects
the solemn star that rises urgently from Cliff Trench.
    It's a beautiful doll for us
it's the Last Reputable Arm.[36]
    But leave it – under the oak.
leave it for a Cook's tourist to the Devastated Areas and crawl
as far as you can and wait for the bearers.[37]

Mrs. Willy Hamilton has learned to draw sheets and so has
Miss Melpomené; and on the south lawns,
men walk in red white and blue
under the cedars
and by every green tree
and beside comfortable waters . . .[38]

Lie still under the oak
next to the Jerry
and Sergeant Jerry Coke.
The feet of the reserves going up tread level with your forehead; and no word for you; they whisper one with another;
pass on, inward . . .][39] Lit by star-shell signs let's rattle his days. Stiff-
flash a photo circa 1933, blinds drawn still face solemn eyes above hard
plaid blankets draped over stumps and the clumsy wheelchair.[40]
Trained in basket weaving, he hold a paper flag.
    Or it's brown bones split all ends up churned indifferently at plough-time,
sugar-beet for the CAP, or trampled vertebrae under motorway tarmac.[41]

Notes on composites, fiction, and imagined people

Appearances notwithstanding, *A trench conversation* is not as radical as it seems.
In the first place the descriptive passages are distinguished merely by a change
of register and voice, or by adopting a style different from the one normally
employed in academic history. The details could all be attested for (e.g., on a

still day large-scale bombardments on the Western Front could be heard clearly but faintly in southern England, East Anglia, in London's parks and in 10 Downing Street; the chalk sides of the trenches were slippery because it had rained over the few days prior to 1 July). Moreover, on the basis of their reading historians frequently employ descriptive invention. No one would be surprised if in a passage on the Russian Civil War an historian were to write: 'the cold arctic winds lashed at the thin uniforms, many men suffered from frostbite' or 'after Winter months in front of Tsaritsyn the Caucasian Spring came as a welcome release'. Footnote references would (and should) follow these phrases, but it would not matter if the actual words used by the historian never occurred in the sources themselves.

Second, historians engage in conversations with the past. Statements like: 'would Lenin have backed Stalin against Trotsky in 1919 had he known what the Commissariat for Nationalities was to do in Georgia a few months later?' invite the reader to displace time, to imagine a dialogue with Lenin, and to draw conclusions. Again, what is happening in *A trench conversation* is a change of style, register and voice.

The issue of 'composites' and imagined people – Private Ball and the unnamed officer – might seem more contentious, but even here a comparison with the standard register reveals kinship rather than difference. In essence, our entire relationship to the past is imaginary. More particularly, historians frequently abstract some attribute from an individual to make a general point: 'like many pre-revolutionary Bolsheviks, Ivan Ivanovich was a Petersburg metalworker'. But, of course, this is not Ivan Ivanovich in the round; what the historian is trying to do here is to conjure up a composite representation of a group by reference to an aspect of one person's life, and so Ivan Ivanovich disappears, becomes fictive, is no longer himself.

A trench conversation makes its fictiveness apparent in a way similar to the method adopted in Conal O'Riordan's 1931 edited collection, *A Martial Medley: Fact and Fiction*. O'Riordan solves the problem of the fictiveness of memoir and the factuality of fiction by refusing to draw clear distinctions between imagination, analysis and reality – between what can be conceived and what might be believed. Thus Grundy, Miles, Brophy and Denison offer fictions about the War which are true because they meditate on aspects of experience; Hancock, Carrington, Pattison and O'Riordan offer memoirs which must be fictive (abbreviation, reported speech, distortions of chronology, etc.), while Southwold, Brophy and Partridge, by choosing to analyse aspects of life on the Western front, leave the reader no less mired in uncertainty (i.e., they create fictions in the reader's mind because they address aspects, not the whole):

Conceivably True
Lost and Found, by C. W. Grundy
Three Episodes of War, by "Miles"
The Perambulator of Wrath, by John Brophy
From Two Angles, by Corie Denison

Concerning the True
Rumours at the Front, by Stephen Southwold
The Soldier's Nostrils, by John Brophy
Byways of Soldiers' Slang, by Eric Partridge

Actually True
War from the Ranks, by Norman Hancock
Capron Copse, by C. E. Carrington
(Charles Edmonds, pseud.)
The Long Way's End, by E. C. Pattison
One More Fortunate, by Conal O'Riordan

Finally (and this relates to points made earlier in the article) so often fiction – outright fiction – speaks volumes in comparison with much academic history, even in terms of cause and consequence, to say nothing of narrative skill and descriptive power:

[Dick turned the corner of the traverse and continued along the trench walking on the duckboard. He came to a periscope, looked through it a moment; then he got up on the step and peered over the parapet. In front of him beneath a dingy sky was Beaumont Hamel; to his left the tragic hill of Thiepval . . .

He went on along the trench, and found the others waiting for him in the next traverse. He was full of excitement and he wanted to communicate it to them, to make them understand about this, though actually Abe North had seen battle service and he had not.

"This land here cost twenty lives a foot that summer," he said to Rosemary. She looked out obediently at the rather bare green plain with its low trees of six years' growth . . .

"There are lots of people dead since and we'll all be dead soon," said Abe consolingly.

Rosemary waited tensely for Dick to continue.

"See that little stream – we could walk to it in two minutes. It took the British a month to walk to it – a whole empire walking very slowly, dying in front and pushing forward behind. And another empire walking very slowly backward a few inches a day, leaving the dead like a million bloody rags. No Europeans will ever do that again in this generation."

"Why, they've only just quit over in Turkey," said Abe. "And in Morocco —"

"That's different. This western-front business couldn't be done again, not for a long time. The young men think they could do it but they couldn't. They could fight the first Marne again but not this. This took religion and years of plenty and tremendous sureties and the exact relation that existed between the classes. The Russians and Italians weren't any good on this front. You had to have a whole-souled sentimental equipment going back further than you could remember. You had to remember Christmas, and postcards of the Crown Prince and his fiancée, and little cafés in Valence and beer gardens in the Unter den Linden and weddings at the mairie, and going to the Derby, and your grandfather's whiskers."

"General Grant invented this kind of battle at Petersburg in sixty-five."

"No, he didn't – he just invented mass butchery. This kind of battle was invented by Lewis Carroll and Jules Verne and whoever wrote Undine, and country deacons bowling and marraines in Marseilles and girls seduced in the back lanes of Wurtemburg and Westphalia. Why, this was a love battle – there was a century of middle-class love spent here. This was the last love battle."

"You want to hand this battle over to D. H. Lawrence," said Abe.

"All my beautiful lovely safe world blew itself up here with a great gust of high explosive love," Dick mourned persistently. "Isn't that true, Rosemary?"]

(Scott Fitzgerald 1986: 66–8)

It doesn't matter that Dicky Diver, Rosemary, and Abe North never existed. Rendered into academic prose Dick's image of the Somme, of the cultural and social background, and of the consequences, would raise no eyebrows. But it would never be expressed as memorably.

Acknowledgements

The first version of this chapter was presented to the Social History Seminar, Department of History, University of Illinois at Urbana-Champaign, in January 1996. My thanks are due to the seminar's participants for their helpful comments and criticisms. The excerpt from *Testament of Youth* by Vera Brittain is included with the permission of her literary executors and Victor Gollancz Ltd., publishers. Excerpts from *Cannon Fodder: An Infantryman's Life on the Western Front 1914–18* by A. Stuart Dolden reproduced by permission of Cassell plc, publishers. Excerpts from *In Parenthesis: seinnyessit e gledyf ym penn mameu* by David Jones reproduced by permission of Faber and Faber Ltd, publishers. The excerpt from *Tender is the Night* by F. Scott Fitzgerald is reprinted with permission of Scribner, a division of Simon & Schuster: copyright 1933, 1934 by Charles Scribner's Sons; copyright renewed © 1961, 1962 by Frances S.F. Lanahan. Every effort has been made to trace the current copyright holder of 'Byways of Soldiers' Slang' by Eric Partridge, from *A Martial Medley: Fact and Fiction*, edited by Conal O'Riordan, published by Eric Partridge at the Scholartis Press, London, 1931, and reissued by Books for Libraries Press, Freeport, New York, 1970. The author will be happy to make arrangements with whoever holds the copyright, should they come forward.

Notes

1 Solzhenitsyn's *Gulag Archipelago*.
2 After the river to the south of the battlefield.
3 The name of the village where the offensive finally ground to a halt.

4 'The very name [Passchendaele],' recalled Wyndham Lewis in 1937, 'with its suggestion of splashiness and of passion at once, was subtly appropriate.' (cited Fussell 1975: 16).

5 And not only for historians. Memory of the Somme inflects the politics of Northern Ireland, for instance. Ulster regiments suffered greatly during the initial assault and for Protestants the Somme is still an important cultural signifier. The deaths caused by the Republican bombing of the Enneskillen war memorial one Armistice Day in the 1980s caused particular anger.

6 Ginzburg on Foucault's study of Pierre Rivière's testimony:

> The possibility of interpreting this text is specifically ruled out because it is held to be impossible to do so without distortion or without subjecting it to an extraneous system of reasoning. The only legitimate reactions to it that remain are "astonishment" and "silence."
>
> (Ginzburg 1982: xviii)

7 See 'Three Episodes of War', a short story in O'Riordan (1970):

> Morris was a cockney of twenty-three, in civil life a clerk in the Foreign Exchange of Barclays Bank. Now a veteran of over three years' active service, he had begun his army life in 1914 in the London Rifle Brigade. Badly wounded at Ploegstreet (Plugstreet) in February 1915, he had returned to his unit in time for the first Somme battle of 1916. Further slight wounds on five different occasions had merely earned him respites in base hospitals, and he had, in accordance with the later procedure of "feeding" depleted units, lost his "crowd," and in turn served with the 2nd Essex, the Royal Naval Division (Drake Battalion), the H.L.I.'s, and on Christmas Day, 1917, he had been sent up with a draft to the Camerons, who were in the line at Monchy in front of Arras. He carried his kilt with the clumsiness of a man in skirts, but such gaucheries had long ceased to be remarked, even in the famous 51st Scottish Division.

8 1916, a September evening on the flat land behind the old German positions: 'The guns were rumbling in one incessant roar on the retiring enemy in front. All the plain was twinkling with myriads of lights from the little shelters.' (Stuart Dolden 1980: 84).

9 In Summer 1759 the Lancashire Fusiliers picked wild rose blooms to garland their hats while pinned down by fire on Minden Heath near Hanover.

10 The first passage is from Jones (1963), an extended prose poem dealing with the author's experiences on the Western Front in 1915–16. With this and other long quotations square brackets indicate a change of voice, from the quoted author to me. The second is from Eric Partridge, 'Byways of Soldiers' Slang', in O'Riordan (1970). Jones served in the Royal Welch Fusiliers in a battalion of 'Londoners with an admixture of Welshman'. The first passage, therefore, should be voiced with a Welsh or cockney accent.

11 Military duties unconnected with actual fighting.

12 Alcohol.

13 Attack.

14 Blighty one: a wound neither maiming nor life-threatening but severe enough to put a soldier out of the combat zone and home to 'blighty'. Men sometimes risked

simulating blighty ones by shooting themselves in the hand or foot, a court-martial offence.

15 Rum, diluted by the officers and dispensed by sergeants, was given to troops in the minutes before they went 'over the plonk' – 'over the top' of the trench and up into the killing ground of No Man's Land.

16 From *The Somme Times*, 31 July 1916, an unofficial front-line newspaper. Reincarnated as *The Wipers Times* (after Ypres) or *The BEF Times* as editors and contributors were moved around the Western Front.

17 William Beach Thomas, the *Daily Mail* war correspondent with the BEF in France.

18 Cf. Toad in Kenneth Grahame's *The Wind in the Willows* (1908).

19 Cf. Wilfred Owen, 'Anthem for Doomed Youth' (1918).

20 A British offensive of March 1915 which also utilized a concentrated preliminary bombardment, though on a much smaller scale.

21 A reference to the trench experience in T. S. Eliot's 'The Wasteland' (1922).

22 Tucker (1978: 10, 201); Robert Graves, 'Recalling War' (*c.*1938); Morgan (1932: 47).

23 Private John Ball is a voice in Jones (1963). Part 7 – 'The five unmistakable marks' – relates specifically to an action on the Somme in the early morning of 10 July 1916.

24 Liverpool Street Station is a stone's throw away from the setting of Dickens' *Our Mutual Friend*.

25 A novel about the First World War published in 1993.

26 One of the best-known war poems in Britain, John McCrae's 'In Flanders Fields' (1915).

27 Popular First World War song: 'Roses are blooming in Picardy'.

28 Excellent, first rate.

29 A large, ungainly and lethal projectile, resembling a coal-box or coal scuttle, lobbed from German artillery emplacements into British trenches.

30 Thoroughly exhausted.

31 The memorial 'To the Missing of the Somme', designed by Sir Edward Lutyens and built in the 1920s. This vast edifice, placed just outside Thiepval, lists on its columns the names of more than 72,000 British, Commonwealth and Empire soldiers who died on the Somme and who have no known grave.

32 'Recessional' was published in 1897 for Queen Victoria's jubilee. The massive loss of life among Dominion troops on the Somme angered many Australians, Canadians and New Zealanders, and probably accelerated the formation of a distinct national consciousness in each of these countries.

33 A long, rambling novel by Umberto Eco which deals playfully with history, chronology and causation.

34 Here the German front-line trench system faced out from the very edge of the wood.

35 The albatross in Coleridge's 'The Rime of the Ancient Mariner' (1797).

36 In the opinion, presumably, of traditionally minded soldiers, and in contrast to newfangled 'disreputable' arms like high-explosive shells, gas and machine guns.

37 Jones (1963) notes:

> This may appear to be an anachronism, but I remember in 1917 discussing with a friend the possibilities of tourist activity if peace ever came. I remember

we went into details and wondered if the unexploded projectile lying near us would go up under a holidaymaker, and how people would stand to be photographed on our parapets. I recall feeling very angry about this, as you do if you think of strangers ever occupying a house you live in, and which has, for you, particular associations.

38 Cf. the 23rd Psalm.
39 Excerpts from Jones (1963), 'The five unmistakable marks'.
40 Nineteenth-century English children's rhyme: 'Rattle his bones / Over the stones / He's only a pauper / That nobody owns'. For many years blinds were drawn in Britain's working-class districts on 1 July in memory of the dead and wounded of the Somme. This was spontaneous and customary. It had nothing to do with the officially sanctioned 11 November two minutes' silence.
41 Cf. Dylan Thomas, 'And death shall have no dominion' (1933). Every year bones and other detritus are still turned up by ploughing. The region is now noted for beet growing, production of which is governed by the Common Agricultural Policy, a cornerstone of the European Union, itself founded in response to the two world wars. A motorway, built in the 1960s, swings across the eastern end of the 1916 battlefield.

References

Brittain, V. (1933) *Testament of Youth: An Autobiographical Study of the Years 1900–1925*, New York: Macmillan.
Carrington C. E. [pseud. Edmonds, C. E.] (1972) *A Subaltern's War*, first published 1931, New York: Arno Press.
Dearmer, G. (1994) *A Pilgrim's Song: Poems to Mark the Poet's 100th Birthday*, London: John Murray.
Edmonds, Sir J. (1932) *Military Operations: France and Belgium 1916*, London: Macmillan.
Eksteins, M. (1990) *Rites of Spring: The Great War and the Birth of the Modern Age*, New York: Anchor/Doubleday.
Fussell, P. (1975) *The Great War and Modern Memory*, Oxford: Clarendon Press.
Ginzburg, C. (1982) *The Cheese and the Worms: The Cosmos of a Sixteenth-Century Miller*, trans. J. and A. Tedeschi, Harmondsworth: Penguin.
Jones, D. (1963) *In Parenthesis: seinnyessit e gledyf ym penn mameu*, first published 1937, New York: Chilmark Press.
Manning, F. (1929) *The Middle Parts of Fortune: Somme & Ancre*, 1916, vol. 1, London: The Piazza Press.
Morgan, C. (1932) *The Fountain*, London: Macmillan.
O'Riordan, C. (ed.) (1970) *A Martial Medley: Fact and Fiction*, Freeport, first published 1931, New York: Books for Libraries Press.
Schama, S. (1991) *Dead Certainties (Unwarranted Speculations)*, New York: Alfred A. Knopf.
Scott Fitzgerald, F. (1986) *Tender is the Night*, first published 1934, Harmondsworth: Penguin.
Seton-Watson, H. (1967) *The Russian Empire 1801–1917*, Oxford: Clarendon Press.
Silkin, J. (1981) *The Penguin Book of First World War Poetry*, 2nd edn, Harmondsworth: Penguin.

Stevenson, R. L. (1892) 'The Lantern-Bearers', *Across the Plains, With Other Memories and Essays*, London: Chatto & Windus.

Stuart Dolden, A. (1980) *Cannon Fodder: An Infantryman's Life on the Western Front 1914–18*, Poole, Dorset: Blandford Press.

The Somme Times, 31 July 1916.

Travers, T. (1987) *The Killing Ground: The British Army, the Western Front and the Emergence of Modern Warfare 1900–1918*, London: Allen & Unwin.

Tucker, J. F. (1978) *Johnny Get Your Gun: A Personal Narrative of the Somme, Ypres and Arras*, London: William Kimber.

AFTERWORD

It is very difficult for me to explain just why I chose to write in an unusual manner about the Somme, not least because I don't really know the answer myself. It is hard for any of us adequately to account for changes in our styles and habits of thought, for shifts of interest or intellectual preference, or for the reasons why we became bored with a given historical topic or approach. And perhaps in the final analysis it is impossible. If we consider the issue at all, we could well convince ourselves that some changes occurred in response to the prevailing social, cultural and political ethos and that others were prompted by the chance mutations and discontinuities of personal circumstances. And in thinking thus sometimes we might seem right, or at least plausible, both to ourselves and our interlocutors. But since in the end we can never know ourselves fully, it follows that we never really know quite why we became different, why our interests changed – or, indeed, stayed the same. The point of all this is on the one hand to flag up the idea that history is personal, and therefore is (or should be) an overtly literary and imaginative exercise, and on the other to distance myself from those who believe that doing history is (or ought to be) a kind of positivistic scientific endeavour which can somehow exist independently of the personalities of its practitioners.

In any event, if like all of us I am unable to give a complete explanation for my actions, I can at least advance some plausible reasons for the way in which the Somme article was written.

First and most important was the growing conviction that the way I was trained as an historian, the *form* of academic history writing I am used to – I'm borrowing this and other terms here from Hayden White's seminal essay (White 1987) – has over-determined the *content* of history writing, or what history writing could be, and therefore narrowed the space for our engagement with the past. To put it another way, it seemed to me that the formal discourse of academic history had in many instances to be abandoned simply to allow us to explore the past more fully. More on this in a moment.

Linked to this was the issue of what could be called 'purpose' or 'intent' in history writing. Looking back at the work I have published over the last decade or so, what strikes me now is the extent to which I and many other historians were not dealing primarily with the past at all. Further, in some cases (though not I hope in my case) several of us were not even particularly interested in the past. So, for instance, if we take a fairly normative, taken-for-granted characterization of what most historians would still claim to be doing with the past (and what I thought I was doing), i.e., narrating events, discovering causes and relating consequences, for most of the time the texts I had written evinced far less interest in events themselves than in causes and consequences. Indeed, events – the very stuff of 'life in the past' – frequently appeared in the text only as a variety of evidential afterthought dragged in to prove some point or other outside the frame of reference of lived experience. To put it more directly, how often have we taught our students not to narrate but to analyze, without pausing to consider that to analyze means to take a very big step away from the past? And how often have I, as a professional academic historian of twentieth-century Russia, lectured on the 'causes' of the Russian Revolution – the ifs, buts and might-have-beens – and passed over effortlessly to the 'consequences' – the one-party state, Stalinism, the Cold War – with scarcely any attempt to address the event itself, the experience of life in the past? Too often, I would hazard.

These were the two main issues I tried to deal with the Somme article. Two sub-sections, *The Somme, experience, and the absence of events* and *The moral and the mechanical: sense and sensibility* – the phrases in the latter section deliberately referential, one to a novel of the First World War sketched lightly in the text (Manning 1929), the other to Jane Austen – indicated ways in which we might escape from the straitjacket of formal discourse, indeed, the necessity of so escaping should we wish to engage more fully with events. In this context what struck me while writing the piece was that time and again I had to turn to *literary* practitioners for that combination of audacity and freshness (which – alas – is so rarely found among ourselves) when searching for new ways to write and think. Consider, once again, the words of Modris Eksteins on the problem of getting to grips with the Great War (see p. 94). Or on the same theme of the limitations of formal discourse and the problem of opening up spaces in the mind, an aside from the literary critic reread Jon Silkin in a passage introducing a selection of Great War poetry (see p. 96).

Of course historians probably can't aspire to be poets, still less to write as wittily as Johnson, but the notion of de-emphasizing intelligence and foregrounding sensation did seem to me useful in the context of Ekstein's criticism, and it was with these ideas in mind that the rest of the article took shape. What I tried to do was to move, step by step, away from formal discourse and towards a literary landscape saturated with the poetry and prose of those who were there in 1916. Thus:

- *Structure of the British Expeditionary Force*, a dry, text-book description of the Army;
- *A narrative*, a heavily ironic 'standard account';
- *The kingdom of the Somme*, a series of lists and meditations on place;
- two pieces on emotion (*Fear, Humour*) intermingled with participant's poetry and prose, in which grammar and syntax gradually disintegrated;

- *Class, subordination, deference, regionalism, battalion loyalty, the fragmentation of the front, the assertion of self-worth and the irony of memory*, passages from memoirs;
- *A trench conversation*, talks with the dead, where time distortions and cross-references became ever more absurd and overt;
- and finally no conclusion, but instead a discussion of the intellectual respectability or otherwise of what had been essayed (*Notes on composites, fiction, and imagined people*).

Let me conclude by returning to Ekstein's worrying criticism. It is a criticism which applies not only to work on the Great War. We all write 'specialized and limited accounts' that 'pale in evocative and explanatory power'. And not only, it has to be said, because we are trained to. Institutions and interests tend to become conservative and we fear the ridicule of our colleagues. I would go as far as to say that while History as a profession may encourage the search for new *content*, it actively penalizes innovations in the *form*. How many postgraduates desperate for a job would be brave enough to challenge 'the historical method', and how many in search of tenure would question what History faculties are actually for? Maybe a book like this can help embolden some of us to take a few risks.

References

Eksteins, M. (1990) *Rites of Spring: The Great War and the Birth of the Modern Age*, New York: Anchor/Doubleday.

Manning, F. (1929) *The Middle Parts of Fortune: Somme & Ancre, 1916*, vol. 1, London: The Piazza Press.

Silkin, J. (1981) *The Penguin Book of First World War Poetry*, 2nd edn, Harmondsworth: Penguin.

White, H. (1987) *The Content of the Form: Narrative Discourse and Historical Representation*, Baltimore, MD: Johns Hopkins University Press.

6 Antonio Foscarini in the City of Crossed Destinies

Jonathan Walker

> Human affairs are not judged according to their true and proper worth or value but on the basis of opinion, even when it is absurd.[1]

1611–12 Antonio Foscarini is elected as Venetian ambassador to England;[2] Giulio Muscorno is appointed as his secretary.

February 1615 Muscorno denounces Foscarini to the Venetian authorities for various improprieties.

March 1615 Muscorno is given permission to return to Venice. Unbeknownst to him, a resolution is taken to detain him on arrival and investigate his accusations against Foscarini.

April–June 1615 Giovanni Rizzardo is appointed as Muscorno's replacement and instructed to secretly collect evidence on Foscarini.

December 1615 Foscarini departs London on his way back to Venice. Like Muscorno, he will be detained immediately upon arrival.

January 1616 to June 1617 Gregorio Barbarigo (Foscarini's replacement as ambassador) and his secretary Lionello interview witnesses in London, gathering evidence for the prosecuting magistrates in Venice.

July 1618 Foscarini is absolved of any improper conduct; Muscorno is convicted.

8 April 1622 Foscarini is arrested on unknown charges.

20 April 1622 Foscarini is sentenced to death. His corpse is exposed hung upside down, implying that he is guilty of treason.

23 May 1622 The spy Gerolamo Vano is rewarded for unspecified services to Venice.

September 1622 Zuanne Facini claims that he was suborned to offer false testimony in the trial of Alvise Querini for treason. Vano (whose evidence was critical in condemning Querini) is questioned. Facini's claims are subsequently judged to be false.

August to September 1622 Vano is arrested and executed on unspecified charges. After his death, questions are raised regarding various prosecutions in which he was involved.

16 January 1623 Foscarini is proclaimed innocent.

There once was a palace where magistrates summoned men and women to tell their stories. Motifs spilled and scattered like playing cards. But I entered the palace in a time of the dead, a carnival of skeletons risen in a last revel before Judgement Day, bones jumbled together promiscuously. In the room where the magistrates who kept the city's secrets safe once met, three ghosts sat in their chairs: Antonio Foscarini; the Countess of Arundel (an English noblewoman); and Giulio Muscorno, Foscarini's secretary. Like Carnival bishops and Dukes, they had borrowed the authority to summon me, an authority no less binding for being part of a game.

I could not give voice to their silence with words alone. Knowing this, they spread a pack of Tarot cards on the table between us in rows like the keys on a church organ. As each in turn pointed to particular images, my words harmonised and clashed with the dumb notes struck by the pictures. Truth and plausibility, fact and interpretation ran counterpoint in three overlapping melodies.

I

Points of Accusation Used in Interrogations During the Trial of Antonio Foscarini, January 1616.

Lord Luca Tron blamed Foscarini for irreverence at mass, having made a fart at the elevation of the Host . . . One day at table when the mystery of the Trinity was being discussed, Foscarini derisively took up three rolls of bread and said, 'I do not think that any one could persuade me that these three loaves are only one.'[3]

[W]hen the ambassador wrote to his Serenity [i.e. the doge of Venice] he made it up out of his own head and he seemed to be introducing characters in a comedy.[4]

When the strength of the republic was praised he likened it to a little drunken ape masquerading as a fierce lion.[5]

When important business had to be dealt with the Ambassador Foscarini . . . had recourse to the drawing of lots [*sorte*]'.[6]

Foscarini kept the cipher and other public documents without any care, leaving them on the table or at the window for days together, where anyone might see them.[7]

Some Catholic Women of very noble birth were invited to dinner . . . Ambassador Foscarini took a glass in his hand, which had the form of a virile member; he filled it with wine and he invited one of the Women [to drink] from it . . . [S]he, inclining her eyes with a modest blush, got up from the table. Sir Foscarini placed the glass in the front opening of her underwear and distressed her by embracing her. As she fled he grabbed her by the shoulders . . . [S]he exclaimed, saying that she would make it known at Court . . . Sir Foscarini responded, 'Excuse me, this is how we behave in Venice.'[8]

KNIGHT OF CUPS

THE CHARIOT

KING OF COINS

THE POPE

The first card is the *Knight of Cups*. It shows Antonio Foscarini, Venetian ambassador in London from 1611 to 1615, perched uncomfortably on a horse ('You ride like a Venetian' was, of course, a proverbial insult at the time). He was a man of distinguished service who had been knighted as ambassador in France; also a man prone to eccentric and licentious behaviour (hence the *Cups*). A member of the hereditary ruling class in Venice, he was also part of a cosmopolitan international community of fellow ambassadors and political sympathisers. Both communities were linked by a network of couriers and messages criss-crossing Europe, as can be seen in the second card, the *Chariot*.[9]

Next comes the *King of Coins*, James I, a monarch known for the pacific foreign policy that, together with anti-Hapsburg sentiments, linked him to Venice. In the traditional symbolism of playing cards *Coins* (like *Cups*) are a 'feminine' suit, symbolising both virgin and whore: the unaggressive stance of England and Venice (the latter a 'Virgin' city unviolated by foreign invasion) and the dubious sexual reputations of both James and Antonio. The proximity of the *King* to the *Knight* also reminds me of the theme of precedence, a critical issue for Foscarini and a central topic of the despatches carried by the *Chariot*. Foscarini's defence of the privileges due to him as Venetian ambassador was insistent precisely because his awareness of Venice's vulnerability was acute.[10]

The theme of high politics is taking shape, leading on naturally to the *Pope*, who had a special importance for Foscarini, defining his place within the mosaic of factional allegiances in Venice. As part of an *anti*-papal group, Foscarini's personal opinions often differed from the official policy communicated to him in despatches by the Senate, the Venetian council responsible for overall direction of foreign policy. Indeed, he pursued independent, informal negotiations without the Senate's knowledge and his official despatches were often openly partisan.[11] The *Pope* also suggests a Venetian antithesis, Paolo Sarpi, a Servite friar with many contacts in England and North Italy, theological advisor to the Republic of Venice during the Interdict crisis of 1605–7. Sarpi and his associates worked behind the scenes to establish an anti-Hapsburg and anti-Rome alliance headed by England.[12]

THE FOOL

The next card is the *Fool*. Perhaps this was Foscarini himself, the farting writer of 'comedies' with his rude novelty glass? Among Foscarini's embassy staff in London there was a real fool, a half-wit Scot who played a part in the obscure origins of a feud between Foscarini and his secretary, Giulio Muscorno.[13] The half-wit had provoked Muscorno into beating him with a stick (a detail obviously not important enough to merit the inclusion of the *Ace of Batons*). Foscarini then incited the man to take murderous revenge, a malicious joke that failed to amuse Muscorno, who opened a prosecution against his superior with an English court.[14]

Muscorno was in fact the most likely candidate for the *Fool* (at least in Foscarini's eyes), on the basis of the 'buffooneries' and 'comedies' he performed at his superior's expense.[15] The atmosphere between them was already poisonous by 1613 and in early 1615 Muscorno left the embassy.[16] The attempts of the two men to undermine each other compromised Venetian interests so that in June 1615 Rizzardo (Muscorno's replacement as secretary) wrote that, 'I have found the whole court and I might even say the city, divided into two parties, one siding with the ambassador and the other with the secretary'; '[m]atters are in such a condition that the friend of the one must needs be the enemy of the other'. Clearly the *Fool* was a malicious figure, suggesting the confusion of strong emotions and the mutual contempt felt by Muscorno and Foscarini. The *Fool* is followed by the *Ace of Swords*, the assassin's knife hovering over Muscorno's throat, or perhaps the sword of legal authority wielded by the court officials who intervened – maybe even Muscorno's dagger, which Foscarini at one point claimed was being sharpened in a plot against James I.[17]

The *Ace* might suggest violence wielded in the name of political and legal authority but the next card makes that suggestion explicit. It is the *King of Swords*, the Council of Ten and Inquisitors of State in Venice,[18] who had heard of the scandal in London and had granted Muscorno's request for repatriation with the intention of arresting and interrogating him on his arrival in Venice.[19] The Council, responsible for the prosecution of political crimes, wielded a princely authority to judge without accountability within the Republican constitution of Venice. In the exercise of that 'royal' authority it directed

KING OF SWORDS

PAGE OF SWORDS

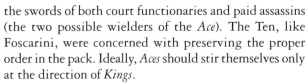

the swords of both court functionaries and paid assassins (the two possible wielders of the *Ace*). The Ten, like Foscarini, were concerned with preserving the proper order in the pack. Ideally, *Aces* should stir themselves only at the direction of *Kings*.

The Inquisitors instructed Muscorno's replacement, Giovanni Rizzardo, to spy on Foscarini, resulting in a parallel series of despatches to the Inquisitors shadowing Foscarini's official ones to the Senate.[20] Rizzardo is the *Page of Swords*, dancing attendance on the *King*. As a secretary he was officially incorporated within the court cards and personalized in a way that the *Ace* was not. A number of other faces were superimposed on the *Page*: for example, the features of the new ambassador and his secretary, who continued investigating after their predecessor's departure. Also discernible are Foscarini and Muscorno themselves, the two most important witnesses in the peculiar 'double' trial developing. Each man sought to be the agent of Justice but each risked becoming its object instead.[21]

The problem facing the Inquisitors of State (who were in charge of the prosecution now underway) and the Ten (who had ultimate responsibility for decisions relating to it) was that they were obliged to conduct an investigation into their own ambassador whilst he was still on the job. Moreover, despite their easy access to Muscorno in custody in Venice, they had to pursue their inquiries at a distance of several hundred miles. Rizzardo was effectively spying on Foscarini, since the Inquisitors could not open the prosecution formally until the latter returned to Venice.[22]

I expected *Justice* to appear next, a woman dressed in the magisterial robes of the Council of Ten, by which all the various swords mentioned so far were dignified. 'Justice wants to know', said the interrogators in court transcripts, meaning themselves. Instead, the *Seven of Swords* was indicated. Unlike the court cards, the *Seven* is an abstract rather than a figurative design, its impersonality suggesting not the anonymous assassin's knife but words on a page. The pen is mightier than the sword but in this case pens served as swords of *Justice*. Distance and delay created a mountain of paper. A series of screens and displacements separated the Ten from their objects of investigation; the accused from the accusers; and the point where a question originated from the point where

it was put to a witness. The *Seven of Swords* represents an interlaced network of sharpened quills, letter openers and secretaries' paper spikes. They prevented Foscarini from regaining control of his own story.

Various levels of communication relating to Foscarini's first trial appear in the *Seven of Swords*. Levels Two, Four and Six are only represented indirectly, in that they affect the content of or are reported in other levels. For example, there are no transcripts of Foscarini's interrogations in Venice, only the summary that was used to prepare the questions put to witnesses in London. Each higher level depends in some sense upon those below it. Sometimes the transition from one stage to the next represents greater awareness (for example, Level Two presumes an awareness of Level One but Level One contains no clue that Level Two exists).[23] However, in some cases it simply represents the passage of time (i.e., what happens in 1617 depends in some sense on what happens in 1615, but not vice versa).[24]

In any case, the appearance of the *Seven of Swords* means that *Justice*, the next card, is free to represent the verdict. Foscarini and Muscorno were weighed in her scales. If one rose, the other fell – the guilt of one being inversely proportional to the innocence of the other. On 30 July 1618, the balance tipped. Foscarini was absolved and Muscorno was sentenced to two years' internal exile in Palma; he was also demoted.[25] This would be a good place for the story to stop. But it continues and, as a result, the meaning of the cards already on the table is retrospectively altered. Judgement is not the end of history, merely an intermediate stage on the way somewhere else, a provisional and (at least for some observers) an unsatisfactory state, subject to revision.

The *Page of Coins* picks up the story, self-proclaimed servant of both the *King of Swords* and *Justice*. This is Gerolamo Vano, a screen and middleman for various informers. Despite his protestations of loyalty, he was bound not by the *Swords* of law but by the *Coins* of reward. The *Moon* was the planet governing his actions. It watched over prison cells and candle-lit council chambers, over the artificial obscurity of cloaks and masks. As Diego Gomez, one of Vano's contacts inside the Spanish embassy put it, 'If I betray my king and my master, if I risk my life and honour, I want money from those big old men.'[26]

XVIII

THE MOON

In 1622, Vano's attention fell on Antonio Foscarini in Venice, or at least this is the most likely explanation for what follows. But before we get to Vano's role we need to consider what Foscarini's contemporaries knew at the time. What were the elements in the sequence to be interpreted and decoded? Foscarini was arrested as he left the Senate and immediately prosecuted by the Inquisitors for revealing secrets to foreign ambassadors – but critically the charges were not made public.[27] Of course, in a sense his arrest as he left the Senate *was* a public declaration and a very dramatic one at that, at precisely the moment when it would make the greatest impact on the maximum number of people.

But what was it a declaration of? The foreign ambassadors in Venice, quick to register every change in the political atmosphere, wrote to their masters immediately but all they could really register was the *size* of the disturbance.[28] They could only speculate on its nature. Their initial reports describe a decisive action whose air of purpose is unmistakable but whose precise meaning is unclear. Most of the commentators had heard some version of the accusations contained in the arrest warrant, but their words reveal a deep uncertainty: 'It is still not known',[29] 'it seems';[30] 'suspicion' is sown;[31] it 'stirs'[32] in the 'shadow'[33] of a crime. Voices run, noises stir. Ambassadors and ex-ambassadors turn up in each other's pockets and each other's reports, their purposes and cross-purposes interwoven. They back each other up, or stab each other in the back. Foscarini had a place in this group. He was someone they took notice of, someone they knew, someone whose actions and fate mattered (i.e. signified in both senses of the word). He was an initiate of their occult world and they were concerned with his fate because it might in some sense foretell their own.

Where does all the rumour come from? Who are the 'probablest voices' referred to by the English ambassador Henry Wotton?[34] They are never identified. No one ever originates, confirms or denies rumours. People just *register* them like litmus paper. 'It is publicly said [*voce pubblica*]'; 'This is what is said, but until now without any certainty'.[35] The Florentine resident tells us that Foscarini went out late at night.[36] This is not a fact, it is a rumour, actually a continuation of accusations dating back to the London embassy. But it *is* a fact that the rumour has now been revived and this reactivation might be significant.

Why have these old rumours suddenly become an issue again (perhaps culminating in the arrest)? What does the fact of the rumour signify, whether it is actually true or not? Was this alleged personal irregularity an important clue, either to Foscarini's actions, or to the intentions of his prosecutors? There are no easy answers, only hypotheses and guesses.

Sexual and political intrigue complement each other.[37] Or rather, sexual intrigue and personal eccentricity are advanced as clues to a deeper political misconduct. What is known is advanced as evidence of what is unknown: the truth lies behind appearances, but corresponds to them. People were seeking a shape for the story. It had to make sense somehow, but it wasn't yet clear which bits of information had to be kept and which discarded. The ambassadors were reshuffling clues not only to determine what had already happened, but to divine possible future repercussions.

The tired old metaphors all apply: we are in a hall of mirrors, or at a masked ball. (Vano is somewhere in the crowd, unrecognizable under his disguise.) The surface of the story breaks apart at the touch, like water. We – and the ambassadors – deal only in reflections. Here we can see a sense in which truth becomes what the story says it is. The ambassadors know that how they interpret is crucial, precisely because their interpretations will affect rather than merely predict the future. For example, their interpretation might determine their ruler's future diplomatic policy.[38]

We are obliged to read the Ten's records in a way that resembles the attempts of ambassadors and spies to decipher information. The problem is that the Ten never make connections explicit and they provide little or no context for resolutions and judgements. Information is strictly compartmentalized in the interests of security. Resolutions are dry as bone.

Foscarini was dead within two weeks of his arrest.[39] The speed and ruthlessness of this prosecution contrast strongly with the slow, poisonous accumulation of evidence between 1615 and 1618. He was strangled in prison, quickly and discreetly, but his body was then 'hanged by one leg on a gallows in the public *Piazza* [i.e. San Marco], from break of day till sunset, with all imaginable circumstances of infamy, his very face having been bruised with dragging on the ground'.[40] Most

THE HANGED MAN

THE MAGICIAN

nobles were beheaded, this being a more honourable death. The inversion here symbolized Foscarini's alleged reversal or inversion of proper values. The corpse was marked with signs that made his dishonour clear, even if the precise cause of that dishonour remained obscure. The Ten were telling the public how to 'read' the corpse, i.e. as the sign of the *Hanged Man* (or *Traitor*, our next card, bringing us back to the table after this long documentary digression), not as a former senator and ambassador.[41] From this point onwards, Foscarini was reduced to a ghostly presence in his own story, whose swinging inverted corpse cast a shadow over those associated with him.

The spill of rumour is figured in the *Five of Cups* (suggesting political as well as sexual impropriety and in the multiplication of the sign, perhaps promiscuity). *Five* also implicates Antonio with his alleged co-conspirators, the ambassadors of France, Spain, the Empire and the Papacy (figures dealt out interchangeably in the rumours).[42] I was reminded again that there are two worlds in this story. There is Venice, a particular city with its own laws, customs and institutions. Then there is an international community of ambassadors and expatriates. Gossip moves, tales are told, on a local circuit, moving from mouth to mouth (the *Five of Cups*) and on an international circuit (the *Chariot*). The movement of information is a constant theme, backwards and forwards, not only from place to place but between speech and writing, between a local circuit where events have one significance and an international circuit where they have another.

Again, I expected this to be the end of Foscarini's tale, but in the artificial 'night' of secret council sessions something was happening, traces of some disturbance bubbled to the surface. Unexplained resolutions prompted further gossip. The turn of events is suggested by the *Bagatto*, perhaps depicting a moneychanger, perhaps a conman running a 'Find the Lady' game. The ambiguous nature of the card mirrors its ambiguous role in the story.[43] The *Bagatto* is an orchestrator of plots who performs sleights of hand in the stories he tells. He is a middleman, a screen, a translator who allows signs and symbols to be interpreted. As a maker of plots the *Bagatto* does not represent any one individual in this part of the story (although Vano, the *Page of Coins*, first suggests him to us). Rather, he is the organizing principle of our story at this point, which is composed of an extended series of plots.

The *Bagatto* was, for example, at work during August 1622 when the Inquisitors of State proposed the arrest of Gerolamo Vano and his associate Domenico for unspecified reasons.[44] Both men were sentenced to hang, a proposal that barely won out over another to drown Vano secretly.[45] An extraordinary meeting of the Ten on the morning of the 22 September deferred the executions until the entire council met later in the day, when a suspension of the sentence was suggested to allow the investigation of 'things asserted' by Domenico, along with a review of the 'necessary' past prosecutions. Again, no details were provided to explain these tantalizing phrases. The proposals failed to obtain the necessary majorities and the executions were therefore carried out as decreed.[46]

On the day of his death, Vano wrote a will in prison (as Foscarini had done a few months earlier).[47] Notes appended to this will in the hours preceding the execution suggest a man with a bad conscience. Their style contrasts with the subtle deployment of light and shade in his earlier intelligence reports, where he specialized in night scenes, using *sfumato* effects and artful imprecision. With death approaching, Vano resorts to crude, broad strokes, bald statements like, 'I Gerolamo Vano do not know the *Clarissimo* Alvise Querini . . . and I didn't speak ill of him to anyone because I've never seen or known him.' This is a very puzzling statement, since Querini, who had recently been convicted of treason, appears regularly in Vano's reports.[48]

What then was the point of Vano's final note? There is a clue hidden in the Ten's registers. In August 1622, Zuanne Facini, one of the original witnesses in Querini's case, had reappeared to claim that his testimony had been suborned.[49] Since this happened at about the same time as Vano's arrest and he and Facini were brought face to face in prison to test their reactions, we can assume that Vano was the man under suspicion. Contrary to what we might expect, Vano was innocent of this charge. The investigation revealed that Querini's brother had bribed Facini to undermine his own testimony in the hope that the case would collapse. In other words, Facini had been suborned to *pretend* that he had been suborned.[50] Despite Vano's suspicious sensitivity on his case, Querini remained in prison (although he was freed by the more prosaic means of a purchased pardon in 1623). Facini got ten years' service in the galleys. Querini's brother, who initiated the whole thing, got off without punishment.[51] Nonetheless, Vano was not out of trouble. Ironically, Facini's false accusation may have raised more searching questions about his credibility. It is surely not a coincidence that a number of cases in which his evidence had been critical were reviewed in the period after his arrest.[52] Doubts spread, cracks in Vano's mask.

One name missing from Vano's 'duty of conscience' (his phrase) was that of Antonio Foscarini. Subsequent events reveal that it should have been there. Wotton wrote to James I in January 1623 to explain why. His story coincides roughly (but not exactly) with those told by other ambassadors.[53] He began with the observation that 'the case of the late Cavalier Antonio Foscarini hath been diversely misreported, and perhaps not the least even by those that were his judges, to cover their own disgrace'. Wotton claimed that Vano had accused Foscarini, citing information allegedly provided by an informant in the Spanish embassy.[54] By early 1622, Vano had already brought about the arrest of various Venetian traitors (including Querini), which no doubt lent him credibility. According to Wotton, a new accusation against Marco Miani was the catalyst for Vano's downfall, since it led to a request by the Inquisitors to interview the informant in question directly.[55] When asked to provide corroboration of Vano's charges, the man denied knowing him, resulting in a sentence of death for perjury against the luckless spy and his accomplice Domenico. There is (of course) no reference to Marco Miani either in the Ten's registers or Vano's reports.

Four months after Vano's execution, the Ten officially announced Foscarini's innocence. How were they persuaded to make this proclamation? In Wotton's version, Foscarini's nephews requested that Vano be questioned about their uncle's case before his execution. Their request was refused,

> either because the false witnesses, being now condemned men, were disabled by course of law to give any further testimony, or for that the Council of Ten thought it wisdom to smother an irrevocable error. The petition being denied, no possible way remained

for the nephews to clear the defamation of their uncle (which in the rigour of this State had been likewise a perpetual stop to their own fortunes) but by means of the confessor, to whom the delinquents should disburden their souls before their death; and by him, at importunate and strong persuasion of the said nephews, the matter was revealed. . . . [T]he nephews have removed the body of their uncle from the church of SS. Giovanni et Paolo, where condemned persons are of custom interred, to the monument of their ancestors in another temple, and would have given it solemn and public burial; but having been kept from increasing thereby the scandal, at the persuasion rather of the Prince than by authority, they now determine to repair his fame by an epitaph.[56]

Again, the nephews and the priest do not appear in official records.

The *Five of Cups* shows Wotton's (unsubstantiated) version of events. He claimed that yes, there were conspiracies, but none of them had anything to do with Foscarini. His 'plot' was a fiction invented by Vano and Domenico. The second plot was that of Vano, who conspired to 'unmask' Foscarini as a traitor. In other words, Vano plotted to conceal the fact that there was no plot. The third conspiracy was that of the Ten, who plotted to conceal Vano's deceit: to conceal the plot that concealed the fact that there was no plot. The fourth conspiracy was that of Foscarini's nephews, anxious to find some way of clearing their uncle's name. Theirs was a plot to reveal the plot to conceal the plot to conceal the fact that there was no plot.

The revelation (allegedly) provided by Vano's confessor furnished the only two specific accusations in this whole tortuous affair, and one of these was indirect (i.e. the confessor accused Vano of accusing Foscarini). It is deeply ironic that the only identifiable (but unnamed) source of information in this (uncorroborated) account is a man who broke his oath as a religious *not* to pass on information he had heard.[57] The Ten piously proclaimed Foscarini's innocence in January 1623,

[s]ince the Providence of the lord God, by means truly marvellous and inscrutable to human minds,

has disposed that the authors and ministers of the falsehood and impostures plotted against our late beloved noble Antonio Foscarini . . . have now *without the intervention or provocation of anyone*, manifested themselves.[58]

Deus ex machina. Details remain 'at large', lost in the gaps between the cards on the table. For example, Foscarini left 6,000 ducats 'to him that should discover his innocency'.[59] Did he? There's no sign of it in the copy of his will registered in the records of the Ten – although this version was certainly censored.[60] Moreover, other commentators constructed different stories, although all used the same basic elements. The cryptic and fragmentary nature of the surviving records does not allow us to determine *which* version is true, only to trace variations and possibilities.[61]

The final image in Foscarini's tale, or at least in our version of it, is placed before us. It is the *Angel* or *Trumpet*, depicting the Last Judgement and the dead rising from their tombs. The outcome of all these plots transcends them all, as the *Angel* hangs untouched above the *World*, seeing all, judging all. Plot follows plot, but the truth comes from God alone (or more likely, the Ten disclaim all responsibility for a truth which is profoundly embarrassing to them). The proclamation of Foscarini's innocence is announced by trumpet, the dead man rises from his grave to be reinterred honourably. Perhaps Gerolamo Vano rises unnoticed with him, to be judged by God rather than the Council of Ten.

II

Despatch of the Florentine resident, 23 April 1622.

. . . is generally agreed that Foscarini went out at night alone, . . . dressed bizarrely, to the house of the Countess of Arundel . . . [T]hey say that Foscarini initially began to visit her as a compliment, and that . . . after a short while meetings with the Imperial resident were arranged, which inevitably led to Spain . . . [I]t is publicly said[62] that the Countess has been secretly ordered to leave Venice within three days.[63]

The second story now commences with the *Queen of Batons* (or *Wands*) at the bottom left corner of the table. The Countess of Arundel can be seen holding the baton that symbolized her husband's authority as Earl Marshal in England.[64] The next card, laid above the first, is the *World*, the community of expatriates, travellers and ambassadorial staff in which the Countess moved in voluntary exile in Venice. This was the same world that Antonio Foscarini lived in, or at least there were many possible points of contact between the two.[65]

What was the Countess doing in Venice? The next card might hold the answer: the *Ace of Cups*, in which the officiating priest at the mass held the wine of communion. The Countess was suspected to be a Catholic (or at least a sympathizer),[66] escaping the restrictions in force in England by having her sons educated abroad.[67] This suspicion was underlined by the fact that the *Ace* now lay just below a card that was already on the table as part of Foscarini's tale: the *Pope*. If the *World* had signified the points of contact between Foscarini and the Countess, the *Pope* might signal their divergence, since they attached such different meanings to the figure. More probably it suggested the rumours that circulated after Foscarini's execution, that placed the two of them together in illegal conversations with various ambassadors, among whom Spain seems rather out of place, given Foscarini's political sympathies.[68]

Sexual intrigue complemented political intrigue under the light of the *Moon*, so it is natural that the next fresh card should be *The Lovers*, followed by the *Three of Cups*, representing the intimate suppers the conspirators were thought to have enjoyed. Venetian tradition says that Foscarini's nocturnal outings were visits to a lover, whose name he refused to reveal when arrested. In this romantic myth, Foscarini's gallantry seals his doom, although it's difficult to reconcile with the image of him sticking a glass dildo down an Englishwoman's knickers.

The *Three* and the *Ace* also suggest the elements manipulated on the board of the *Bagatto*, covering and moving (deferring the revelation of) the single seed of truth. The tales of Foscarini and the Countess crossed each other, even if the same elements might assume

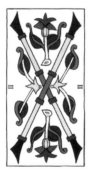

different meanings in each, although in fact these connections were only made by observers *after* Foscarini's execution, which we now cross over to in this story. The *Hanged Man* comes into particularly sharp relief because it possesses the same meaning in the Countess' tale as in Foscarini's: potential disgrace.

The card after the *Hanged Man* was also already on the table: the *Fool*. This was another card with the same meaning in both tales, even if the *identity* of the Fool is quite different here. For the Countess, the *Fool* was Henry Wotton, the English ambassador, 'a fabler, or, as the devil is, father of lies',[69] the man whose malicious or ill-informed advice nearly proved disastrous for her.[70] In April 1622 Wotton sent to tell the Countess that her arrest was imminent, and that she should leave Venetian territory without delay, advice that she did not take. The Countess at the point of decision, faced with Wotton's ultimatum, can be seen in the next new card, the *Two of Batons*, a crossroads. It also shows the roads over which news of her predicament travelled (by means of the *Chariot?*) to the courts of Europe, and in particular to that of James I.[71] The secretary Lionello, who was familiar with Foscarini's tale from his previous experience in the London embassy, had spoken with the Countess' steward.[72] He had confided that

> she is very angry with Wotton, not only for making her believe as certain what the republic never thought, and by the bad advice to flee and so create an indelible impression of guilt, but because she is not without reasonable suspicion that he had something to do with the origin of this false report, because he objected to her staying in this city, fancying that she watched his proceedings, and was a weight on his arms, preventing him from acting with such freedom in public affairs as he desired.[73]

Wotton predicts the Countess' imminent arrest (or perhaps he pretends to believe the rumours for his own purposes? Every interpretation has a shadow alternative that follows it, every outward appearance conceals or hints at an inner reality.) He warns the Countess not to return to Venice. If she had run away as a result of this advice, she would have ended up fulfilling Wotton's prophecy. However, none of the prophecies and divinations regarding the Countess come to pass because she took continual and decisive action to frustrate them. Thus it *was* possible to swim against the natural 'flow' and momentum of the story.

Gossip flows like blood from a wound (or spills like wine from the various *Cups* before us?) and Foscarini died before he could staunch it. But the Countess was in a stronger position, and moreover was a woman of determination, as suggested by *Fortitude* (or *Strength*). Wotton's warning led her to seek an audience with the Venetian cabinet on the morning of 22 April to protest officially her innocence regarding the rumours linking her with Foscarini.

Reputations depended on stories. The critical point here is whose version would be heard. Who could muster enough backing to make their version stick? The struggle for reputation was a struggle for publicity. The Countess knew that '[a]s the rumour against her was public', 'it concerned her honour to give some public satisfaction of her innocence, and likewise to receive some public reparation'.[74] The Ten ruthlessly suppressed information about Foscarini, leaving his reputation open to every malicious rumour. The Countess initially had the same problem. The Florentine resident interpreted her actions as further evidence of her guilt, the opposite of what she had intended.[75] (Similarly, some years before, Paolo Sarpi had warned the English ambassador not to defend their mutual friend Antonio Foscarini before the Venetian cabinet as this would be more likely to sow suspicion than dispel doubt.)[76]

We might ask in what sense the rumour regarding the Countess was 'public'? It was publicly known, but relayed only in private conversations and ciphered despatches. The Florentine resident has a delicious phrase: it 'is publicly said that the Countess has been secretly ordered'. A paradox: secrets (or rather rumoured secrets) are publicly known and public rumours are whispered secretly. There are two levels in politics, just as there are two circuits of information. There is what is said publicly, what is official policy. The Doge says in the audience of 22 April, 'We know nothing about any of this! We are shocked and troubled by your suggestions.' Then there is the second level, that of signs and clues. The Countess intended her visit to the cabinet to be read as a straightforward complaint and statement: I am innocent.

But the Florentine resident, used to devious hints, reads it on another level, because the subject of the audience was not publicized.

A week later on 29 April, Wotton and Arundel were requested to attend another audience. The messenger (Lionello) read their reactions. Wotton said he was happy but changed colour when told that the Countess would also be there.[77] (Clearly the cabinet wanted to 'read' the relationship between Wotton and Arundel just as much as the community of ambassadors wished to 'read' the hints and clues regarding the possible relationship between Foscarini and Arundel.) The Countess had actually been summoned to receive notice of the 'public reparation' she desired but,[78] since she didn't know this, she brought a prepared statement with her, which Wotton also circulated in manuscript to make sure everyone knew its contents. Moreover, she was accompanied by honourable witnesses to make sure the real subject of the audience was publicized. *Strength* might therefore also represent Colonel Peyton, an English mercenary captain in Venetian service, waiting outside the Council chamber where the Countess was in audience, his presence symbolizing her moral authority and ability to command support.

During the audience Wotton read out the Countess' statement, in which she claimed complete innocence of any association with Foscarini and explained the circumstances behind the audience of 22 April. Now this is rather odd, since it was hardly complimentary to him. What are we to make of this, and of the earlier sign of Wotton changing colour? What better way was there for the Countess to justify herself, and head off the possible threat represented by Wotton, than to force him to tell *her* story, which brought little credit to him, rather than his own? Wotton was a ventriloquist's dummy here and, after reading out the Countess' account, his odd behaviour suggested the deep discomfiture he felt.

> The ambassador, who throughout the audience had made constant interruptions, again broke in saying, 'I have to justify myself also in this matter, because, as I told your Serenity, I have been deceived. Rumours against the Countess came to me from every quarter after the sentence on that unhappy gentleman [i.e. Foscarini]'. . . . [The Countess]

appeared as contented as the ambassador was confused, as he feared that he had utterly ruined his fortunes and his prospects at the court by this business.[79]

In fact, Wotton was recalled to England shortly after these events (a piece of information that might or might not be connected to one of the cards on the table).

Fortitude prises open the jaws of a lion, just as the Countess compelled the mouth of Henry Wotton to speak her words and brought forth tokens of victory from the jaws of the Lion of St. Mark. Wotton's humiliation (the *Fool* made to appear foolish) was obviously instructive in itself but it was also intended as a message to the cabinet, as were the echoing footsteps of Colonel Peyton outside. The cabinet understood it, as the final card in this tale suggested: the *Sun*. The deliberation read to the Countess on 29 April awarded her various gifts, an escort during public festivities and other signs of respect.[80] The Florentine resident said in May that she had 'been totally cleared and has justified herself to the public fully'.[81] Why did these things 'justify' her to him, when the earlier audience had merely provoked his suspicion? In this case, the state publicly and unambiguously expressed its support, both with words *and* signs (i.e. the gifts). In publicly honouring the Countess, the Republic committed its honour to her innocence. To continue to assert her guilt was therefore to offend the Republic's honour.[82] The Countess finished her tale in the warm light of public approval. It was a tale whose destructive suggestions (running from the *Moon* to the *Fool*) had been contained by a show of *Strength*.

III

Points on which Defence Witnesses were to be Questioned on Behalf of Antonio Foscarini, February 1617.

> If Muscorno said publicly, speaking of the mass of the Nobility[83] . . . [that] two or three hundred [were] his friends and patrons . . . [R]aising his posterior parts and smacking them with his hand, he said, 'I hold all the others here'.[84]
>
> If Muscorno never did anything but make mischief, turning Foscarini's house upside down. If during the whole time of his stay in England he kept Foscarini in a constant state of disquiet.[85]

That Muscorno negotiated with the ministers of the king and the ministers of other princes without ever informing Foscarini about it.[86]

Our final tale takes us back to the London embassy and begins with a card already upon the table, the *Bagatto*, representing Giulio Muscorno, who had played the part of the *Fool* in Foscarini's tale. However, in his own tale, Muscorno was not the performer of 'buffooneries' but the master manipulator of plots.

In London, Muscorno was *Page* both to Foscarini's *Knight* and to the brimming *Cups* of rumour in the London court (hence the following *Five of Cups*, with the *Page* in ghostly potential behind it, unused because it was too obvious for the devious mind of the *Bagatto*). The next two cards were also already on the table and the first, the *King of Swords*, signalled the same event in Muscorno's tale as in Foscarini's, the initial intervention of the Council of Ten.

The *Ace of Swords* was Muscorno's tongue, a double-edged weapon by which he himself was wounded. His tale now branches out with fresh cards, since he had left London and terminated all contact with Foscarini. The first is *Temperance*, which Muscorno had lacked, but which the Council of Ten displayed in their slow accumulation of evidence. In his willingness to play the *Ace of Swords* in both London and Venice lay Muscorno's undoing. For while he wished to use the *Ace* to chop off Foscarini's head,[87] he did not understand that his fate was still inextricably bound to that of his master, a situation shown in the inter-twined *Two of Swords* (the same situation suggested by the scales of *Justice* in Foscarini's tale). Both men still possessed the power to hurt each other but not the power to save themselves. Muscorno failed to realize that the appearance of the *King of Swords* denied him full control of the *Ace*, which no longer represented his tongue but a notary's pen. The sword of *Justice* was not his to command. His accusations no longer belonged to him but to the state.

This gradual loss of control is represented by the next card, the *Wheel of Fortune*, an image that fore-tells Muscorno's conviction by the court. The final card in Muscorno's tale is the *Old Man* (also called the *Hermit*), his isolation when stripped of his official

identity as a secretary, banned not only from the Ducal Chancery but from a future role in the tales of others, watching the sands slip through the hourglass he holds in obscurity.

Or rather, this is how the tale *should* have ended. Unfortunately, I know that off the edge of our grid of cards, in a bathetic coda that undermines the dramatic conclusion to his story, Muscorno was pardoned and accepted back into the Ducal Chancery with a demotion in 1620. This produced a farcical situation in which he lacked the security clearance to index and edit his own correspondence from London.[88] This absurd insistence on snipping up identities and refusing to re-integrate them is symptomatic both of the way in which the Council of Ten controlled stories and of the difficulties they faced in sustaining the judgements with which they concluded them.[89] There is no card for this final development because it does not fit. It is a false note in our melody.[90]

IV

> [The] Lord God, moved by my undeserved disasters and most humble prayers, inspired Your Serenity and the most excellent Council of Ten, . . . to give weight not only to my poor tongue, but also to my reverent silence.[91]

In the grid of cards, Foscarini's tale includes cards that are also used in both Arundel's and Muscorno's, but the latter two stories do not cross each other. Muscorno had no opportunity to cross Arundel, since he was off-stage in 1622 when the shadow of the *Hanged Man* fell over her tale.

What are the morals of our three tales? I offer you a choice. Stories built on nothing might nonetheless have real consequences; gossip creates its own facts; in some cases it is possible to be guilty of acting suspiciously. The truth sometimes matters less than who has access to information, or who can shout their story loudest, or who can get other people to tell their story for them. In short, *how* you tell a tale matters.

Foscarini's tale appears as a fantasy here but other genres may be discerned within it. Perhaps it's a detective story, or a spy story, a story of intrigue and conspiracy (although who exactly is doing the intriguing and conspiring is rather complicated and, as I've already said, its initial interpreters were concerned with prediction as much as with detection). Maybe, in our terms, this works better as a spy story than as a detective story. Its subject is not the truth that must be revealed so much as the successive onion layers of deceit surrounding it.

Foscarini's many surviving words emphasize his silences, the last of which was imposed upon him by the executioner's garrotte. The images placed between the evidence and my words serve as a mask, a screen that separates the 'real' Foscarini from the various 'pseudo-Foscarinis', protecting his identity in much the same way that Vano protected his informants. In other words, the cards protect the truth by emphasizing artifice. Only in this way can I respect Foscarini's silence whilst still allowing him to be heard.

Acknowledgements

This chapter began life as a lecture for a course at the University of Wales, Swansea called 'Telling Tales', largely inspired by Davis (1988). My thanks are due to Stuart Clark and John Spurr, who conceived this course (but should not be held responsible for what I have done with their idea here). The students who had to sit through my original lecture ('What's he talking about?', 'Are you writing any of this down?') also deserve a mention. Richard Mackenney's conference paper 'A Plot Discovered'?: Myth, Legend and the 'Spanish Conspiracy' against Venice in 1618 provided early inspiration, while Jason Scott Warren suggested numerous improvements.

Notes

CSPV is the *Calendar of State Papers and Manuscripts Relating to English Affairs, Existing in the Archives and Collections of Venice* (1905, 1907, 1908, 1909, 1911) London: HM Stationery Office. The following abbreviations refer to material from the *Archivio di stato di Venezia* (but note that some archival sources are quoted indirectly *via* the translations given in *CSPV*). X, *Consiglio dei Dieci*, followed by Co., *Comuni*; Cr., *Criminali*; Sec., *Secreti*; Inq., *Inquisitori di stato*; reg., *registro*; b., *busta*.

1 Paolo Sarpi to Dudley Carleton, 19 Dec. 1613, in Sarpi (1969: 652).
2 The outline of Foscarini's story is well known to Venetian historians, although the standard accounts omit various details discussed below. See, for example, Romanin (1858: 164–99); Bartoccini *et al.* (1997: 361–5); Secchi (1969); and Preto (1994), particularly pp. 66, 129, 605 (I am indebted to Preto's work for invaluable references to primary sources). A useful selection of primary sources can be found in *CSPV*, vols 12–15 and 17, Smith (1907) and Romanin (1858: 584–606).

3 This first point is actually quoted from testimony collected by the Venetian ambassador in Paris, rather than the interrogatories cited below. See *CSPV*, vol. 14, 26 Sept. 1615: 29–30.

4 Point no. 13 from the interrogatory relating to the accusations against Foscarini, quoted from the paraphrase in *CSPV*, vol. 14: 593.

5 No. 19 quoted from *CSPV*, vol. 14: 594.

6 No. 49 from Inq., b. 155.

7 No. 78 from *CSPV*, vol. 14: 596.

8 No. 80 from Inq., b. 155.

9 Hence, during enquiries into Foscarini's activities as ambassador in London, the Inquisitors of State were authorized to write to 'all foreign courts and whithersoever they shall think fit, so as to come at the truth' (*CSPV*, vol. 13: 556). A selection of material collected by the Venetian ambassador in France to establish details relating to events in London can be found in *CSPV*, vol. 14: 29.

10 For arguments over precedence involving Foscarini, see *CSPV*, vol. 12: 351 and *CSPV*, vol. 14: 66–7, 76, 90, 96–8. His oversensitivity to this issue was a consequence of his allegiance to the anti-papal *giovani* party, who favoured a more active, interventionist foreign policy for Venice. Foscarini may be obliged to carry a 'feminine' sign in my tale, but perhaps he would have been happier with the assertive suits of *Swords* and *Batons*.

11 See Secchi (1969); Bartoccini *et al.* (1997: 361); Wootton (1983: 65).

12 On Sarpi and his associates (including Foscarini) see Wootton (1983: 93–4, 98); Lievsay (1973); Cozzi (1979).

13 Muscorno replaced the previous secretary, Scaramelli, who had also fallen out with Foscarini (*CSPV*, vol. 12, 4 June 1612: 369, see also p. 389).

14 See Rizzardo's despatch of 18 June 1615 in *CSPV*, vol. 13: 481–3. Foscarini insisted that he had been misrepresented, see *CSPV*, vol. 14: 597.

15 *CSPV*, vol. 14: 599 and the interrogatory for Foscarini's defence. Point 126 queries 'If Muscorno began to make comedies of Foscarini in the Exchange, with lords and ladies, with the ministers of princes and finally at the court of their Majesties and the prince'.

16 *CSPV*, vol. 13: 467, 482–3.

17 *CSPV*, vol. 14: 595–6 for the latter point.

18 On the Inquisitors, see Preto (1994); Canosa (1989); Fulin (1868).

19 *CSPV*, vol. 13: 391–3. In Sarpi (1969: 661 and note 7), Cozzi claims that Muscorno submitted an official denunciation against Foscarini in mid-1614, but the surviving index of material relating to the trial in Inq., b. 155 indicates that the investigation was only opened in February 1615, and the formal trial only began after Foscarini's return to Venice.

20 For Rizzardo's initial report on 11 June 1615, see *CSPV*, vol. 13: 467. On 22 October 1615, Rizzardo explained that

> the Ambassador Foscarini is collecting proofs of his charges against the Secretary Muscorno. He attaches importance to this and has frequently spoken to me about it, occasionally asking my opinion. I have been obliged to answer and conduct myself in conformity with your commands, in order not to excite his suspicions.
>
> (*CSPV*, vol. 14: 48)

21 What should have been a rigorously inquisitorial prosecution actually took on characteristics of an accusatorial prosecution, with the Inquisitors and the Ten acting as a middleman or screen between the two parties who, after their separation in London, probably never confronted each other directly again, at least during the trial. On inquisitorial prosecution as used by the Council of Ten, see Cozzi (1988); Maranini (1974: 458–72); Povolo (1997); Walker (2002a).

22 Since Rizzardo could not appeal to formal judicial procedure to authenticate the material sent to Venice, he was acutely conscious of being personally accountable for its accuracy and obsessively asserted *his* (as opposed to the *witnesses'*) reliability. On 18 June 1615 he claimed 'By comparing the things said by . . . various people I have unearthed the truth' (*CSPV*, vol. 13: 483); on 23 July he clarified that 'I have written nothing which I have not verified by the testimony of more than one person' (*CSPV*, vol. 13: 535).

23 'Awareness' is slightly misleading, since texts rather than authors are indicated here. The Foscarini who writes despatches to the Senate at Level One is obviously aware of the Foscarini who pursues his own private strategies at Level Two but the Level One despatches do not at any point betray that awareness. Among the most vivid examples of the discrepancies between different levels (in this case between Levels One and Two) are Foscarini's letters (to the Ten rather than the Senate) in support of Muscorno's requests for repatriation, which betray nothing of the conflicts racking the embassy (see e.g. *CSPV*, vol. 13: 193, 275).

24 Level Four involves a hypothesis which is neither demonstrable nor, perhaps, even likely but it raises interesting questions that certainly must have occurred to the Inquisitors. *If* Foscarini was aware that Rizzardo had been sent to spy on him, then this entirely changes the meaning of the documents relating to Levels One, Two and Three, despite the fact that their content remains exactly the same. The hypothesis is valuable, whether or not it is true, because it shakes the kaleidoscope (and therefore illustrates a more general point). Nothing in the rest of the narrative depends on its truth.

25 See *CSPV*, vol. 15: 277–8. The *CSPV* paraphrase of the sentence against Muscorno is incomplete. For the original see X Cr., reg. 35 (1618), 44r–v. In August he was permitted to convert his sentence to imprisonment in Venice and he was released early with a pardon in July 1619 (*CSPV*, vol. 15: 285, 561).

26 Inq., b. 636, report of Gerolamo Vano to the Inquisitors of State, 8 or 9 July 1620. For more on Vano's reports, see Walker (2002b, 2003).

27 *CSPV*, vol. 17, 8 Apr. 1622: 284. The Savoyard ambassador reported on 23 Apr. 1622 that 'Tomorrow the sentence will be published in the Great Council; and then the causes of this affair will be revealed' (see Romanin 1858: 589). However, there is no note regarding any such publication in the Ten's criminal register. In what follows the distinction between what the Council of Ten knew and what the foreign ambassadors who commented on the case knew is critical. The Ten were working on the basis of a specific accusation from a trusted informant that was legally acceptable because 'matters of state' allowed judicial discretion in the interpretation of evidence (treason, like witchcraft, was a *crimen exemptum*, and for much the same reasons). Foscarini was convicted and executed *unjustly*, but *legally*. His condemnation by public opinion, based on the gossip relayed by ambassadors, was a distinct process (but one which the Ten were willing to take advantage of).

28 The text of the relevant reports can be found in Romanin (1858: 584–606).

29 Despatch of the Tuscan resident Nicolo Sacchetti, 9 Apr. 1622 in Romanin (1858: 584).

30 Sacchetti, 16 Apr. 1622, Romanin (1858: 585).

31 Sacchetti, 12 Apr. 1622, Romanin (1858: 584).

32 Letter of Henry Wotton, 15 Apr. 1622, in Smith (1907: 232).

33 Sacchetti, 16 Apr. 1622 in Romanin (1858: 585).

34 Smith (1907: 232).

35 Sacchetti, 23 Apr. 1622 in Romanin (1858: 586).

36 Despatch of 12 Apr. 1622, Romanin (1858: 584).

37 'He is said likewise to have led a courtesan to Monsignor de Leon's [the French ambassador's] house vizarded, and then calling himself Bernardo Tiepolo; which change of name doth stir suspicion; for otherwise the fact itself *se ne va con l'acqua santa*' (Smith 1907: 232). For further reminders of Foscarini's 'eccentricity', see the despatch of the Savoyard ambassador dated 23 Apr. 1622 in Romanin (1858: 589).

38 Given the possibility for error, it was all the more important that the information on which interpretations depended be accurate. In 1615 Muscorno had played on this sensitivity (and on the existence of the various levels of awareness depicted in the *Seven of Swords*) by claiming that Foscarini's despatches to the Senate were 'not true but capricious inventions of his own', or second-hand gossip (see *CSPV*, vol. 14: 19–20). On 9 Oct. 1615 Rizzardo partially confirmed this: 'the news sent by His Excellency is mostly obtained from the ambassadors of other princes, and when I have suspected him of speaking on his own authority, especially in important matters, I have indicated so much' (CSPV, vol. 14: 40). Needless to say, this is not the impression gained from Foscarini's despatches.

39 See X Cr., reg. 39, 12v, 14r–v and *CSPV*, vol. 17: 292.

40 Smith (1907: 262).

41 Sacchetti noted that the sentence was

> executed with greater consternation among this nobility than has ever been seen, since the body of a principal Senator has been exposed all day in this manner. The investigation was carried out in such a secret manner, that the reasons for this rigorous sentence are still apparently not known precisely.
>
> (Romanin 1858: 586)

On the 'icon' of the 'Hanged Man', see Edgerton (1985).

42 These are the five possible conspirators mentioned by contemporary commentators; the Ten probably had another group of five in mind, if the prosecution was based on Vano's reports. He focused on a group consisting of the Imperial resident (Nicolo Rossi), the secretary of Spain, the Mantuan resident and Rossi's secretary Giulio Cazzari, who was also a crony of Spain and Mantua. Foscarini would, of course, be the hypothetical fifth man. Giluio Cazzari was assassinated in July 1622 as a result of evidence supplied by Gerolamo Vano. See Walker (2003).

43 Sixteenth-century Italian sources often use the name *Bagatella*, but this variant of uncertain etymology is now established in Italy. There are various possible derivations for the card's name. *Bagattelliere* means someone who performs card tricks, but also a Mountebank (the name of the card is sometimes translated thus into English from the French variant, *bataleur*). Such men were often accompanied by a *Fool* in early modern Italy. *Bagatella* (related to *bagattino*, a small coin) means a

thing of little value (the card is always the lowest trump), but also a card trick or fraud (although the card ranks lowest, it often has a high point value in games). A number of puns in Aretino (1992) suggest possible connections between the figure of the *Bagatto* and the verbs *barare* and *barattare*. The former means 'to trick at the game of cards or dice'; the latter means 'to exchange' (see Cortelazzo and Zolli 1979: 113, 117 under *barattare, barattiere* and *baro*).

This (fruitful) confusion with regard to the card's name led to confusion in its iconography. Sometimes the man behind the table appears to represent a money-changer with a supply of coins; sometimes he is explicitly holding a playing card; at other times he appears to be shuffling the cups involved in a 'Find the Lady' game.

44 X Cr., reg. 39, 61v. Domenico was an ex-employee of the Spanish embassy who had previously worked for Vano as an informant. See Walker (2002b).

45 The corpses of Vano and Domenico were not to be hung upside down by the foot, as Foscarini's had been. This suggests that they were not accused of treason, or at least that the Inquisitors did not wish to label them as traitors.

46 X Cr., reg. 39, fos 76r–77r. It is clear from the formulae used that Domenico was *not* seeking a pardon in exchange for the information he had to offer. Was he seeking to make a final confession and unburden his conscience?

47 See X Cr., filza 49, entry under 5 Oct. 1622 for Vano's will. For Foscarini's will, see X Cr., reg. 39, 15r–17r and below.

48 Arguably, perhaps, in such a way that he could claim to be passing on someone else's comments and usually only by surname, so it was left to the Inquisitors to work out exactly *which* Querini was guilty. See e.g. reports dated 4 July, 18 July and 31 Aug. 1620 in Inq., b. 636.

49 Zuanne Facini was almost certainly 'Zuanetto' (a.k.a. Zuanne), one of Vano's informants in the Spanish embassy during 1620.

50 Vano was arrested on 22 August and Facini did not physically turn himself in to the Ten until 3 September. However, Facini had written to them earlier and it *may* have been this initial denunciation that led to Vano's arrest on charges relating to Querini, *not* Foscarini. The Ten voted to view records relating to the prosecutions of Alvise Querini and Zuanne Minotto as part of the investigation into Facini's allegations (Minotto had also recently been involved in an attempt to get himself pardoned on spurious grounds) but there is no mention of Foscarini's case. [Additional note, April 2003: The connection between Alvise Querini's case and Vano's downfall is more complicated and involved than this summary suggests, as I have subsequently discovered. I shall provide a fuller account in my forthcoming book about Foscarini and Vano.]

51 On Querini and Zuanne Facini, see X Cr., reg. 39, 69r–70r, 72v, 73v–74v, 79r–v, 115r–v. On the former's pardon, X Co., reg. 73, 5v–6r, 8v. [Additional note, April 2003: I have subsequently discovered numerous sources relating to Querini's involvement in a Spanish plot to take over the Venetian fortress of Peschiera. Full references will be provided in my book.]

52 See X Sec., reg. 17, 10 Mar. 1623, 111v (Lodovico Rho); X Co., reg. 73, 24 Apr. 1623, 59r–v and X Cr., reg. 40, 24 July 1623, 52v–53r (Andrea Alberti); Luzio 1918: 148 (Alessandro Grancini).

53 See, for example, the reports of the Mantuan resident, reprinted in Luzio (1918: 146–8).

54 Smith (1907: 261–2).

55 This was normal practice. Diego Gomez had, for instance, been similarly interviewed. The Mantuan resident mentioned other intended victims. One of these, Francesco Emo, is listed as the victim of a false accusation in 1622 by an eighteenth-century index of material in the Inquisitors' archive (see Museo Correr, Venice, MSS. P.D. 171C, 'Specifica dei Processi che si trovarano nell'Archivio degl'Inquisitori di Stato dal 1573 fino all'anno 1774 e 75. Compilata da Gius.e Gradenigo').

56 Smith (1907: 262–3).

57 The priest Christoforo Orseti, attached to the confraternity responsible for ministering to prisoners, is recorded as a witness for Vano's will and presumably took his final confession. See X Cr., filza 49, entry under 5 Oct. 1622. Of course, this kind of hearsay evidence was totally unverifiable. A priest acted as an even more effective screen than a spy.

58 X Co., reg. 72 (1622), 16 Jan. 1623, 234v (my emphasis).

59 Smith (1907: 263).

60 The Ten noted on 29 April 1622 that it was not 'appropriate . . . that the will made by the late sir Antonio Foscarini . . . is released in the form in which it is found and has now been read to this council'. Consequently, they released only portions of it, keeping the full text 'under seal'. See X Cr., reg. 39, 15v–17r.

61 One of the most popular versions, with obvious affinities to Wotton's, can be found in an early form in Siri (1679: 380–1). Here an unknown member of the Ten going through trial records notices that an unnamed man (Vano?) condemned for perjury some months after Foscarini's death appeared as a witness in the earlier trial. When challenged on the details of his testimony against Foscarini, the perjurer confessed its falsity. A similar version much closer to the events can be found in Museo Correr, Venice, Codici Cicogna 3782, G. Priuli, *Pretiosi Frutti del Maggior Consiglio*, vol. 2, 29r–30v. Here the outline is even more vague: the execution of unnamed false witnesses leads by unexplained means to Foscarini's posthumous absolution.

62 *Voce pubblica*.

63 Romanin (1858: 586).

64 Alethea Talbot, third daughter and heiress of Gilbert, earl of Shrewsbury, married Thomas Howard, second earl of Arundel, in 1606. He was appointed Earl Marshal of England in August 1621. The Earl had many international contacts due to his activities as an art collector.

65 Foscarini had in fact tried to meet the Countess in London, but had been refused an audience (see *CSPV*, vol. 13: 507). The fact that she was interviewed as a defence witness for Muscorno in June 1617 suggests that she was not well disposed towards Foscarini (see Inq., b. 155, Difese per Muscorno and *CSPV*, vol. 14: 603).

66 Her husband was raised Catholic but converted to Anglicanism in 1615.

67 See Sacchetti's despatch of 21 Apr. 1622 in Romanin (1858: 585).

68 A point made by Siri (1679: 380–1).

69 The quotation is used for Wotton's entry in Leslie and Lee (1900: 53).

70 Wotton had been suspected of 'bad faith [*poco fedeltà*]' in England for some time, as Lionello wrote to the Ten in August 1617 (*CSPV*, vol. 14: 574–6).

71 *CSPV*, vol. 17, report of Lionello dated 26 Apr. 1622, pp. 297–8: 'the injury was public, *not only in Venice but in all the Courts*' (my emphasis). Similarly, news of Foscarini's absolution was officially sent 'to all the Courts' by the Venetian government (see Priuli, *Pretiosi Frutti*, 30v).

72 The steward had previously worked for Gregorio Barbarigo, Foscarini's successor and Lionello's erstwhile master in London.

73 *CSPV*, vol. 17, report of Lionello dated 26 Apr. 1622, pp. 297–8.

74 *CSPV*, vol. 17, 22 Apr. 1622: 293, 302; Smith (1907: 233–4).

75 'The Countess of Arundel went to the cabinet meeting yesterday morning supported by the English ambassador; it is said that she wanted to obtain an extension [i.e. on her alleged notice to depart Venice], she being surprised to receive an affront of this sort: she was unsuccessful, and the cabinet treated her very brusquely (or so it is understood)' (from Sacchetti's despatch of 23 Apr. 1622 in Romanin (1858: 586)).

76 Sarpi (1969: 661–2).

77 *CSPV*, vol. 17: 300.

78 See the resolutions at *CSPV*, vol. 17: 299–300.

79 *CSPV*, vol. 17: 303–4.

80 The Senate also sent official notification of these awards to the Venetian ambassador in England. See *CSPV*, vol. 17: 299–300.

81 Despatch of Sacchetti, 7 May 1622 in Romanin (1858: 587).

82 The Senate's instructions to the Venetian ambassador in England stated that 'Should . . . noblemen of the Court discuss the topic, you will repeat these assurances, which by admitting the news to be false and announcing our regret will clear the private character of the Countess and that of the entire English nation' (*CSPV*, vol. 17: 299). [Additional note, April 2003: In fact, the Countess left Venice not long after the Foscarini affair. I may have overestimated the extent to which public declarations of her innocence were able to offset private suspicions.]

83 It is not clear if Venetian or English nobles are intended, but probably the former.

84 Point no. 103 from the interrogatory relating to Foscarini's defence in Inq., b. 155.

85 No. 106, quoted from the paraphrase in *CSPV*, vol. 14: 599.

86 No. 169 from *CSPV*, vol. 14: 600.

87 'Muscorno had several times uttered the threat that if the ambassador would not let him alone he would have his head chopped off' (*CSPV*, vol. 14: 7).

88 See X, Co., reg. 69 (1619), 74v–75r, 94v; reg. 70 (1620), 82r, 89r–v. Foscarini presumably composed the letters but Muscorno physically wrote most of them.

89 The use of blank pardons, offered as rewards for the arrest or killing of outlaws and other services to the state and sold to the highest bidder by the recipient, was a common expedient in Venice.

90 And this is not all. In 1625, there was another reversal in Muscorno's fortunes. He was accused of repeatedly beating his servant Aurelia, resulting in her death, then attempting to bury her without anyone seeing the body. See X Cr., reg. 42, 56v–57r, 62r, 66r, 69v–70r, 72r–v.

91 The quotation is from Foscarini's report on his embassy in England, delivered to the Senate after his release in 1618 and reproduced in Romanin (1858: 179).

References

Aretino, P. ([1543] 1992) *Le Carte Parlanti*, Palermo: Sellerio.

Bartoccini, F., Caravale, M. and Pignatelli, G. (eds) (1997) *Dizionario biografico degli italiani*, vol. 49, Rome: Istituto della Enciclopedia italiana.

Canosa, R. (1989) *Alle origini delle polizie politiche: Gli Inquisitori di stato a Venezia e a Genova*, Milan: Sugarco.

Cortelazzo, M. and Zolli, P. (1979) *Dizionario etimologico della lingua italiana*, vol. 1, Bologne: Zanichelli.

Cozzi, G. (1979) *Paolo Sarpi tra Venezia e l'Europa*, Turin: Einaudi.

Cozzi, G. (1986) 'Venezia, una repubblica di principi?', *Studi Veneziani* n. s. 11: 139–57.

Cozzi, G. (1988) '"Ordo est ordinem non servare": considerazioni sulla procedura penale di un detenuto dal Consiglio dei X', *Studi Storici* 29(2): 309–20.

CSPV (*Calendar of State Papers and Manuscripts Relating to English Affairs, Existing in the Archives and Collections of Venice*) vol. 12 (1905), ed. H. F. Brown, London: HM Stationery Office; vol. 13 (1907), vol. 14 (1908), vol. 15 (1909) and vol. 17 (1911), ed. A. B. Hinds, London: HM Stationery Office.

Edgerton, S. Y., Jr. (1985) *Pictures and Punishment: Art and Criminal Prosecution during the Florentine Renaissance*, Ithaca, NY: Cornell University Press.

Fulin, R. (1868) *Studi nell'archivio degli Inquisitori di stato*, Venice: Marco Visentini.

Leslie, S. and Lee, S. (eds) (1900) *Dictionary of National Biography*, vol. 63, London: Smith, Elder & Co.

Lievsay, J. L. (1973) *Venetian Phoenix: Paolo Sarpi and Some of his English Friends (1606–1700)*, Lawrence, KS: University Press of Kansas.

Luzio, A. (1918) 'La Congiura Spagnola contro Venezia nel 1618 secondo i documenti dell'Archivio Gonzaga', in *Miscellanea di Storia Veneta*, ed. R. Deputazione Veneta di Storia Patria, third series, 13, Venice: R. Deputazione Veneta di Storia Patria, pp. 1–204.

Maranini, G. (1974) *La costituzione di Venezia dopo la serrata del Consiglio Grande*, vol. 2, Florence: La nuova Italia.

Povolo, C. (1997) *L'intrigo dell'Onore*, Verona: Cierre Edizioni.

Preto, P. (1994) *I servizi segreti di Venezia*, Milan: Il Saggiatore.

Ricoeur, P. (1978) *The Rule of Metaphor: Multi-Disciplinary Studies of the Creation of Meaning in Language*, trans. R. Czerny with K. McLaughlin and J. Costello, London: Routledge and Kegan Paul.

Romanin, S. (1858) *Storia documentata di Venezia*, vol. 7, Venice: Naratovich.

Sarpi, P. (1969) *Opere*, ed. G. and L. Cozzi, Milan and Naples: Riccardo Ricciardi.

Secchi, S. (1969) *Antonio Foscarini: Un patrizio veneziano del'600*, Florence: L. S. Olschki.

Siri, V. (1679) *Delle memorie recondite*, vol. 5, Lyons: Anisson and Posuel.

Smith, L. P. (ed.) (1907) *The Life and Letters of Sir Henry Wotton*, vol. 2, Oxford: Clarendon Press.

Walker, J. (2002a) 'Political and Legal Discourse in Seventeenth-Century Venice', *Comparative Studies in Society and History*, 44: 800–26.

Walker, J. (2002b) 'I Spy with My Little Eye: Interpreting Seventeenth-Century Venetian Spy Reports', *Urban History*, 29(2): 197–222.

Walker, J. 'Pistols! Treason! Murder!: A Political Assassination in Seventeenth-Century Venice', *Rethinking History, The Journal of Theory and Practice*, 7(2): 139–67.

Wootton, D. (1983) *Paolo Sarpi: Between Renaissance and Enlightenment*, Cambridge: Cambridge University Press.

AFTERWORD

This is a pastiche of Italo Calvino's *The Castle of Crossed Destinies*, a novella in which mute characters lay out cards from a Tarot pack, while spectators have to guess their story from the images chosen and the order in which they are displayed. It functions like a comic strip in which the cards serve as individual frames.[1] I should stress that no prior knowledge of card games or occult philosophy is required (the arrangement and interpretation of the cards are determined exclusively by the demands of the story).[2]

I wanted to construct my stories in such a manner as to suggest and exaggerate the way in which ambassadors constructed theirs, to make *my* artifice obvious in writing about the artifice of stories told by people in the past.[3] The stories people tell to themselves to explain past events, whether they are true or not, subsequently have a life of their own and a decisive influence on future events. Echoes, distortions, reflections and misunderstandings superimposed on events are real objects of study, not smeared lenses which have to be removed in order to see the past clearly.

Moreover, for ambassadors and spies, interpreting political information was an occult science akin to cartomancy.[4] I mean that they shuffled apparently unconnected fragments of information, laid them out and tried to link them by placing them within a sequence or story, threading details like beads onto a string. These details had to be interpreted (or labelled) in a variety of ways from the banally literal to the obscurely symbolic to be convincingly related to each other.[5] Snippets acquired *new* meanings as they were placed in different sequences or as new information came to light. For instance, the ending of a story might retrospectively alter the meaning of its beginning.

The game of interpretation was more complex when the intention was not just to reconstruct events in the recent past but to project their future consequences. Although ambassadors were able to identify what they considered to be portentous details, they were often unsure exactly *what* they foretold. Foscarini's contemporaries filled in silences and gaps by moving from fact to interpretation (or from literal meaning to hidden meaning). In a similar way, I have explained written sources by connecting them to symbolic images.

I do not mean to imply that my interpretations are somehow 'in' the sources.[6] On the other hand, I strongly disagree with Hayden White's statement that 'No one and nothing *lives* a story'.[7] This ignores the extent to which people process and present their own experiences as stories and record them in that form within the sources, creating/discovering their own metaphorical truths. Meaning does not inhere automatically in events but it may be put there by participants as well as by retrospective interpreters. As the work of Natalie Davis and Thomas and Elizabeth Cohen has taught us, the choices of people who participated in events and the perceptions of those who wrote primary sources are just as subject to 'emplotment' as the work of historians.[8] This affected what happened in the past *as it was happening*. Telling the story is an intervention in the story.

My dramatization of these themes is an explicitly metaphorical one, which simultaneously implies an 'is not' at the same time that it asserts an 'is'. I assume that the fantastic nature of the frame narrative is obvious, but I have gambled that it reveals more than it conceals about the storytelling practices of ambassadors and spies. The point is that stepping outside a 'historical' perspective (or the conventions of academic discourse) can illuminate what happens *within* the historical world one leaves behind.[9] The central conceit in no way invalidates or contaminates the evidence cited in the notes because it operates on a different epistemological level.

I wanted to acknowledge the gap between narration and evidence but simultaneously offer the possibility of bridging it, if only by the leap of faith or suspension of disbelief involved in the assertion of a metaphorical equivalence. The clash between two different registers in the piece (the academic and the fantastic, the literary and the vernacular) is therefore not a fatal flaw. Instead, it is central to how the piece works. Indeed, it is what it is *about*.

The point of this is to *play with meaning* in the way that Gadamer defined play:

> Play [unlike science] places something in the world rather than abstracts something from it . . . In the case of painting, for example, the aptness of its playful presentation means that the thing represented 'experiences an increase in being' . . . Unlike a mere sign for something else, 'the picture does not disappear in pointing to something else but, in its own being, shares in what it represents'.[10]

Art represents its chosen objects but this does not mean that it must exactly reproduce them, for what would be the point of that? I am attempting to acknowledge that time has passed since my sources were composed, by *adding something to them*.[11] I do not, of course, mean that I have added words that cannot be found in the originals, except insofar as this is occasionally necessary to clarify the grammatical sense of a quotation.

The rules of writing history were not brought down from the mountain on tablets of stone by Von Ranke; nor are they determined by PhD examiners – nor even by journal referees. Examiners and referees merely determine the qualifications necessary to be a 'professional' or academic historian. As graduate students we are initiated into a particular way of writing that we are led to believe functions like a universal language, as Latin once did, but what we are really learning is a particularly obscure dialect, one whose limitations I have found increasingly frustrating. I do not wish to suggest that there should be *no* rules: just to point out that a rule is not the same thing as an axiom. Academia is full of people happy to discuss the relation between literature and history, but only in abstruse theoretical terms, and in essays whose entirely conventional form ironically reinforces the rigid disciplinary boundaries that their content is allegedly challenging.

By contrast, I believe that we should learn by *doing*, by actively incorporating ideas from the culture around us (not only literary fiction, but graphic novels, cinema, contemporary art, photography, popular music, etc.) and allowing them to transform the way we think and write. We have to be prepared to step off the edge of the map, even if it means floundering around in the undergrowth and being shot at by border guards. (One does occasionally run into a fellow explorer, or pick up a trail left by someone else.)

Notes

1 Story-telling in this manner is not a normal use for Tarot cards and in early modern Europe they were used almost exclusively to play games (although some relevant early modern literary conceits are described in Pratesi 1988). The exact mechanism by which the sequences of cards are deciphered is deliberately vague in Calvino (1978), allowing the narrator/interpreter considerable freedom. Let me be clear that here the choice of cards is mine, as are the interpretations; further-more, I am using the cards to interpret stories told about Foscarini by others, stories existing in written form before being translated into images.

2 I have, however, explained some of the more suggestive iconographic and etymological traditions in the footnotes. Since no complete pack of Tarot survives from seventeenth-century Italy, with the exception of specialized local variants from Florence and Bologna, my illustrations are based on a pack made by Jacques Vieville in Paris sometime in the period 1643–64 (for a detailed discussion, see Dummett 1980: 205–11).

3 Artifice should not be taken to mean deceitfulness. On story-telling in history, Hayden White's work is of particular importance (and its influence should be obvious).

4 There is, it should be stressed, *no* evidence of the use of Tarot cards for fortune-telling in the sixteenth and seventeenth centuries.

5 Compare White (1978a: 125).

6 On historical narrative as allegory, see White (1987).

7 White (1978b: 111). See also White (1999: 9): '[S]tories are not lived; there is no such thing as a real story. Stories are told or written, not found.' I would argue that the first sentence does *not* follow necessarily from the second.

8 Davis (1988); Cohen and Cohen (1993).

9 Compare the opening to Davis (1995), which takes place in 'Thoughtland'.

10 Quoted in Hamilton (1996: 88). See also Gadamer (1979: 91–150), especially pp. 124, 132.

11 See Gadamer (1979: 121): 'The world which appears in the play of representation does not stand like a copy next to the real world, but is the latter in the heightened truth of its being.' I am also interested in how particular kinds of representation *take something away* from the reality they describe or depict, i.e. in representation as a form of reduction – or rather, I am interested in how taking away and adding to can sometimes amount to the same thing.

References

Calvino, I. (1978) *The Castle of Crossed Destinies*, trans. W. Weaver, London: Pan Books.

Cohen, T. V. and Cohen, E. S. (1993) *Words and Deeds in Renaissance Rome: Trials before the Papal Magistrates*, Toronto: University of Toronto Press.

Davis, N. Z. (1988) *Fiction in the Archives: Pardon Tales and Their Tellers in Sixteenth-Century France*, Cambridge: Polity Press.

Davis, N. Z. (1995) *Women on the Margins: Three Seventeenth-Century Lives*, Cambridge, MA: Harvard University Press.

Dummett, M. (1980) *The Game of Tarot*, London: Duckworth.

Gadamer, H. G. ([1965] 1979) *Truth and Method*, 2nd edn, trans. W. Glen-Doepel, London: Sheed and Ward.

Hamilton, P. (1996) *Historicism*, London and New York: Routledge.

Pratesi, F. (1988) 'Italian Cards: New Discoveries 7. Venetian Tarot in the 16th Century – Evidence From Specific Literature', *Journal of the Playing Card Society*, 17(2): 58–64.

White, H. (1978a) 'The Fictions of Factual Representation', in *Tropics of Discourse: Essays in Cultural Criticism*, Baltimore, MD: Johns Hopkins University Press, pp. 121–34.

White, H. (1978b) 'Historicism, History, and the Figurative Imagination', in *Tropics of Discourse*, Baltimore, MD: Johns Hopkins University Press, pp. 101–20.

White, H. (1987) 'The Metaphysics of Narrativity: Time and Symbol in Ricoeur's Philosophy of History', in *The Content of the Form: Narrative Discourse and Historical Representation*, Baltimore MD: Johns Hopkins University Press, pp. 169–84.

White, H. (1999) 'Literary Theory and Historical Writing', in *Figural Realism: Studies in the Mimesis Effect*, Baltimore, MD: Johns Hopkins University Press, pp. 1–26.

7 Narrating a southern tragedy

Historical facts and historical fictions

Bryant Simon

Historical facts

Gaffney *Ledger*, March 29, 1912

MAYBE LYNCHING AT BLACKSBURG

Gaffney *Ledger*, April 2, 1912

ANGRY BLACKSBURG MOB LYNCHED TWO NEGROES

NEGRO'S AWFUL TREATMENT OF WHITE MAN IS AVENGED

Made Him Intoxicated and Forced Him to Commit
Fearful Crime

Blacksburg is the Scene of Double Lynching. Two Negroes Being Put
to Death for Their Treatment of a Respectable Laboring White
Man Who Was Put Into an Intoxicated Condition and Then Taken
to a Cemetery Where Crime Was Committed

Spartanburg Herald, March 30, 1912 (Special to the Herald)

"*T*he first blot on Cherokee county's fair name came last night when two negroes, Frank Whisonant and Jim Brinson, were lynched by a mob in the peaceful little village of Blacksburg, eight miles from Gaffney."

"Although the sheriff of Cherokee County, W. W. Thomas, and Deputy Watkins have been here all day making valiant efforts to get some trace of the posse or its leaders, as yet not a scrap of evidence has been secured."

"Brinson and Whisonant were being held in the city jail here on serious charges. Selling liquor, carrying concealed weapons, highway robbery in the night-time and assault and battery with intent to kill, are some of the charges, while a third serious charge was also lodged against them."

"It is alleged that these two negroes met a white man named Jim Childers Wednesday night about 11 o'clock and forced him to drink quite a quantity of whiskey, after which they took him to a cemetery, robbed of him of his money and at the point of a pistol forced him to a most horrible action."

CHILDERS DRUNKEN

"*C*hilders was interviewed by a reporter yesterday. He stated that he had come to Blacksburg on Wednesday night from Gaffney and that he was here expecting to get work with the Whittaker cotton mill. Shortly after he left the train, he was approached by the two negroes and asked if he would like to buy a pint of whiskey. He stated to them that he did not care for the whiskey, but they persisted and he finally told them that he would purchase it. They led him to a deserted spot and one of the negroes drew a gun from his breast and forced Childers to drink all of the pint with the exception of two drinks. They told him that they would kill him if he did not obey them. They then took the rest of his money, only a small amount of silver, and then stated that he would have to give up his clothes. In this they did not persist, but forced him to the cemetery, where the most revolting part of the crime was completed. When he escaped from the negroes, Childers went to the police and reported the matter. Early yesterday morning the two negroes were arrested by the Chief of Police Allison and lodged in the city jail, following which they were given a trial before Mayor Ramseur on the charge of selling whiskey. During the trial the other crime was necessarily touched upon and both the negroes acknowledged that it was true, but each laid it upon the other. After hearing the case, the mayor adjudged them guilty and sentenced them to a fine of $20 apiece. They were then placed back in jail."

N. W. Hardin to Governor Cole L. Blease, March 29, 1912, Blease Papers, Box 11, Folder—Cherokee County, 1911–1913, South Carolina Division of Archives and History, Columbia, South Carolina.

> *Hon. Cole L. Blease*
> *Governor,*
> *Columbia, S.C.*

> *Dear Governor:*

> *Doubtless you will hear much from news-papers and otherwise about the lynching here last night, some of which will be true, but most of it exaggerated. These are about the facts: Two trifling negroes, not worth killing, came up with Childers, a white man, and factory operative, sometime Thursday night and Childers engaged them to get him some whiskey. He was to meet them in outskirts of the town and receive it, which he did. The three drank whiskey freely, then the negroes drew their pistols and commanded that he drink the balance of the quart or die. Childers did the best he could, but could not drink it all. They then drew their pistols, cocked them and told Childers to open his mouth and keep it open, that if he closed it, he would be shot on the spot, when Whisonant, one of the negroes, pushed his penus (?) into the mouth of Childers. Soon as Childers could release himself from the Negroes, he sought a policeman, who arrested them, took their pistols away from them and preferred charges for selling liquor and carrying concealed weapons, for which they were tried and convicted in the Mayor's court. Yesterday afternoon a warrant was sworn against them for sodomy, and they were confined in the City guard house last night, a very substantial structure of stone and brick, waiting a preliminary this morning. There was much imagination yesterday morning when the character of the crime was made known, but Dr. Ramsseur, the Mayor, and myself took the matter in hand, and it quieted down, so in the afternoon, we could hear nothing and felt secure. The negroes, as well as whites were mad in the morning, though. I was astonished this morning to the find the negroes lynched, hung from a cross beam in Caldwell's shop. Am satisfied that nearly all the citizens of the town, if not all, were surprised as much as myself. The lynching must have occurred late this morning, about 4 or 5 o'clock. There were half a dozen residences within 100 yards of the lynching, and no one knew anything about until this morning. I am told that people, on horseback, came from Gaffney, Cherokee Falls, Hickory Grove and King's Mountain.*

> *My idea is that as Childers was a factory operative, the lynching was done by the operatives of the surrounding mills, trying to take care of their class. I am sorry that it happened, but I had no idea, not even suspicion that it was going to happen, or, under the circumstances, had I known it, would have had them sent to the County jail. Some of the d——d fools are already saying: this is Bleasism.*

> *Hope you are well and will continue in good health until you thresh Ira B. Jones.*

> *Yours truly*

> *H. W. Hardin*

According to the manuscript census of the United States, Joe Brinson was born in North Carolina. In 1910, the twenty-one-year-old African American man lived in a rented house in Blacksburg, South Carolina, with his wife of four years, Nancy, and their three-year-old daughter. Neither Joe nor Nancy could read or write. He worked odd jobs, apparently pretty steadily. He told the census takers that he was employed every single week the previous year. His wife was not so lucky. A laundress, the record said, she worked only 28 weeks over the same time period.

There is no one by the name of Frank Whisonant listed in the 1910 census of Cherokee County. There are several Whisonant families that are African American. One of the Whisonant men, in fact, was quite prosperous, owning a house and a rather large farm. There were also several white Whisonant families in Cherokee County in 1910. But again, there is no one named Frank Whisonant, black or white.

There was no one named Joe Childers, as one paper called him, listed in the census for Cherokee County in 1910 either. There was a thirty-five-year-old James Childers—several papers referred to the white man in the Blacksburg drama as Jim Childers—working in the mills in Blacksburg, but according to most reports the Childers involved in this story did not live in that town. There was another Childers, who lived in Gowdaysville Township, and worked in the mills, yet it is impossible to make out this man's first name in the census. It seems that his first initial is J, but that is all that is clear. This Childers was twenty-three years old in 1910. He and his twenty-six-year-old wife, Martha, had been married for five years in 1910. They had three children, all daughters, ages, 4 and 2 years old, and 10 months.

Historical fictions

Jim Childers looked just like all the other white men in the Limestone Mill Village. He was wiry, kind of tall, and real thin. His face seemed to be pulled by something in the back of his head tight around his colorless cheeks. He wore faded blue overalls, thinning at the knees and spotted in the front and back with grease. His gray shirt used to be white. Jim's thick black hair, cut at home by his wife to save money, stuck straight up in places on the top and sides, and it was sprinkled with lint making it look like salt and pepper mixed together, which made him look older than his age, twenty-five years old in 1912.

Again, like most people in the mill village, Childers wasn't born there, but in the countryside. His parents had owned a plain four-room wood house that listed a little to the right on a seventeen-acre farm twenty miles northeast of the Limestone village in York County. Usually the family rented another patch of land just across the red clay road—path was probably a better word—that ran right in front of their house. Mostly they grew cotton, but they also planted corn, potatoes, and peas and they had some pigs and chickens, and an ox, goat, and cow.

Just about every day, Childers got up with the sun and followed his father around the fields and into the sheds pretending to be just like him. When he was eleven, his uncle—his father's brother—who lived next door and helped the family out, died; of what, Childers couldn't remember. He did recall the hushed conversations around the kitchen table that took place over the next several nights. "You can't raise those girls here," he heard his father say to his sister-in-law. A couple of weeks later, Jim's family—his mom, his dad, and two sisters—stood outside and waved good-bye to his aunt and cousins as they headed off to the Orr Mill Village near York. Others in the area had left long before for the mills, but they were first of the Childers to go. Jim's family was soon to follow. A year later, in 1904, cotton prices dipped again, and Jim's father threw up his hands, sold the ox and the cow, and decided to take a chance on the mill.

Childers had been to town with his dad a few times before they moved to the mill. They went a couple of times a year to buy clothes and shoes. They had gone once to get some parts to fix a broken wagon, and another time to the doctor's office when his mother was sick. But really he hadn't been off the farm much and each time he did go to town, the strange noises, the commotion, and the smells thrilled him, but they scared him too. He felt like his clothes, his hair, and his voice made him stand out, that they were like a stamp that said here is a countryman and he doesn't belong here. His father looked and acted no more at ease than he did. When Jim first came to the mill village, he felt the same way, like an outsider. Although he was twelve years old, he clung to his mother's print dress like he was still a child. Everywhere he looked, people were racing around, running up and down the tight, narrow streets. It was, he would later understand, just when the day shift let out and the night shift began. Men and women most about his parents' age, and lots of children, some his own age, although they seemed older, moved in every direction. They seemed to know where they were going. Yet he could not imagine how. Most of the action took place just in front the mill. It was the biggest building Jim had ever seen, three stories tall, as wide as a dozen houses back home, and made of reddish, maybe rust colored, bricks. It had long narrow windows and an even longer chimney with big white letters going from top to bottom, spelling Orr Mills.

At first, only Jim's parents worked in the mill. They told him he was too young to work, so he went to school. The Orr Mills School, as it was called, looked brand new and it was much bigger than the country school he had gone to back on the farm. The teachers were different too. They were younger and they spoke in a more educated, even high-brow, tone. At first, Jim liked going to the new school, but pretty quickly, within a year or so of moving, Childers, like most of the other boys in the village, wanted to get out of the classroom and into the mills. By this time, the screech of the morning whistle, the grinding of gears, the pounding of looms, and the confusion of the shift change were all familiar to him. Lots of times, he skipped school and took supper to his parents in the mills. He would hang around for as long as they would let him, helping with their jobs. That's where he learned to tie a weaver's knot and run the looms. He couldn't wait to start working himself, to get some money, to be in the mill everyday, hearing the stories, talking about the machines, making fun of the foreman, meeting girls, throwing dice, and acting like the other men.

The older Childers got, the more he pestered his parents to let him quit school and start working. Finally they said okay. They needed the money anyway. Just before his sixteenth birthday. Jim got his first job sweeping up in the weave room where his dad worked. Not long after, he met Martha Westbrook. They flirted. He asked her to a dance, and then to a concert, and then to another dance. She said yes three times. Two years later he asked her to marry him, and she said yes again. A magistrate read them their vows. No rings were exchanged. They were too expensive. After the quick ceremony, the newlyweds, and a few friends and relatives went back to Martha's parents' mill house, where Jim and Martha planned to live until they saved enough money to buy some furniture of their own. They ate cake and ice cream. The men sat on the front porch, talking about work, kidding Jim about how things would change now he was married, and sipping some nasty corn whiskey. Everyone went home early, because everyone—Martha and Jim included—had to get up when the first whistle blew the next morning, an hour or so before the sun rose.

Like all the mill houses, Martha's parents' house was small, it was just three rooms. The kitchen was set off the back porch detached from the rest of the house. There wasn't really enough room for everybody, especially not with Jim and Martha expecting a baby and Jim and Martha's dad not getting along that well. Childers was ready for a change, ready to strike out on his own. Just about that time, Jim heard that the Limestone Mills in Gaffney—not really too far away—were looking for people. He also heard that they paid more than the Orr Mills and that the houses there had four rooms, not three.

Jim decided to take the train over to Gaffney and have a look around. This was the first time he had been on a train. He tried to act like he rode them all the time. He studied what the others did and that's what he did. He gave the conductor a nickel and followed the other white people to the white car. He spent the entire ride looking straight ahead, afraid that if he looked out the window, like he wanted to, someone would know that this was his first time.

The Limestone Mills looked just like the Orr Mills. It was a wide, three-story, red-brick building with long narrow windows. The only difference was that the tops of the windows had some decorations on them, making them, Jim thought, look like those big churches over in Europe that he had seen in the books back in school. Someone from Limestone told Childers to get in touch with a secondhand named Mr. Bonner. Childers found the man without much trouble. Bonner asked Jim a few questions—Did he drink? No, Jim lied, he didn't. Could he start soon? Yes, tomorrow, Jim answered. Bonner hired him on the spot. Before dark, Jim and Martha moved the few things they had managed to buy—a hand-me-down bed, a couple of chairs, a wobbly wood table, an assortment of dented pots and pans, some clothes, and a couple pictures of their families—into a four-room house on brick stilts in the middle of a block of identical four-room houses on brick stilts.

The shriek of the factory whistle woke Jim Childers up the next morning at 5:45 AM. He rubbed his eyes, ran his fingers through his hair, and pulled his overalls over his gray shirt without a collar buttoned to the top. Now that he had a new job, he thought to himself, he would buy some new clothes. He sat back down on the bed and listened to Martha rattling dishes in the kitchen and singing a sweet tune under her breath. He hoped that they would be happier here. Lately, things hadn't been going too well for them. Maybe this place would work for them. He felt a flash of pride looking around his new house; there wasn't much there, but it was his first house, and he was in charge. The second whistle blew. Jim jumped off the bed and walked into the kitchen. He smelled the gristle of the fatback and the bitter aroma of the coffee. He ate quickly. He wondered if Martha was also excited about this new place. He didn't get to ask her. The third whistle blew. That was his signal. He ran out the door and joined the flow of women and men streaming to the factory. At 6:30 AM the final whistle of the morning sounded. By this time, Childers was standing at his new post in the weave room, the same place he would stand Monday through Friday until sundown, and until noon on Saturday, for the next three years.

When Childers wasn't working, he was either in church or at the ball game or hanging out in front of the company store at the far end of the village. He didn't spend much time at home, and he didn't really spend that much time in church, certainly not as much time as his wife did. Usually he would go with her on Sundays to the Orr Mills Baptist Church in the village, and every once in a while to the prayer meetings at the preacher's house on Wednesday evenings. But he didn't really like to go to church; it wasn't that he didn't like the preacher—he was okay and sometimes he made sense and the singing was nice—but still he didn't like to go to church. This worried him. He worried that there was something wrong with him, that he didn't have God in him. Sometimes he wanted to get God, to feel him, the way his wife said she felt God, but he couldn't feel it, and he didn't like to go to church because it reminded him that he didn't have God in his life.

What he did like to do was to drink. He told himself that these two things were not related. He didn't think that he drank because he didn't have God in his life, although he knew that's what some people thought of him. He drank because he liked to drink. That first taste was the one he liked the best. He loved the way the whiskey tingled the roof of his mouth, coated his throat, and burned sweetly in his stomach. He made sure he got drunk every Saturday. Right after his shift ended and after he stopped by the pay office, he bought a bottle—usually a pint, but a quart if he could afford it—and went somewhere—the store, a juke joint, the ballgame, uptown, or just out in the woods by himself, and drank. Sometimes he would head home after he finished the bottle and go to sleep or make love to his wife, and other times, he would buy another bottle and sit up and listen to a fiddle player or sneak over to a house just outside the village where there were card games and women.

Childers tried as hard as he could to drink only on Saturdays. That was his day. Sundays were the Lord's day and the rest were the company's. Try as he might, every once and in while, he needed to have a drink on company time and even God's time. Sometimes he got drunk on Sundays. Tuesdays, Wednesdays, and Fridays; never, he didn't know why, on Mondays and Thursdays. He had nothing against those days, they just weren't drinking days in his mind. The drinking, even he admitted, got worse the longer he stayed at Limestone. He thought about that first taste almost everyday. Usually he started to imagine the whiskey just after lunch. He would close his eyes and think about the moment when his tongue and the liquor met, the melody of saliva and corn mash. As the looms rattled and creaked, he thought about whiskey: who he would drink it with, where he would drink it, and how he would keep his wife from finding out about it. Then he would think about the money and the next morning's headaches and he would tell himself he wasn't going to go behind the store and buy a pint from Mr. Lattimer, the guy who always seemed to be there and always seemed to know where to get a drink.

Most days, Childers went straight home after work, but he did have to admit that Mr. Lattimer knew him by name and always gave him exactly what he wanted without him having to say anything. Usually he managed to answer the morning whistle, but there were days when he just couldn't get out of bed. He would send one the neighborhood kids down to the mill to tell the foreman that he was sick and not going to make it to work that day. No matter what, even if he really was sick, the next morning, the secondhand would ask him kind of suspiciously how he was feeling, if his cold or sore throat had gone away. Then he would smile and walk away laughing like he knew something. Childers hated that.

On the first Saturday of 1912, Childers got really drunk, much worse than usual. How he didn't really know. But he was surely drunk. He stumbled around the village, puking on a neighbor's front porch and screaming at his wife. Later, he picked a fight at the house outside the village where there were women and dice. They threw him out, literally. When he got home, he and his wife had another fight, they yelled and cursed. She made him sleep on a blanket on the floor in the front room. Of course, the supervisor heard about all of the fussing. He seemed to know everything. Really it was his spies who knew everything and they told him most of it. Anyway, the boss sent word to Childers on the Monday after his bad drunk to come to his office.

Childers knocked a little sheepishly on the slightly ajar wooden door. Without looking up, the superintendent waved him in and motioned for him to sit down. Childers followed the silent instructions. Then nothing happened for a few moments. Eventually, the boss stood up rather slow and looked Childers up and down, again real slow. "Do it again and you're done here, hear?" That's it. He sat back down and started back to doing what he was doing when Childers first walked in. Jim waited a few moments, maybe even as long as a minute. He did not know what to do. The boss gave him no clues, he never even looked up again. Finally, Childers slipped out of his chair as quiet as he could and snuck out of the office.

Jim was scared that he would lose his job, scared that Martha wouldn't forgive him this time for messing up. He was mad too, mad that the boss had treated him like that, and that he had let him do it. His stomach was growling and he was sweating under his coat. A drink was what he wanted, what he needed, and he walked over toward Mr. Lattimer's usual spot, but he thought better of it and turned up the street to his wife and two children and a bland meal of dumplings and cornbread. All week long he stayed away from whiskey, taking only one short drink on Wednesday to celebrate a neighbor's son's engagement to a girl down the street. Saturday was a different story. That was still his day, and no matter what the man said, he was going to buy a pint, the question was where. Mr. Lattimer wasn't a good idea. He could go back to York. Then he remembered that when he went to Blacksburg the previous summer to visit his aunt and cousins that he had bought a couple of quarts near the train station from two young black guys. He didn't usually like to buy whiskey from niggers, but he remembered that their whiskey was pretty good. He got on the train in Gaffney at 2:00 PM and he was in Blacksburg at 2:23 PM.

The station was at the end of town. From the raised platform you could see the edges of the town square not too far away. Jim stood and looked out. He didn't care about the town or what was going on, he was looking for the black guys. At first, he didn't see anyone who looked like they were selling whiskey, and he wondered if he remembered it right. Still he was in no particular hurry and with no place to go, he waited for a while. He hadn't really noticed it before but it was a nice day out, the sky was blue and the air was crisp and cool, you could see your first breath, but after that you got used to the air. He didn't have to wait long, a few minutes, maybe ten, and then they came out from behind the station. That was them, he could tell from their eyes, the way they looked around waiting for people to notice them. He walked toward them. The two black guys were about his age, maybe a little younger. They took a quick glance around, surveying the scene, and then waved him, nodded actually, behind the station. The sale went smoothly. Childers bought a pint of whiskey. The price was right. Trying to act patient, like he didn't really want a drink—he did— he didn't open the jar right away.

He thought about stopping by his cousins, but then he thought he would rather be alone and think about the fight he had had with Martha, and how he hated the superintendent. He waited for the train and went back home and walked out into the woods and sat down and got drunk. The next morning he went to church. On the way, he told Martha that he had gone to Blacksburg the day before, and that he was thinking about taking a job at the Whittaker Mills there.

Childers went back to Blacksburg every Saturday for the next month or so. Each time he bought a pint from the same two guys. He never said much to them, and they never said much to him. The whiskey was good, and he even found a few spots in Blacksburg to drink it, so he didn't have to wait until he got back to Gaffney to have that first taste. He had, he thought to himself, a nice thing going—the train, the whiskey, and the secret. All week long, he looked forward to going to Blacksburg.

On the last Wednesday of March at about 4:00 PM, the Limestone mill shut down early. Somebody said something about a broken belt. Childers didn't stay around long enough to hear exactly what had gone wrong. He ran out of the mill to the train station. He just made it. He settled into a seat and closed his eyes. He wondered if the two black guys would be there on a Wednesday. He got to the station and didn't see them. Without really thinking about it he headed toward Blacksburg's niggertown, two dirt streets of shot-gun houses and country shacks some well kept and some not so well kept on the other side of the tracks. He walked up one street and then down another, trying to fend off the suspicious looks thrown his way by keeping his head down and walking a straight line. Then he saw the two black guys sitting on the porch of a newly painted house in the middle of the block. They didn't seem the least bit surprised to see him, so he tried not to look surprised or even relieved to see them, but he was both surprised and relieved. As soon as he saw them, he started to taste that first drink.

"How about drink, mister?" the tall one asked with a big smile on his face.

Joe Childers could not stop thinking about him. Not everything was clear. He could remember paying him and he could remember the firm contours of the muscles around his shoulders, strong and powerful even through a couple shirts. He remembered his smell, the tastes of whiskey and the strength and agility of the nigger's callused hands. Over and over again, he heard those sounds: the grunts, groans, gasps, and muffled words. He couldn't stop thinking about the spot in the woods near the Blacksburg train station where they went. He pictured himself leaning up against that scrub pine tree, bark digging into his back, his overalls down around his ankles, his dirty white socks peaking up over his clothes, and the nigger on his knees before him sucking his cock. He couldn't stop thinking about the nigger sucking on him. He couldn't stop thinking about it at home in bed with his wife. He couldn't stop thinking about it in front of his looms at work. He couldn't stop thinking about it when he was standing out in front of the company store with the other guys cursing the boss. And he couldn't stop thinking about it in church even when he was sitting there right next to his children. He tried to push the nigger out of his head. He tried to think about other things, but the nigger would just pop right back into his head, he wouldn't go away, and Joe hated him for that.

It wouldn't happen again Joe told himself. He wouldn't do it—he never actually said what it was, not even to himself—with another man ever again. It had been a couple of years since the last time it happened. It wouldn't happen again. He wouldn't do it again. He promised himself, he promised God. Anyway, he'd been drunk. There must have been something weird in that whiskey that the nigger sold him. It was the nigger's idea. He told himself over and over again that it wouldn't happen again. He wouldn't think of it. No, he wouldn't think of it or that nigger that way again. Anyway he hated that nigger. He was a sick fuck, he told himself, a pervert. He wouldn't have anything to do with him.

Almost as soon as he got done making all these promises to himself, it started all over again. He thought of Joe Brinson's shoulders, his wet lips, and his hot breath. He thought of sucking off Brinson. No, Childers said to himself, stop thinking this way. He squeezed his eyes shut as tight as he could, scrunching up his face, trying to push Brinson out of his thoughts. It worked for a moment, but then Brinson was right back in his head kneeling before him sucking his cock.

A couple weeks after that day that he had gotten drunk and paid Brinson to give him a blow job, Childers went back to Blacksburg. He told himself he would never go back there, but on the second Saturday of March 1912, he left work at the end of his half-day shift and headed over to the office to pick up his paycheck. He bought a bottle of Coca-a-Cola and slipped behind the company store to pick up a pint of whiskey. He went to the same spot in the woods where he usually went on Saturdays. He sat down on a stump and studied the pint-sized mason jar, running his fingers over the slightly raised letters on the glass surface that spelled out the name, SAMCO. He unscrewed the cap and pried off the lid. He took a sip of the whiskey, then a sip of Coke, then a sip of whiskey, then a sip of Coke, and so on until the Coke bottle was finished and the whiskey jar was half full. He was thinking about Brinson. He got up and walked down to the Gaffney train station and bought a round-trip ticket to Blacksburg. He boarded the train around 2:00 PM. Twenty-three minutes later, he was in Blacksburg. Only a few people, two men and a family of four, got off the train with him there.

Childers walked quickly through the small train station to the front entrance. He looked around. He didn't see Brinson. He waited a few minutes, took a sip of whiskey and walked away from the train station toward Blacksburg's niggertown. He got to the foot of an unpaved street. He looked up and down the row of painted and unpainted houses, and went no further. He turned around and walked back to the station. He looked around again. He didn't see Brinson. At the station, he took another sip of whiskey. He still hoped that Brinson would show up, but also he was also relieved that he hadn't seen him. Another sip of whiskey. Then he went inside the station and waited for the next train. It came forty minutes later. Childers tried not to think of anything, not Brinson, not his wife, not his shame, not his fear that something was wrong with him, or his hidden urges. He just sat there, trying not to think. He got back to Gaffney at 4:52 PM. He was home a little after five. He told Martha something about the basketball game he didn't see. He was in bed by nine, saying he was as tired as he could be. He went to church the next day. He didn't say anything to God, he figured he already knew about Joe Brinson. No sense reminding him.

The following Wednesday, knowing that his wife was at prayer meeting and that his daughters were with a neighbor, he caught the train to Blacksburg again. He tried to sleep, but every time he closed his eyes Joe Brinson's lips, buttocks, and hands danced real slow in front of him as if they were playing on a nickelodeon screen on the back of his eye lids. Entering the station, the train rattled from side to side before it settled to a stop. Childers opened his eyes and looked outside. There was Brinson. He felt nervous, a flash of something shot through him and he could feel his penis rise. He thought about staying on the train, but only for a split second. He knew what he was going to do, so he started to rehearse how he would approach Brinson, what he would say, and what he would do.

As he walked out of the station, aware of each step, he looked right at Brinson. The young black man looked right back at him. Then he jerked his head toward the back of the train station. Childers thought that he might even have winked at him. Brinson started off first. Childers followed ten or twenty steps behind. As they reached the tree line, he walked faster closing the gap. He was breathing heavy. "Calm down," he told himself. "Calm down."

They got to the place in the woods where he had gone last time. This time Brinson wasn't alone. Another man, a shorter, stockier, darker black man with bright brown eyes and an easy smile was with him. This man, Childers would later find out, was Frank Whisonant.

Whisonant looked Childers over. He smiled and cracked a nasty joke about a guy who couldn't get it up. He laughed again. Then he pulled out a big jug of whiskey. All three men drank from it. They passed it around three, four, maybe five or six times. Childers couldn't remember what they talked about. At some point, Brinson moved closer to Childers. Childers gave him some money. The white man unhooked his overalls. Brinson pulled them down and started to suck on his penis. Childers closed his eyes and bit his lip. He heard Whisonant laughing and talking, cocking a pistol over and over again. His eyes were still closed when he heard the white voices.

Brinson jerked his mouth away from Childers's penis, hurried to his feet, and raced off. Whisonant must have run too. A couple of seconds passed. Childers's overalls were still down around his ankles. He looked behind him to where the voices were coming from and saw two white teenagers coming toward him. He couldn't see them clearly, but he was pretty sure he did not know them, and that they didn't know him. They were 15, maybe 17, he guessed.

"What were those two nigger boys doing?" one of the white kids asked as Childers yanked up his pants.

"I know them. That one is Brinson—seen him working over at the Turner place . . . that place over on the Gaffney road . . . The other . . . his name . . . is . . . Whizz-on-something . . ."

"What were those two niggers doing to you? You okay?" the other boy interrupted, looking at Childers.

Thinking what he should say, Childers stood there adjusting his overalls. Quick, quick, he said to himself, think of something. Then he blurted out—sound mad he reminded himself—"Those nigger sons-of-bitches attacked me, they just attacked me."

"The fuckers attacked me," Childers shouted again, louder this time, before the boys could answer. The words hit them hard, they almost jumped back when they heard them. Childers stared at them in the darkness, trying to figure out whether or not they had believed him.

Before the boys could say anything, Childers grabbed them and yelled, "Let's get the law. Let's get those nigger bastards. Those fuckers attacked me."

Childers started to run, grabbing the boys by their shirts and jerking them along. After a few steps, he let go and the boys continued to run after him. That made Childers feel better, like maybe they believed him.

Blacksburg was a small town. The United States Census reported that there were only 1232 residents in 1910. Childers didn't care about this fact at that moment. It was the distance that he was concerned with, and he quickly found out that it didn't take long to get from behind the train station to the center of this small town. Once he got there, he looked around until he spotted the police sign on the municipal building tucked in the northeast corner of the square.

Without hesitating, he ran over to the office. The boys followed. A policeman, a short, unassuming man not much older than Childers, wearing a plain blue uniform, was in. He was sitting behind a big brown desk that made him look even smaller than he was. Only later would Childers think that he didn't look much like a policeman, but as soon as the law officer looked up that night, Childers greeted him with an explosion of words and gestures.

"I came over here looking for a job at the Whittaker Mills, nothing else," Childers said quickly. (Don't sound guilty, he reminded himself, don't sound guilty.) "Two niggers attacked me," he continued a bit louder and more assertive. "These two boys saw it, right, boys?" The policeman tried to say something, to get him to slow down a little, but Childers wouldn't stop. "What were their names, boys? Brin, Brin . . . something and the other one, what was his name, boys?"

"Whisonant," both boys said at the same time.

The policeman studied all three of them. He ran an inventory: the two boys he knew. They were pretty good kids, went to school, helped out around the farm, and raised hell on weekends; Brinson, good with his hands, did odd jobs, drank a little, and sometimes sold liquor by the train station; and Whisonant, he didn't seem to work too much, definitely drank too much, and occasionally got into a fight, but nothing bad, nothing that a 19-year-old nigger boy didn't do. The white man he didn't know, he wasn't from Blacksburg.

"Attacked? What do you mean, attacked?" he asked trying not to sound too skeptical. And before Childers could answer, he said as politely as he could, "I'm sorry, I don't know you, do I?"

"No, no, you don't, I don't think so. I'm Joe Childers from Gaffney. I work at the Limestone Mills over in Gaffney. Like I said, I was looking for work at Whittaker. My aunt and uncle live a little ways past the square—Sam Childers, you know them, don't you?"

"Yes, yes, sure do," the policeman responded, still trying to sound professional and not at all intrigued or alarmed by the situation. Still he wanted to ask

Childers what he was doing applying for a job at night—Whittaker didn't run a night-shift—but he didn't. Something about this guy just didn't seem right.

Sensing the policeman's uneasiness, Childers, still red in the face from running, yelled: "I was attacked by those bastards. Those—those niggers attacked me."

The policeman looked at him, but didn't say anything. "They attacked me," Childers screamed.

"What do you mean? Did they take your money or anything like that."

"Yeah, but they attacked me too, they attacked me," Childers answered, accenting the last word, adding a vowel or two to it.

Then Childers looked over at the boys and leaned forward and whispered to the magistrate, "They attacked me, made me . . . uhm . . . It was . . . bad . . ." He couldn't say the word rape, even though he kind of wanted to, knowing that this would get the policeman's attention.

"They attacked me . . .," Childers said again, putting a lot of emphasis on the last word.

The policeman pulled his head back. Now he understood what Childers was talking about and anyways he couldn't stand the sour smell of Childers's whiskey-soaked breath for another moment. He thought again about Brinson and Whisonant. He had never heard anything about them going off with men for money or anything else like that before. Now there were some around that people said did stuff like this, but not these two. He didn't really know about Childers and he didn't know how to ask the boys about it. Hard to question a white man, even a Gaffney linthead, about something like this. Think, he told himself, what should I do? Better listen to this white man.

Childers kept looking at him, waiting for him to say something. Finally, the policeman stood up. He looked even smaller now: "Let's go find those two nigger boys and talk to them." Looking over at the teenagers, he commanded them, sounding for the first time like he was in charge of the situation, "You boys can go home. I'll talk to your parents tomorrow about why you're coming home so late, but tell your momma and daddy everything is okay."

The boys left. He looked over at Childers.

"Childers, you stay here. Sober up a bit, why don't you? We'll go and find those two nigger boys. They can't be too far."

Here's what Joe Brinson told his cousin from his jail cell on the morning of March 30th:

Now don't tell anyone any of this, especially not my wife. I don't really want no body knowing what happened, but I got to tell someone. I hated that low life linthead, piece of shit just about the first time I saw him. He came down here calling me nigger, calling me boy, and shit like that. Who the fuck was he? He was a fucking linthead, shit-bug, she-boy, faggot. That's what he was.

I can't remember exactly when; it must have been sometime in the winter that I first saw him. He was standing around the train station looking for whiskey. I had never seen him before. He wasn't from Blacksburg. At first he only came around on Saturdays. He didn't say much. Just stuff like, nigger get me this, nigger get me that, and he had a mean way of saying it. Then he started coming around during the week. I didn't care that he did, I always liked making a little money off of white people. Shit they never pay us black folk enough for doing their jobs anyway, so we got to get it other ways. Selling whiskey works. Yeah, the white guy. Like I was saying, he started coming during the week, usually the same time, around seven, eight o'clock at night. It was about then that he started asking me queer shit, stuff like, "did I want to make some extra money, did I want to go with him?" He'd say this shit over and over again.

To tell you the truth, I didn't get it at first. I didn't know what he was talking about. I mean, why would a nigger boy like me want to go anywhere with a piece of shit linthead boy like him? Really, I didn't get it. I mean, I had heard about faggots and she-boys, but I ain't never seen one up close before. Ain't one never said this kind of shit to me before. Cocksucker. I was mad. Why was he saying this kind of shit to me? What did he think? That I was like him? I kept thinking of ways to get back at that white piece of shit. Ain't no one going to talk that kind of faggot shit to me. White people think they can say anything they want to us niggers, anything they want. They think we are scared of them. But I ain't scared of no she-man, faggot, I don't care if he is white. Anyway that's what I thought.

I mean, I thought about hurting the faggot, but I didn't really plan nothing. That just sort of happened. Really. I got up early that day, right when the sun came up. Mr. Thomas, that white guy from over on the other side of town, had hired me and a couple other fellows to help him clear away some brush around his farm. He said it would take all day and that he would give us fifty cents for the job. Well, it didn't take that long and that meant he didn't think he had to pay us. Ain't that just like a white man? We were done early, I don't know, around three o'clock I guess. Just because we were niggers, Mr. Thomas tried to take our money. He said he wouldn't give us the whole fifty cents.

"You boys finished early," he told us. "I'll pay you thirty-five cents, that's it. You didn't work a full day, you don't get paid for a full day."

Fuck this, I thought, we did the work we deserved the fifty cents, but what's the use of saying anything, white people do what they want. But, I don't know, I just didn't feel like taking it that day. I just wanted him to know that I knew he was stealing from us. As I walked up to him to get my pay, I said real low, not wanting to get him too mad, "Mr. Thomas, uh . . . sir, we done the work you wanted us to do, so we deserve the pay, right?" He just handed me the thirty-five cents, and pretended that he didn't hear me. I took the money and didn't say nothing else, but I was pissed off and I couldn't stop thinking about it as I headed over to the train station. Frank was there. We stayed by the station way past suppertime, drinking and talking. We sold a few pints. Made a little money. I was telling Frank about Mr. Thomas, and we were talking about white folks, about how they think they are all big and all, and how they treat us like shit, but that we ain't shit anyways. You know, we were talking big like we always do when we are drinking. I guess we were drunk when the linthead, faggot showed up. It must been about eight o'clock.

"Hey, nigger," he hollered over to me. Hearing his voice, seeing his face was like having someone stick me with a pin or something sharp in my back. "Hey, nigger," he said a little louder, "got any more of that rot-gut shit that you niggers call whiskey and that you are always selling over here?"

Now those pins were being shoved even deeper into my back. I could feel the anger and meanness rising inside me I thought about doing mean stuff to him, like spitting on him, kicking him hard in the balls, and sticking him with a sharp pitchfork in the ribs. I still hadn't answered him.

"Hey, boy, I said, got any of that nigger whiskey left?" He was even louder now. Usually, you know, the law didn't bother us, but no use advertising what we were doing. I was worrying that the linthead was fucking things up. He was already drunk; how far gone I couldn't tell, because I was pretty loaded up on whiskey myself.

"Shhh," I said putting my finger to my lips without thinking.

He looked mad, the way white people do when they don't like what niggers are doing. "Who you shushing?" "Got any of that whiskey?" he called out again before I had time to answer the first question.

"Yeah, sure, sure I got some, got some back over there. Same as last week. You want a pint jar or a quart jug?"

"Quart!" he said real quick, sharp like.

I nodded to the linthead, pointing him toward the back of the station. I called out to Frank, "Let's go." We didn't say anything. Nothing, I swear, was planned ahead of time. The linthead followed. We got to the spot where we kept the whiskey. He gave me some money. I could see, then, that he had some more left. That's the first time I thought about taking his money. I don't know, I guessed I wanted the money Mr. Thomas owed me. Frank didn't know anything about this.

"How about a drink boys?" the linthead asked kind of nice, kind of like he was trying to be friendly now. I wanted to take his money and go, but Frank—Frank did not know about the other time when he asked me if I wanted to make a little extra money—said sure, why not. Drinking with white people always made me nervous. Something, anything, could go wrong with white people, especially drunk ones like this one, but Frank didn't give a shit. "A drink was a drink," he would say. The bottle went around for a while. I was drunk I could feel it now. I was rocking back and forth trying to catch my balance. The linthead, and Frank too, looked drunk and they were laughing about something.

The way he laughed set me off. I was staring at him, feeling like I wanted to do something to him. Maybe he could tell what I was thinking because he yelled at me, "What are you looking at boy?"

I looked right at him. I hated that prick at that moment, but I didn't say nothing.

"Good thing cause I'd cut your balls off nigger as easily as I'd kill a god-damn bug." He laughed all evil, showing his teeth making him look even more evil.

The bottle went around a few more times. The linthead was really drunk now. The sound of his voice started to change. He starting talking, I don't know, sweet like. Fucker. He was asking us all sweet and funny if we wanted to earn a little extra money. He started rubbing himself and trying to touch us, saying how he knew us niggers could never get enough. He was saying all kinds of stuff, stuff I can't remember. Frank was laughing real loud now, but I was getting madder and madder. I guess I sort of lost my way. I pulled my pistol out, you know the one I always carry, and stuck it against the side of his head. He glanced over at me, moving his eyes, but not his head. He laughed that evil, ugly laugh again.

"Shut the fuck up," I said. Frank laughed.

"Nigger what are you doing?"

"Don't look like there is but one nigger here now, and that's you." Frank laughed some more.

"I'll kill you, nigger."

"How you gonna kill me, linthead, when I got a gun pointed at your head?" Truth is, though, I was scared now. I didn't know what I was going to do. Lots of times, I had wondered what it would be like to stick a gun to white man's head and make him do what I said, and now I was doing it, and I got to tell you I was scared, real scared. I mean, I was shaking inside, but I still felt mean, real mean, mean deep down so that I felt it in my stomach, on face, and in my hands.

I pressed the gun harder against his head. I could tell by the way he jumped a little that it hurt. I liked making the white boy jump. Frank slurred all drunk, "Wha, wha, what you gonna do Joe, kill him?" Then he laughed, but this time he laughed kind of evil. Everybody was kind of evil like by then, I guess.

Frank's laugh gave me time to think. That's when I first thought about it—I thought I'm going to bring this fucker down.

"Give me your money," I yelled.

"Fuck you," he yelled back.

"Get it Frank, get his money." Frank went over and reached into his right pocket and pulled out some change. He laughed.

"I'll kill you fuckers," the linthead screamed. I don't know why, but then I kicked him in the side as hard as I could. I could tell it hurt him pretty bad. He groaned.

"Let's go," Frank said.

"Not yet, not yet," I answered, "We're not done with this cocksucker yet."

"On your knees," I ordered the linthead. He didn't move so I pressed the gun tighter to his head. Then, he dropped to the ground in a quick motion that made a funny kind of thud sound. I can still hear it.

I cocked the gun and pressed it even harder still against his head. "Suck his cock, you she-man faggot," I said. The linthead tried to turn around to look at me, but I kept his head still with the gun.

Frank let out his biggest laugh yet. "Pull down your pants, Frank. Let's bring this fucker down." He laughed kind of nervous this time. Our eyes met and he knew I was serious. He laughed and pulled his pants down. The linthead tried to turn his head toward me. I pressed the metal against his head and nudged him forward.

He still won't do it so I stuck the gun—I mean I rammed it—into his back real hard. I could feel him twitch. Then I moved real, real close to him. My lips almost touched his ear. I'm sure he could hear my breathing. I screamed: "Suck his black cock, you piece of shit faggot." Then I shoved him. He opened his mouth. I heard sucking sounds—slurp, slurp. Frank heard them too. He laughed. I laughed too. You should have seen that faggot on his fucking knees sucking Frank off. He wasn't talking shit any more.

I must not have heard them coming. All of the sudden, I heard a young white boy's voice, saying, "What are you boys doing?" That was the signal for Frank and me. We ran as fast as we could, I mean we ran our asses off until we were out of breath. We made it down the tracks about two miles or so and ducked into the woods. That's where they found us.

"Are you coming or are you going to sit there like a chicken-shit, piece of shit?" That's what Lester Burns asked me.

A few hours before we had been sitting in front of the company store at Cherokee Falls. I came over there just about every night after my shift at the mill to talk to the fellows before dinner. That night, it must have been around half-past five or so when I got there because it was just starting to get dark. Peter Copeland from down the street was with me. A couple others were already there when we walked up. They were facing us, sitting down on a bench and a few wooden chairs just to the right of the door leading into the store. In front of them was Lester.

Lester was a regular-looking man, not too big, too small, normal hands, normal feet, just regular. But he didn't act regular. He was always acting like a politician up there on the stump, pacing one way and then turning right around and going back the other way. That night, he was looking all serious, staring real hard straight ahead. There was something about Lester that always seemed to be smoldering. He never really flamed up, just burned orange and bright without going out, like the end of a lighted cigarette.

"There goes Lester again," Peter said as we walked up to the store. Lester was going on as usual about stuff that happened to him and stuff he heard about happening to other people. Before I go any further, there are two things about Lester you should know: he loved baseball and he hated niggers. It was March 30th when we saw Lester in front of the store, so the baseball season hadn't started, so that left him with only niggers to talk about.

It didn't really matter what you were talking about before it was baseball season, when Lester came up you just automatically started talking about niggers. I mean he just had to say stuff about niggers. Peter said Lester was crazy going on about niggers all the time. I don't know, I kind of agreed with Lester and I liked listening to him go on and on. I don't know if I hated niggers like he did, but I sure didn't like them much.

"Niggers," he would say, "want to be just like white folks. You see them going around acting white." "Niggers," he would say other times, "want to work in the mills. I'll die before I let one of those animals—you ever smell them?—take my job or get in there next to my wife and daughter." "People," he would say, "think niggers are stupid. Well, they ain't right. I don't care what they say. Niggers ain't stupid, they ain't stupid at all. They just think with their dicks all of the time. That ain't just my opinion, that's science talking here."

Peter and I got up next to the store and took our seats next to the others. The fellows nodded in our direction, but Lester just kept talking not even looking at us. Peter was right, he was talking about niggers, saying nigger this and nigger that. But he seemed a little more agitated, a little wilder, and a little angrier than usual that night. We were about to find out why. When we sat down, he was just starting to tell a story. It was about something that had happened the night before in Blacksburg. It was about Jim Childers, a good friend of Lester's cousin and a couple of niggers. No one interrupted Lester for a good while. The longer he went on telling the story, it was funny, the calmer he got, like telling it made him feel better or something.

"This Childers fellow lives over at the Limestone mill in Gaffney. Last night, he went over to Blacksburg, looking for a job at the Whittaker Mills. You know that place, that little spinning mill where Peter's brother used to work. They pay decent wages, I hear. He gets there about six or seven at night. He took the train there. Just as was he leaving the train station heading over to that mill hill, a couple of niggers, one named Brinson and the other one was called . . . uh . . . I can't remember—he had some kind long name—followed him."

"'Don't you want some whiskey, mister?' they said to Childers. He didn't want none, but they wouldn't leave him alone. They just kept pestering him to buy their nigger whiskey."

"Was Childers a drinking man?" one of the fellows wondered.

"I dunno, I don't think so, no. And it don't matter, does it?" Lester snapped back, kind of like he was mad at the guy for interrupting him. "Like I was saying," he continued, "the niggers just kept pestering him. Finally he says, okay boys, give me a pint, but it better be good. That Brinson fellow—I hear he is a low-down criminal—looked at him kind of mean when he called him boy. Childers followed the niggers into the woods behind the train station. That's where they said the whiskey was."

"'We only got quarts, so now I guess you're going to buy a quart,' one of them told him. Childers said no. Now he was mad. 'A pint's what I said I'd buy and that's what I'm buying.' But then all the sudden the nigger Brinson pulled a gun. 'You buying a quart, now, white boy. You know what else? You going to drink that quart right now.' Then the nigger stuck a gun to his head and told him to drink the whole thing. The niggers started laughing and making fun of him, and calling him names. He knew they were drunk—and now, you know there ain't no accounting for what a nigger will do when he's got liquor in him. That Childers was afraid now, afraid that they would shoot him if he didn't finish the bottle. Now, remember he isn't a drinking man, but he tried to finish that every drop of that liquor, and he couldn't. He almost threw up trying."

One of the guys at the store spoke up, "Shit, I couldn't drink a quart of nothing, not even with two niggers sticking a gun to my head."

"Yeah," one of the others added.

Lester took advantage of the talking to catch his breath, then he started again: "Childers couldn't finish the bottle. The niggers got mad. They started yelling. Then the real mean no-good one, Brinson, stuck that pistol hard into Childers's ribs and told him to take his overalls off. Then those sick son-of-bitches made him take off his britches too. Imagine that—niggers making a white boy strip down to nothing."

Lester's eyes were bulging. I'd seen him riled up before, but not like this. You could see the veins in his neck pumping real fast, and his face getting red all over. All the fellows were leaning forward listening real hard now. It was almost like no one was breathing any more.

"There was Childers out there in the woods," Lester was saying, "buck naked, with a couple of low-down niggers. The niggers just sat there laughing, while he shivered. 'Cold boy,' they said, and then they laughed. Now here's the worst part. Those nigger boys raped that Childers."

The word rape hit us like buckshot, knocking us back away from Lester. "Yeah, the fuckers raped him," he said, not shouting, but in a low, real, real serious kind of voice. "They raped a white man. Niggers, I been telling you, they think they are white. Niggers, like I been telling you, can't control themselves, that's why they're niggers, they're not like us, they ain't been civilized yet."

Lester was wild like a tent preacher now, all fired up and kind of crazy, like a spirit was in him. He leaned forward and got real close like he was trying to pull us in even closer. "There are some boys over on the mill hill in Hickory Grove that's friends with my cousin," he hissed, "and they say that Childers is a good man, a hard-working, and decent man. They're planning to go over to Blacksburg tonight and set those niggers straight. Ain't no nigger going to treat a white man that way. Niggers raping white men, what's next? That's what they say and that's what I say. I'm going over there—any of you going to join me?"

I had never done nothing like this before. Once when I was kid, me and a friend jumped a nigger boy. We took him to the woods, tied him to a tree, hit him hard with a stick, and fired two shotgun blasts past his head. I don't really remember why we did it. I don't think he really did anything in particular to us, I guess we did it just because he was a nigger and we wanted to let him know he was a nigger.

When Lester asked if any of us was going with him, my hand shot up, like I had no control over it. Then I heard myself say, "I'm in, Lester, I'll go . . . yeah I'll go." No one else raised their hands or said they would go. That made me feel good, like they was chicken, I wasn't. Lester stared at them. Soon they all set off in different directions to their houses to tell their wives and children the story of Jim Childers and the niggers and to tell them that Lester and I were off to get those two niggers. I imagined these women hearing about it, I imagined that they would look at me different next time they saw me. I guessed that they would be scared of me and that they would look up to me. I liked thinking about this.

Lester's stern voice caught me off-guard. "Johnson, I'll be by your house at ten o'clock. Be ready and don't be drunk." How'd he know that's what I planned to do? Sometimes Lester was funny that way. Sometimes he seemed to know just what you were thinking. On the way home, I picked up a pint of whiskey. I wasn't scared, not then at least, I was still imagining what people would think of me for killing those nigger boys.

Lester was right on time, maybe even a few minutes early. I had finished the pint an hour or so before and I was sitting on the porch waiting for him. By then, I was getting nervous. I could tell that I was nervous by the way my throat went dry, my stomach was churning, and I felt a little sweaty under my shirt, even though it was cool out. I was starting to worry. What if we get caught? I didn't really think too much about that, but you had to think about it now that there were these politicians—mostly rich ones—running around talking about not killing niggers any more. Mostly, though, I worried that I wouldn't be able to do it, that we would get there and I wouldn't be able to do it. Then what? I ain't never killed nobody ever, not even a nigger. I kept telling myself the stuff that Lester said, trying to make myself feel better: "No nigger is taking my job. No nigger is working next to my wife. Niggers got to be taught a lesson." I especially liked that last part, I liked thinking that I was the one teaching those niggers how to act. But, I don't know, going out in the night still made me nervous. What if something went wrong and I couldn't do it? Then I would look like a pussy.

Lester must have smelled my nervousness. Was it that easy to tell? He hadn't even got to the first step of the porch, when he said, "Are you coming or are you going to sit there like a chicken-shit, piece of shit?"

That did it. I was going. I wasn't going to be no chicken-shit, not me. I wasn't going to have people say I backed out; that was worse than not even saying I would go. I said to Lester in a whisper just loud enough for him to hear, "Let me get my shotgun. I'll meet you out back."

AFTERWORD

This story of history and fiction, narrative and experimentation began in the archives. It began, more specifically, at one of the dozen or so long thick wood tables in the book-lined reading room of the South Carolina Division of Archives and History in Columbia, South Carolina. It was the summer of 1993. I was just out of graduate school and coming back to South Carolina from my first job in Los Angeles to work on the early chapters of my manuscript. One thing you have to know about the South Carolina archives, it was open long hours, 9 am–9 pm, Monday through Friday, and 9 am to 6 pm on Saturdays. Of course, this was both a blessing and a curse: a blessing in the sense that you can get a lot done in a short period of time, and a curse, if you are like me— that is, plagued by guilt—and feel like you have be in the library every single moment that it is open.

So that's the setting—an archive in South Carolina open for just about half of every day. The night my story begins was a hot summer night. (This is a southern story, so it must be a hot, right?) On this muggy night where the heat made you feel like you were wearing a scratchy wool blanket, I was sitting in the archives as the cruel South Carolina sun was finally coming down. With the exception of a quick lunch and periodic coffee breaks, I had been sitting there on a hard wood chair since the building opened. My back ached and my eyes burned. This was not the best of time for research for me. I felt like I often did often when I worked at restaurants. By the end of my shifts, I usually just went through the motions waiting for quitting time. In the library that night, I was rather mindlessly going through the papers of Governor Coleman Livingston Blease—an early twentieth-century South Carolina politician and demagogue—waiting for the archive to finally close for the day.

The truth is I was really hoping not to find anything. I didn't want to write out yet another colour-coded note card. So there I was—if anyone asked— looking for clues about workers' ideas toward politics but really I was just flipping through the files of mostly hand-written letters on small sheets of coarse paper asking for clothes, jobs, clemency and advice, watching the clock and hoping it would move faster. Then it happened. I made one of those great "finds" historians always hope for.

At first glance the only thing that made this letter different from the other letters was that it was typed. I had never heard of the correspondent, N. W. Hardin. His stationery said he was a Spartanburg lawyer and magistrate—a kind of judge and that made him, in addition, a low-level political appointee.

I started to read Hardin's letter to the Governor with the same dull detachment that I read everything at that hour. But the words—lynching, white, negro, penus—jumped off the page. I read Hardin's letter over and over again. I made another researcher read it and then I made the attendant read it (she thought I was crazy). I did not want to leave the archives that night or put the remarkable letter back in the box and risk never seeing it again. I wanted to keep the letter; I wanted to think about it; I wanted to know the story behind the startling words. But soon it was nine o'clock and I returned the letter to the file and walked back to my un-air conditioned rented room to eat a frozen pasta dinner and watch late night re-runs of *Hill Street Blues*.

The next day I ordered a copy of the letter. The letter is reprinted in its entirety on p. 158.

This amazing letter was my first clue—and what would remain my best clue—about this grizzly tale of murder charged with political partisanship, class resentments, and homoeroticism. Over the next few days, I looked at the newspapers from the area where the killings took place to see what they said about the murders. I learned that the murders took place in Blacksburg, a small mill town just South of the North Carolina border along what is now interstate I-85. I also found out a bit more about Joe Childers—the white man involved in the mystery. One paper described him as a "respectable laboring man" with a "good reputation." I discovered the names of both victims: Joe Brinson and Frank Whinsonant. The papers said that the two men were gagged and then hanged with a piece of rope taken from the community well and that the murder took place at a blacksmith's shop near the jail. Also I determined that the larger community was divided over the crime. "Law and order," worried the editor of the Gaffney *Ledger*, the local paper of record, "has been flaunted" as "passions [became] inflamed and reason dethroned". "Every good citizen", he was certain, "deplored the crime". The newsman, however, had no sympathy for the dead: "Those were two bad negroes who were lynched in Blacksburg", he conceded. "But", he added, "those who outraged them became worse whites".[1] Finally, I learned that the newspapers addressed the homoeroticism of the crime, but they spoke about it in a coded language. The press wrote that Childers was the victim of an "unmentionable act"—a phrase usually reserved in the South for the alleged rape of a white woman by a black man. This made me more curious—was the paper acknowledging the sexual dimensions of the murder? Was this something people were talking about? Nonetheless, I had reached a dead-end with the newspapers. They had filled in a few gaps and gave me some key details, but they provided no answers.

In the days after I found Hardin's letter, I talked about the Blacksburg lynching non-stop. I asked everyone I knew or ran into at the archives if they had ever heard about the killings. No one really knew much about it except John Hammond Moore. At the time, Moore was finishing a book on lynching in South Carolina. He said he thought he had seen a photograph of the Blacksburg lynching at the Historical Center of York County. This was, he said, the only known double lynching in South Carolina at the time and there were two men in the photograph he saw. I wrote Sam Thomas at the Historical Center, and he wrote back and said yes he did in fact have a faded picture showing two men—apparently African American men—hanging from the rafters of what looked like an outdoor shop.

They say a picture is worth a thousand words, and maybe it is, but this picture (see Figure 7.1), while it provided more painful details, revealed few answers. It said little about the killings and the events behind the killings. It spoke, instead, in a sparse grammar of frozen silence.

Next, as I said previously, I went looking for Childers, Brinson and Whinsonant in the US manuscript census records. The only one I found for certain was Joe Brinson. According to the census, Brinson was born in North Carolina in 1889. Two years before he was killed, the 21-year-old lived in a rented house in Blacksburg, South Carolina with his wife of four years, Nancy, and their three-year-old daughter. Neither Joe nor Nancy could read or write. He worked odd jobs, apparently pretty steadily. He told the census takers that he was employed

Figure 7.1 A lynching in the South Carolina upcountry sometime before World War I

Sources: Historical Center of York County, York, South Carolina; and John Hammond Moore, 'Carnival of Blood: Dueling, Lynching, and Murder in South Carolina, 1880–1920' (unpublished MS)

every single week the previous year. His wife was not so fortunate. A laundress, the record said, she worked only 28 weeks over the same period of time.

There is no one by the name of Frank Whisonant listed in the 1910 census of Cherokee County or the surrounding counties. There are several Whisonant families that are African American. One of the Whisonant men, in fact, was quite prosperous; he owned his own home along with a rather large farm. There were also several white Whisonant families in Cherokee County in 1910. But there is no one named Frank Whisonant, black or white, listed in the census.

There was no one named Joe Childers, as one newspaper called him, listed in the 1910 census either. Yet there was a 35-year-old James Childers—several papers referred to the white man in the Blacksburg drama as Jim Childers—working in the mills in Blacksburg, but according to most reports the Childers involved in this story did not live in that town. There was another Childers, who lived in nearby Gowdaysville Township, and worked in the mills. However, it is impossible to clearly determine this man's first name in the census. It seems that his first initial is J, but that is all that can be made out for sure. This Childers was 23 years old in 1910. At the time, he and his 26-year-old wife, Martha, had been married for five years and they had three daughters ages 4, 2, and 10 months.

I kept looking in the archives for more details, more evidence, but this is all I could find. I wanted to tell the story of the Blacksburg lynching, but how could I? I wanted to explore what happened—I wanted to understand desire and sex in the turn-of-the-century south; I wanted to understand why people killed other people. I want to know why people loved and hated. I wanted a story—with a plot and characters and drama—but I couldn't find the evidence to tell a story—that is what we conventionally think of as a historical narrative or straightforward non-fiction story.

Unable to find enough evidence to tell the story I wanted to tell, I told another story about the Blacksburg lynching in the opening scene of the first chapter of my book, *A Fabric of Defeat*.[2] It was a story full of questions, full of perhaps and maybes—lines like "depending on who told the story"—and it was a story used in the service of another story—in this case the story of why textile workers—people like Childers, and Brinson and Whisonant's murders—supported a demagogic politician like Cole Blease. This was a story built around the symbolic meaning of the details of the killings, not a story of what happened that gruesome night in Blacksburg.

After finishing my book, I keep looking for information about the murders. I talked to a few genealogists and other South Carolina historians—but still I could not find anything—anything that a historian would deem to be clear and compelling evidence. At this point, I made a decision—I was going to tell the story, and I was going to tell it as fiction. To help me do this, I enrolled in a fiction class in the adult learning division of my home university—the University of Georgia. (I almost dropped the class the first night when the older, somewhat prim-looking southern woman teaching the class announced that we could read anything aloud—anything, that is, but stories about sex. Finally we came to an agreement. I could read what I was writing; it just couldn't be too graphic—whatever that meant [I should add that the rather prim-looking southern woman turned out to be a wonderfully generous and open teacher].

Now the question was how to tell the story as fiction. I knew I wanted to talk about the South, violence, sexualities and class. I also knew I wanted the fictions to raise at least implicitly some questions about how we—academically trained historians—talk about the past. Then I asked myself, who was it that I was writing these fictions for? Who, in other words, was my audience? I quickly decided that I was really writing for university-based historians more than the other fiction writers in my class, and I knew I wanted to tell a "true" story—that is I wanted to use what I knew about the South and South Carolina, white mill workers and African Americans at this time and in this place combined with what I had found out about the lynching in the archives, newspapers, and census to talk about what might have happened in Blacksburg. Put another way, I was interested in fiction as a way to explore the past, not as a way to distort or misrepresent the past. I wanted, to paraphrase the historian David Farber, to beyond the evidence to tell a story truer than what the archives revealed.[3]

Once I made the decision to write fiction, I started to think about the links between my imagined audience and the structure of the story. How, I kept asking myself, could I write fiction and at the same time engage historians about questions about writing about the past—especially about how to write scenes where the silences in the archives speak louder than the sources? At one point, I thought about giving the documents I found in the archives to other scholars and asking them to interpret them as fiction or any other way they wanted. I thought I would then assemble these various accounts and somehow put them together as an essay. I imagined these contradictory accounts would speak to the power of interpretation in history. But at that time I was already engaged—embroiled might be a better word—in one editing project, so I decided against this plan. Then I considered writing fiction with footnotes. My idea was to have two texts going on at once in columns running along the same page. On one side would be the fictional story, on the other would be an extended discussion about why I decided to tell the story the way I did complete with detailed annotations and historiography. Actually, this is how I started my re-writing of the Blacksburg story. Quickly, however, I found out the annotations overwhelmed, rather than meshed with the story. Each sentence it seemed generated a paragraph of supporting text. So, finally, I decided to take a page or a frame from *Rashomon*, John Dos Passo and Norman Mailer. What I did was present the evidence—the letter that appeared earlier, a few newspaper articles and some of the information from the census—at the front of the essay. I called this section "historical facts".

Then I presented what I labelled "historical fictions". These consisted of four fictional accounts of what I thought could have happened in Blacksburg. These versions of the story overlapped and contradicted each other. What I was trying to get at was what was possible at that moment; what, in other words, was the geography of same-sex, inter-racial sex in the early twentieth-century South? How did people express and repress desires? What was on the minds of the lynchers? In the end, I was trying to push beyond the limits of the evidence and the silences in the archives to explore the possible meanings—both at the time and today—of this episode. Again, I wanted to use fiction to make sense of the past, not to distort the past.

Let me at this point add a final confession: I confess I was tempted by fiction. I say this with a certain amount of guilt and maybe even shame. I was tempted by the freedom and imagination of fiction; I was tempted by how fiction gave me the chance to wander through the heads of my historical characters; I was tempted by the simultaneous ambiguity and certainty of fiction; and finally, I was tempted by the interior perspective of fiction—an interior perspective of people's private thoughts and anxieties that historians rarely explore in print because the evidence rarely gives us access to these worlds. In the end, I was tempted to say what I really thought was happening. Isn't this what all historians do when we are sitting around talking and thinking? We imagine past our sources into the shadows where things are going on that we can't quite see and make out but we know they are there. I wanted to put these imagined thoughts onto paper. I wanted to put a light to the shadows and see what appeared.

Notes

1   Gaffney *Ledger*, 2 April, 4, 1912.
2   Simon, *A Fabric of Defeat: The Politics of South Carolina Millhands, 1910–1948*, Chapel Hill, NC: University of North Carolina Press, 1998, pp. 11–15.
3   Farber made this comment at the Narrating Histories Workshop held at the California Institute of Technology in the spring of 1994. For a report on the conference, see Robert Rosenstone, Bryant Simon and Moshe Sulhovsky, "Experiments in Narrating Histories: A Workshop", *Perspectives* (September 1994), 8.

8 Reconstructing the voice of a noblewoman of the time of Peter the Great: Daria Mikhailovna Menshikova

An exercise in (pseudo)autobiographical writing

Robin Bisha

Did Peter the Great sponsor a revolution for women in Russia in the early eighteenth century? This is a question that scholars and aficionados of Russian women's history have been debating since the end of the nineteenth century.[1] I spent several years gathering material for studies of Russian women in the first half of the eighteenth century, particularly focusing on evidence about Russian noblewomen, as they would have been more affected than other women by Peter's legislative efforts to revamp Russian society. I planned a prosopographical study of Peter the Great's female contemporaries and women of court circles who were born during his reign. I have identified numerous women for such a study, but evidence for the details of their lives remains elusive and difficult to uncover. I suspect that, rather than freeing women from the subjugation of the *terem*,[2] Peter harnessed them to the needs of building his modern Russian state, for as long as he needed them, and that women's lives returned to normal—paternal or spousal control—after a brief period during which Peter's personal, patriarchal control allowed a certain sort of initiative to Russian noblewomen who were savvy enough to recognize the opportunity.

Daria Mikhailovna Arseneva and her sister Varvara were two such women. Born into a noble family of long standing and distance from Moscow, through Daria's relationship to Aleksandr Danilovich Menshikov, the Arsenev sisters catapulted into Peter's inner circle.[3] They remained firmly at the center of the ruling elite until Menshikov's fall from power in 1727, shortly after the death of Peter I's widow Empress Catherine I; later the Arsenev men were able to make good careers in imperial service because of Daria's advantageous marriage. Peter recognized Menshikov's abilities early in his reign, promoting him through the ranks of the "play regiments" he created at the royal family's estate in suburban Moscow. Menshikov, whose social origins are shrouded in legend, gained Peter's confidence and became a loyal assistant to the young Tsar. Peter's protégé showed great talent as a military strategist in the war against Sweden which occupied much of Russia's energy in the early eighteenth century. Menshikov introduced the Tsar to a peasant woman, a refugee of the war, who would become his second wife Catherine.[4] Through his service to the Tsar, Menshikov acquired great power and wealth. After Peter's death, Menshikov acted as one of Empress Catherine's chief advisors. His aspirations for even more power eventually led to his disgrace and exile after Catherine's death. Menshikov's wife, sister-in-law, and daughter are all prominent figures in his political success and failure. Varvara Mikhailovna Arseneva advised him, Daria Mikhailovna Menshikova cleaned up his messes through traditional Russian female politics, and his daughter Maria was the pawn in his final, disastrous scheme to increase his power by becoming the reigning tsar's (the grandson of Peter I) father-in-law.

Despite the importance of women in the cultural and political life of Petrine Russia, it is a task of amazing difficulty to learn about the actions, let alone the thoughts, of prominent women of Peter's court. The Arseneva sisters are no exceptions to this general rule. Daria Menshikova carried on a voluminous correspondence with her husband and his patron, many letters of which have been published in the monumental collection of Peter the Great's papers,[5] along with letters to and from other key female members of Peter's entourage, including his favorite sister Natalia Alekseevna. Yet, this correspondence reveals little of the inner world of the correspondents. A recent Russian biography of Prince Menshikov does little more to illuminate the role of the women of his family in the affairs of society and state, yet both suggest that there is much more to the story than the surface view reveals.[6] Given the paucity of sources to conduct studies that would reveal the real roles of women in Peter's era, numerous unsubstantiated legends have guided the thinking even of reputable scholars. It is my wish to avoid rumor, yet despite extensive investigations in Russian archives and published materials I remained frustrated in my ability to learn more from the women themselves about their thoughts and actions.

Puzzling over this problem and immersed in the materials I had been scouring for information about the Arseneva sisters, I conceived the idea for a pseudo-autobiography;[7] I decided to write the autobiography Daria Mikhailovna Menshikova might have written, had it occurred to her to do such a thing.[8] In many ways Daria Mikhailovna's life, as deeply as I know it, epitomizes the life of the supposed "New Petrine Woman." Bold in her youth, she served the Tsar-Reformer well as Menshikov's consort, but the majority of her activities were confined to the so-called private sphere.

Daria Mikhailovna writes while on the final leg of the journey toward the place of the Menshikovs' exile in Siberia. The work remains unpolished, and perhaps even unfinished, because she died before reaching their final destination of Berezov. Daria Mikhailovna was last mentioned in the guard's report of 5 May 1728. She passed away somewhere between Nizhnii Novgorod and Laishev. It is rumored that her grave is located in Kazan.[9]

If only she had spoken for herself . . .

I, Princess Daria Mikhailovna Menshikova, humble servant of the Lord, have appealed to my Sovereign for mercy for my husband His Most Serene Highness Prince Aleksandr Danilovich Menshikov. His cold heart has allowed him, instead of treating my husband less harshly, to extend the sentence of exile to include our entire family, including the innocent children. Since God has not seen fit to lift the burdensome sentence of exile from our family, since our Sovereign's heart remained hard before my pleas on behalf of my husband, His Most Serene Highness Aleksandr Danilovich Menshikov, until recently prince of Izhora and . . . , I now set down on paper for my children and my grandchildren, the story of my life. When I have left this life, they will have this document as proof of our innocence before the charge of treason. These memories will help them to establish the injustice of this punishment and to restore the name of Menshikov to the honor it deserves in the Russian empire and the Western world. Perhaps there may be blemishes on the service record of Aleksandr Danilovich, he is an impetuous man, large in spirit, given to excess in all, including in love for his sovereigns. If I have done wrong, it was not against my sovereign. Since I first set foot on the grounds of Preobrazhenskoe, I have served my Sovereign, may he rest in peace, with devotion. The present Tsar, also Peter Alekseevich, but the son of a true traitor to his homeland, sees fit to punish me and the innocent children and in spite of my pleas and the pleas of those he holds in esteem, he will not revoke the sentence imposed upon our family by the Privy Council. Let him punish me, but spare Aleksandr Danilovich, who is sick near death, and the futures of these innocent young people.

Is this the way to treat a mother who has borne seven children and given four up to the Lord? Now, those who fawned on my husband while his patron, Petr Alekseevich, was among the living have stripped the remaining three of their family's honor. Thank the Lord that our first-born, Luka-Peter, and Samson, who died at the breast, and Varvara and Ekaterina do not have to suffer the indignity and shame of unjust punishment. I pray that our Aleksandr, only thirteen years old as I write, will be able to restore the family's honor so that his sisters Maria and Aleksandra will be able to marry appropriately. And they tell us Maria Aleksandrovna was not a suitable bride for a tsar. No matter that this goes against the wishes of the Tsar's step-grandmother, the late Empress Ekaterina Alekseevna, who wanted to join our families in matrimony.[10]

What will become of my daughters? Their father's good name would get them married, but that name is now sullied by exile. Our Peter Alekseevich valued his Prince; these people punish him for his work. And how will they make good marriages from Berezov? Whatever will become of them when we are in the grave? I raised my girls to be the kind of women the great Peter Alekseevich wanted Russian women to be—European, cultured, the best wives for any Russian man—suitable for a Tsar because they were molded by the Tsar. And here we are, sent into exile because the other nobles envy my Maria's success.

My poor, poor children, God grant their fond memories of childhood sustain them now when they have lost all comfort in the world. If only they could see the letters I saved for them. Instead, we were forced to abandon all of our belongings when they came for us.[11] If only they could read how Maria sent gifts to her father at the front and letters describing how she learned to walk. If only her sister and brother could read how she congratulated them upon their births.[12] If only Aleksandr could see how his father considered him the man of the family and how much trust he has always placed in his third son.[13]

I first saw the esteemed Peter Alekseevich and his beloved Aleksashka (Peter's nickname for Menshikov) when I came to Preobrazhenskoe some twenty-nine years ago.[14] The soldiers were so dashing. Such entertainments I had not seen in Siberia! Such weapons! Such uniforms! Varvara, my sister Varvara Mikhailovna, whom the Privy Council has so cruelly included in our Menshikov family sentence and then stripped from my presence even more cruelly along the way to the distant, desolate hut in which we are to live, so undeservedly taken, I know not where while she remains blameless.[15] Two figures stood out from the rest, Peter, who towered above all men, and a young man about his age who seemed ever at his side. We and the other *boiar*'s daughters watched their war games when we were not busy with the Tsarevna, Her Majesty Natalia Alekseevna in the drawing room.[16] She had a fondness for dramas which she occasionally wrote herself and which we women would act out for her in her chambers.[17]

His Most Serene Highness first noticed me in these family skits; his presence in the household was accepted unquestioningly. Already he was closer to our great Father than any other human being. Such a man as Aleksandr Danilych took an interest in me, a humble *boiar*'s daughter from Siberia, and he so handsome and so intimate with His Majesty the Tsar. One day, Her Majesty the Tsarevna called me to her chambers. She told me the Tsar desired my presence at an audience. I was awed and frightened by such a command. Natalia Alekseevna, seeing my obvious distress, deigned to comfort me with the news that her royal brother desired to present me to his associate, Aleksandr Danilovich Menshikov. My fear was replaced with delight!

I practically ran out of the room to consult my wise sister Varvara as to how to conduct myself at this meeting. We were raised to cover our faces and bow before men. I had seen these exalted persons in large companies, but was still not used to the ways of Preobrazhenskoe. I did not know what to expect from the men I had seen joke informally with my mistress, the Tsarevna. What should I do? Bow demurely? I so desperately wanted to please my Sovereign. Varvara told me that although he was the Tsar of All the Russias, this Peter Alekseevich was a different sort of man. She reminded me that he spent his time in the company of foreigners, and of foreign women. She knew of his displeasure with his wife Evdokhia, who was a girl like us, a girl from the provinces.[18] Varvara told me to show my teeth proudly and to laugh at the Sovereign's jokes. She told me to look directly at Aleksandr Danilovich, but not before bowing. I feared my shyness would prevent me from taking such a bold action.

I was conducted to the Tsar's apartments. When the guard announced me, the Tsar jumped out of his seat and bounded to the door of the chamber. He took my hand and all but dragged me before Aleksandr Danilovich in his enthusiasm. I attempted to wrest my arm from His Majesty's grasp to execute my bow, but he would not release me. I lowered my eyes. I felt Aleksandr Danilovich's gaze upon me and I blushed. He said I was indeed the girl he had noticed, at which point Peter passed my hand to his friend and said, 'For God's sake, woman, look at him!' My schooling in the German way escaped from me in the presence of the Tsar and his dashing young man; all I could do was bow deeply in the old Russian style. I could not comply with His Majesty's command to look at Aleksandr Danilovich. I feared that he would beat me, as I had seen him do so many times to others at Preobrazhenskoe, instead, he laughed and turned my head up with is long index finger under my chin. What a picture I presented, doubled over in obeisance, staring straight into the eyes of the object of my awe.

After this meeting, Aleksashka, as His Majesty called him, began to visit me and bring me gifts. For a worldly man who spent so much time among Germans, his gifts were quaint: pears and apples from the trees around Preobrazhenskoe, fish he caught while accompanying His Majesty on trips to the river. We walked on the grounds. Aleksashka paid attention only to me when he accompanied his royal companion on his visits to Natalia Alekseevna's court. While he spent many evenings with Peter in the German Suburb, he assured me that I was the only woman whom he fancied. I learned from Her Majesty Natalia Alekseevna how to conduct myself in this unfamiliar circumstance. I, unused to the company of men, was now thrown headlong into relations that I enjoyed, and feared, and understood to be my duty. If the Tsar himself had presented me to Menshikov, he must have meant for him to have me. Varvara and I concluded this without anyone's assistance. We saw our Tsar make matches for his favorite courtiers, something he did throughout his days. Thus, I have served my Sovereigns for some thirty years, only to be rewarded with penury in Ranneburg and this horrible journey to distant exile.

His Most Serene Highness volunteered for His Majesty's trip to Europe. He returned more knowledgeable of the ways of the Germans. He supported most whole-heartedly the reforms in dress for all the nobles and would no longer tolerate the very sight of an old Russian caftan. He insisted that my sisters and I be among the most fashionable. We put all the resources we had, and then some, into our new German wardrobe. At first, I felt awkward in the close-fitting bodices of the German gowns, but I soon grew accustomed to them, and to the new dances Aleksashka and His Majesty brought with them from their travels. What merriment they must have committed in the courts of Europe! And they were a merry company! My happiness at the Embassy's return was marred only by the treachery of the Tsarevna Sofia Alekseevna and the *streltsy*.[19] Danilych was, as always, at the side of his Sovereign, so angry his face was as red as the blood that flowed outside the Kremlin walls. And now my sister, loyal pillar of the family of the one who served so constantly has been locked away just like the traitorous Tsarevna Sofia, and the servant himself sent to ignominious exile. Through all the changes of Emperor Peter's reign one thing remained constant, loyalty. Only now does the antichrist truly roam the land when loyalty stands for nothing.

Oh, the excitement that came in the spring! The courtiers of Preobrazhenskoe donned the uniform of the Tsar's new army. European they looked! The peasants arrived from across the land to learn the new European techniques of arms for the glory of Russia. We traveled to Voronezh to witness the launching of the first naval vessel, built largely by the hands of our Sovereign and his loyal Menshikov. We women considered this the fruits of the sovereign's education in Germany and Holland. But in July, we gasped one night at the fireworks celebrating the peace with the Turks and the next day at the declaration of war against Charles XII, the Swedish Emperor.

The year was 1700 by the new calendar. Aleksashka threw himself into the war with all his soul, as he did everything. He filled my heart with fear for his safety. Through all the twenty years of the Swedish war I wrote him letters. We sent each other gifts. I risked life and limb to travel to the front to comfort him, and through this to strengthen our great Tsar Peter. Peter relied on Danilych, and Danilych brought him our dear Little Mother Ekaterina Alekseevna, may she rest in peace . . .

Katia, as we knew her in those days, came to live with us in Moscow.[20] My sister and brothers and I lived then with Aleksandr Danilovich's sisters.[21] Varvara and I looked after Aleksandr Danilovich's youngest sister Anna.[22] His other sisters were not capable of it. Anna traveled with us to visit her brother in the theater of war, as did our great friend Anisia Tolstaia.[23] During the war we rarely stayed in Moscow, or even St. Petersburg; we lived first in Smolensk, then Briansk and Kharkov, following the war. We could not stand to be far from our companions.[24] Varvara already showed her talent for household administration and Katia brought joy to the house. She was also a companion for the trips we made to the front.

Year after year the war dragged on. The Sovereign was so taken with Katia that he could not bear to be parted from her. We went together to visit him whenever he could find a few days to take rest in a safe place near the front. We traveled to him and also to Danilych, who commanded many of our forces. I saved dozens of letters from that time, all lost to me now; it was a time of great fear and also great happiness. At first, we learned only that Aleksandr Danilovich was still among the living from his letters. Varvara and I sent him, the one who so generously had taken us all into his household, gifts of clothing. Once, in the second or third year of the war, she sent him ties and I sent a shirt and heart-shaped diamond. The response warmed my heart. I still remember it, 'the diamond heart is not dear to me, your affection is.'[25] I had come to love him so. Love that I so little understood, but felt with all my heart. I wrote him constantly, thinking only of his safety, fearing that he would be taken from me. I sent him presents. He so loved the berries that I myself grew. He tried to comfort me, always assuring me that he would not enter the battle himself, always insisting I should be just as joyful without him as I was when he was there, but I could not find peace.[26] The Lord Himself gave me knowledge of the danger Danilych was in. I was content only when I could be with him near the front, to see the reality of his continued existence; this he would not permit me often. He was probably right in not allowing me to travel through such danger.[27] I remember one trip, we were to meet in Minsk. A lone rider on horseback arrived, telling me to hurry, travel as fast as the horses would carry the carriage, giving General Menshikov's authorization to take the best post horses at every station. And finally, telling me to go back and take the road to Smolensk. He did come; the enemy had moved unexpectedly. We spent the first weeks of March together, not yet spring, light snow on the ground, a rare moment of peace during the fighting. How I did not want to let him go back, but he was bound to serve his Sovereign. He was careful, but still I feared for his life. The angel of death awaited him in those days. I knew in August 1708, by the new calendar, that he was in mortal danger. How I wished to see him, but he would not permit it.[28]

Of course, my gifts to him meant little in his success, his great abilities would shine without new shirts and Hungarian wine. But his gifts to me meant the difference between deep longing and fear and a certain contentment that something of him was near me. He sent Polish girls to entertain me and Swedish deserters to work for me. One year in May he sent Luka-Petr and me each a team of horses he had captured from the Swedes. How do rusks, oatmeal, chickens, pickles, and buns compare to such gifts?[29]

In the year 1706, by the new calendar, my life changed at the order of my Sovereign. Peter Alekseevich, so much the Little Father to us all, gave me in holy matrimony to my beloved Aleksandr Danilovich Menshikov. We married in Kiev, in the summer. The Tsar called him back from the campaign, which was quiet at that time.[30] Now, I thought my life would be devoted to serving my husband, but my Sovereign needed me for other tasks. I soon left Aleksashka to accompany Katia on her journeys to visit our Peter Alekseevich. I learned only later that my spouse had promised his Sovereign to provide him a matron with whom she could travel, in order to quiet the whispers flying about Moscow and the new city of St. Petersburg. Thus, even in my marriage to my dearest Prince Aleksandr Danilovich, I served my Tsar and country.

During the winters and after the peace, I served at home in St. Peterburg. I enjoyed running the house, especially since my sister helped me. She was good with the children and helped with the callers. She had a quick mind, of the masculine sort, so different from my humble, female being. She was always more comfortable with the men who gathered at our house than I was. I relied on her and left her to her own affairs. My trust in her allowed me to pay attention to the kitchen, which I so loved, and what a kitchen it was . . . The Tsar himself had little interest in entertaining the diplomats from foreign lands but he wanted them well fed and their thirst quenched with only the best spirits. He loved to attend the parties, but his Prince Menshikov provided the ballroom and fine cuisine. Danilych built the most amazing palace on Vasilevskii Island; the most important men to visit Russia passed through those doors, ate from our kitchen, and drank from our stock of wine.[31]

And how they all loved to drink! They drank and drank, not only at the Assemblies in our halls, but at every chance. They particularly loved the launching of new ships. We ladies would have our own quarters on the new ship while the admirals, generals, and diplomats celebrated the achievements of the Russian navy. Sometimes late at night, or on the second day of the celebration, I would be summoned to the deck where the men were having their party. There, amid the revels, I would find my Aleksandr Danilovich on the floor, in need of reviving so he could continue on with the party. If he did not revive, the Tsar would fly into a rage and threaten to throw him overboard. I massaged his head and hands. I wiped his face with wet cloths and always avoided losing my husband to the currents of the Neva.[32] And what would have become of us all if the Tsar had lost his right hand? What gratitude the young Tsar, the grandson of the great Peter Alekseevich, shows to Menshikov now in allowing his rivals in the Privy council to send him into exile.

Exiled, he who guided the hand of Empress Ekaterina after her beloved Peter, our Emperor of All the Russias, had passed his crown to her. Prince Menshikov, Peter's right hand, so essential to him. Aleksandr Danklovich used to talk with sister Varvara for hours about affairs of state; they would play games and drink and talk. I never had a taste for intrigue or spirits. Varvara aided him, but I did enjoy his trust when the task suited me.[33] Once he entrusted to me two cannons he had captured from the Swedish army. I turned them over to the Tsar on his visit to Kharkov. There we presented Luka-Petr to him also. Such a handsome boy and only a few months old. Danilych wanted his friend and Sovereign to know his first-born son. Had he not met the boy that autumn, he would never have met him at all. Aleksandr Danilovich also required my assistance with presents. I gladly supervised the making of a blanket for Peter Alekseevich and a goblet for the King of Prussia.[34] These things I could do, and try to keep trouble from stalking my Prince as well.

Such a man is the father of my children. Always in the center of everything, always talking his way out of an incident. He came from nowhere and but for a quick wit and a loyal Russian wife, he would have returned there. When he was accused of theft from the treasury, I petitioned the wives of both his supporters and detractors in the Senate. I pleaded with the Empress, who owed us so much. Alas, the efforts of Russia's best women have failed to gain mercy for Prince Menshikov now that she is gone. The times have changed and loyalty means little. Position means everything. The lives of my daughters depend so much more on a good name than did mine. In my time, the time of Peter Alekseevich, deeds carried great weight. Now, rewards come only to those who have already been rewarded and women once again marry for names and position.[35] The Swedish War has ended, and we have become like the West.

Notes

1   Works on the women of Peter I's era (1682–1725) proliferated around the turn of the century including D. L. Mordovtsev (1902) *Russkiia zhenshchiny novago vremeni:*

Biograficheskie ocherki iz russkoi istorii, St. Petersburg, is a multi-volume work covering famous Russian women in all periods; while it has an air of scholarly respectability about it, Mordovtsev does not reveal the sources for the biographies he recounts. Sigizmund Librovich (1993) "Zhenskii krug Petra Velikogo," reprinted in *Smena* vol. 6. This article was originally published in St. Petersburg in 1904. Librovich, like so many who write on Peter's circle, focuses on the most sensational aspects of the relationships. Contemporary Russian work on women of the Petrine era has, in the main, consisted of reprints and recounting of the same undocumented biographical tales. The most recent of these works is Larisa Vasil'eva (1997) "Zhenskaia revoliutsiia Petra Velikogo," *Nauka i religiia* 1997, no. 1–5. Natalia Pushkareva's general work on women in Russia avoids the obvious pitfalls of this approach, but does not focus specifically on this period. See Pushkareva (1997) *Women in Russian History: From the Tenth to the Twentieth Century*, trans. Eve Levin, Armonk, NY: M. E. Sharpe. For another view of the Petrine period, see Lindsey Hughes (1990) *Sophia: Regent of Russia 1657–1704* New Haven, CT: Yale University Press.

2 The separate apartments for women that were standard for Russians of high rank in the seventeenth century.

3 Aleksandr Danilovich Menshikov was of far less exalted background than his wife, having more than likely, begun his career as a stableboy at Preobrazhenskoe. The Arsenev sisters were the daughters of Mikhail Afanasevich Arsenev who was a *stolnik* (a rank in the middle of the hierarchy of the Muscovite nobility, a few rungs down from the top rank of *boiar*) and *voevoda* (governor) of Iakutia, a Siberian province. See "Arseneva, Varvara Mikhailovna," in *Russkii biograficheskii slovar*, t. II, ch. 1, 315; "Arsenevy," in V. M. Karev, M. N. Khitrov and S. A. Bolshakova (eds) (1991) *Entsiklopedicheskii slovar' Brokgauz i Efron: Biografii*, Moscow: Sovetskaia entsiklopediia, vol. 1, 478; K. A. Averianov (1994) *Dvorianstvo Rossiiskoi imperii. Spravochnik*, Moscow: [s.n.], vol. 1, 33; and N. E. Volkov (1900) *Dvor russkikh imperatorov v ego proshlom i nastoiashchem*, St. Petersburg: Pechatnia R. Golike, 208.

4 Martha Skavronskaia took the name of Ekaterina Alekseevna at her coronation. She succeeded Peter I to the throne, becoming Russia's first empress (r. 1725–1727).

5 Akademiia nauk SSSR. Institut istorii (1887–1985) *Pis'ma i bumagi Petra velikogo* (*PiB*) 12 vols. St. Petersburg and Moscow: Gos. tip.

6 N. I. Pavlenko (1988) *Poluderzhavnyi vlastelin: istoricheskaia khronika o zhizni spodvizhnika Petra Pervogo A. D. Menshikova*, Moscow: Izd-vo politicheskoi literatury. Other works on Menshikov include B. D. Porozovskaia, "A. D. Menshikov, ego zhizn' i gosudarstvennaia deiatel'nost'," in N. F. Boldyrev (1994) *Ioann Groznyi, Peter Velikii, Menshikov, Potemkin, Demidovy: Biograficheskie ocherki* Cheliabinsk: Ural, 221–26; Grigory Esipov (1875) "Kniaz' Aleksandr Danilovich Menshikov," *Russkii arkhiv*; N. I. Kostomarov (1992) "Kniaz' Aleksandr Danilovich Menshikov," in *Russkaia istoriia v zhizneopisaniiakh ee glavneishikh deiatelei*, Moscow: Kniga i biznes (reprint of 1876 edition), 843–866.

7 While I borrow Andrew Wachtel's term "pseudo-autobiography," I use it in a substantially different manner. Wachtel uses it to refer to the genre of autobiographical fiction, rather than to work imagined in the voice of another. See Andrew Wachtel (1987) *Russian Pseudo-Autobiography and the Creation of Russian Childhood*, Berkeley, CA: University of California Press, and (1990) *The Battle for Childhood: Creation of a Russian Myth*, Stanford, CA: Stanford University Press.

8 The style in which this "pseudo-autobiography" is presented draws on extensive

reading in memoirs of the Petrine era and early Russian women's autobiographies. For example, N. Iu. Trubetskoi (1870) "Zhurnal sobstvennyi Kniazia N. Trubetskogo po vozvrashchenii v 1717 g. iz nemetskoi zemli," *Russkaia starina*, t. 1, 8–15; G. P. Chernyshev (1872) "Zapiski grafa G. P. Chernysheva, 1672–1745," *Russkaia starina*, t. 2, 791–802; and V. A. Nashchokin (1842) *Zapiski Vasilia Aleksandrova syna Nashchokina*, St. Petersburg. The earliest autobiographical writing by a Russian woman is Natal'ja Borisovna Dolgorukaia (1977) *The Memoirs of Princess Natal'ja Borisovna Dolgorukaja*, ed. and trans. Charles E. Townsend, Columbus, OH: Slavica. Dogorukaia wrote of her exile (originally published in 1767), as a newlywed, with her husband's family. Natal'ja's parents advised her to give up the match, but she insisted on marrying Dolgorukii. Few members of Russian society attended the wedding; Dolgorukaia and her new husband were arrested almost immediately afterwards. Their crimes, like those of Menshikov, were connected with an attempt to marry a daughter to Peter II. When Peter died shortly before the wedding was to take place, the Dolgorukiis tried to place the bride-to-be on the throne in her own right. While Russian succession law allowed the Tsar to choose his successor, Peter II had not. Since he died at the age of twelve and unmarried, he left no obvious heirs, causing a crisis for the ruling house. A council of high-ranking nobles offered the crown to Peter I's niece Anna Ivanovna, who was then Duchess of Courland.

9   Pavlenko, 356–57.

10 Pavlenko, 351.

11 The family was confined near Moscow, at first. They lived much as they had before, having taken many valuables with them (these were used to pay the guards to obtain luxuries for them). Menshikov continued to oversee his financial affairs from confinement. He was later deprived of his estates, the majority of his serfs, the right to correspond, and sent far to the east only to ensure that he would not interfere with the coronation of Peter II in Moscow. Pavlenko, 352–55. In 1732 the Imperial government gave the Menshikovs' palace on Vasilievskii Island to the Corps of Pages for a new campus. See Iu. M. Denisov and Iu. V. Trubinov (1970) "Dvorets Menshikova ili Kadetskii Korpus," *Stroitel'stvo i arkhitektura*, no. 5, 39 and "Opisanie doma kn. Aleksandra Danilovicha Menshikova, v S. Peterburge, 1732 goda," Petr Ivanovich Shchukin (1909) *Shchukinskii sbornik*, Moscow: A. I. Mamontov, vol. 8, 137–141.

12 Pavlenko, 328. Adults of the Menshikov family wrote letters and sent presents in the names of their children.

13 Pavlenko, 329. Menshikov always listed Aleksandr first in his letters to his three children and reminded him that he was his sisters' guardian while their father was away.

14 Daria Mikhailovna Arseneva and her sister Varvara came to Preobrazhenskoe in the 1690s as companions of Peter's sister, Natalia Alekseevna. See Robert K. Massie (1980) *Peter the Great: His Life and World*, New York: Knopf, 373.

15 Varvara Mikhailovna Arseneva bore responsibility for the upbringing of the Menshikov children. Her apartments in the palace on Vasilevskii Island (in St. Petersburg) adjoined the children's rooms and were nearer to Menshikov's than were his wife's rooms. This may lend credence to the rumors that Arseneva was Menshikov's most trusted political advisor. Should this prove to be the case, it would explain why Arseneva was forcibly tonsured (in the Aleksandrovskii Uspenskii Women's Monastery in Vladimir province) at her brother-in-law's fall.

A maid-of-honor to Empress Catherine I, she had attained the highest court rank available to a woman on 22 May 1727 at her niece Maria Aleksandrovna Menshikova's betrothal to Tsar Peter II. She received villages and a stipend of 2,000 rubles annually. On 29 July 1727 she received the Order of St. Catherine. Arseneva lost all of this when Menshikov fell. For the floor plan of the palace, see N. B. Kaliazina, L. P. Dorofeeva, and G. V. Mikhailov (1986) *Dvorets Menshikova. Khudozhestvennaia kul'tura epokhi. Istoriia i liudi. Arkhitekturnaia khronika pamiatnika*, Moscow: Sovetskii khudozhnik. For Arseneva's biography, see Pavel Fedorovich Karabanov (1870) "Stats-damy i freiliny russkago dvora v XVIII st.," *Russkaia starina*, t. II, 469.

16 Massie, 373.

17 Pushkareva discusses Natalia Alekseevna's private theatricals in *Women in Russian History*.

18 Peter forced his first wife Evdokhia Lopukhina to enter a convent so that he could obtain a divorce from her. A spouse's calling to a religious vocation was one of the few grounds for divorce accepted by the Russian Orthodox Church.

19 By the end of the seventeenth century, the *streltsy* made up the tsar's bodyguard. They had become a conservative group, anxious about the effect of reforms in religion under Peter I and his father Alexei's rule. The force was originally created by Ivan IV in the mid sixteenth century as an elite unit of musketeers.

20 Peter also entrusted the care of the children he had begun having with Catherine (Ekaterina) to the Arseneva sisters, instructing them to "make sure he [Peter's son] has enough to drink and eat," in a letter of March 1705, *PiB*, t. III, 275.

21 Peter reported to Menshikov the good health of all the household after his visit there in December 1705. *PiB*, t. III, 536.

22 According to Librovich, Menshikov was preparing Anna Danilovna to marry the Tsar. For this, he insisted that she obtain a good education. Daria Mikhilovna was to supervise this. Librovich reproduces the text of a letter from Menshikov to his wife, "For God, Daria Mikhailovna, make my sister study earnestly, both Russian and German, so that time is not wasted." Librovich, 95.

23 Pavlenko, 321 and *PiB*. Before Daria's marriage, Peter seldom addressed a letter to one of the three (Daria, Varvara, and Anisia) without addressing it to all of them.

24 Pavlenko, 317.

25 Pavlenko, 56. Pavlenko reproduces a fragment of Menshikov's thank you note of 27 March 1703.

26 Pavlenko, 57. Daria Mikhailovna wrote, "I can no longer remain capricious against Your Worship. I sincerely wish to see you, my joy, and to be ever in the presence of Your Worship." (Tol'ko ne mogu bol'she blazhit' protiv milosti tvoei. Zhelaiu serdesh'no vidit' tebia, radost' svoiu, i neotluchno byt pri milosti tvoei vsegda.) He cites TsGADA (now RGADA) f. 198, d. 1169, l. 100, 22.

27 For example, on 29 October 1708 Aleksandr Danilovich wrote Daria Mikhailovna, telling her the enemy was approaching and she should return to Briansk. He also included greetings to Anna Danilovna (his sister), Varvara Mikhailovna, Anisia Tolstaia, and Ekaterina. *PiB*, t. VIII, ch. 1, 250.

28 Pavlenko, 318.

29 Pavlenko, 319. In fact, Daria Mikhailovna's gifts helped to provision the General and his army. Peter I approved and encouraged her, writing in 1707, "Keep feeding Danilovich this way so that I never see him as he was at Merechi," (Takozh otkormite Danilovicha, chtob ia ne tak evo videl kak v Merechakh) *PiB*, t. 6, 144.

30 Pavlenko, 75. Menshikov married Daria Mikhailovna Arseneva, 18 August 1706.

31 Berkhgol'tz says that Menshikov's kitchen was the most advanced in Russia in this period. He praises the food served at Menshikov's as the best he ate on his sojourn in Russia. See *Dnevnik kamer-iunkera Berkhgoltsa 1721–1725*, translated from German by I. F. Ammon, and published in *Russikii arkhiv*, 1902–1903. Menshikov's palaces were among the most beautiful new buildings of St. Peterburg and its suburbs. Peter used them for entertaining since he had no splendid palaces of his own. Pavlenko claims, essentially, that Menshikov did not lose his head for his crimes because he threw such good parties.

32 Kliuchevski reports, without citing sources, the results of drunken parties on board ship: Admiral Apraksin cried and bemoaned his loneliness while Menshikov, dead drunk, ended up under the table in need of his wife's ministrations ("his frightened wife Princess Dasha"). See V. O. Kliuchevskii (1958) *Peter the Great*, trans. Liliana Archibald, New York: Vintage Books, 45.

33 Karabanov, 469. Karabanov writes that Varvara Arseneva was unusually bright and loved science. The assessment of her use of these skills is most unflattering, and typical of writers of the late nineteenth century.

34 Pavlenko, 315.

35 Aleksandra Menshikova and her brother Aleksandr survived to be released from exile in 1731. Pavlenko reports that some of their father's effects were returned to them; Peter II had given the most valuable items to his sister Natalia Alekseevna (Pavlenko, 346 and 348). Aleksandra, who had lost her Order of St. Catherine on 8 September 1727, became *kamer-freilina* (maid-of-honor of the chamber) at Empress Anna Ivanovna's court. Anna Ivanovna betrothed her to Gustav Biron on 3 February 1732. Aleksandr was made a colonel of a regiment of the prestigious Life-Guard. See Volkov, 208 and 228.

9 A prologue for La Dame d'Esprit

The biography of the marquise Du Châtelet

Judith P. Zinsser

Prologue: 1749

From the window of the Queen's apartments at the palace of Lunéville, *allées* of trees shadowed the gravel walks, and borders of yellow and red zinnias brightened the vista. Fountains and the series of circular reflecting pools suggested some relief from the late summer heat, particularly in the early hours of the evening. On August 29th, 1749 Gabrielle Emilie le Tonnelier de Bréteuil, marquise Du Châtelet, the forty-two year old mathematician and authority on Leibniz, worked at this window amidst the apparent chaos of her scholar's tools. All around her, piled on the parquet floor, the shelves of cabinets, and on the tables were the mathematical and astronomical charts, the books of physics, and Newton's *Principia* and his *System of the World* that she had translated and on which she was now writing a commentary. Bits of paper, sealing wax, a compass, the cup of trimmed quill pens, the ink pot, a shaker of sand—littered the desk. Her quarto-sized notebook lay open. She had indicated in the margins the calculations to be corrected. Now, explanations must be clarified, page proofs revised, line after line of complex equations checked.

On that Saturday evening in August, she must have pushed all the papers aside. She found a blank sheet of her stationery with its delicate hand-painted border, folded it in half, and began a letter to the marquis de Saint-Lambert, her young lover and the man responsible for her pregnancy. The summer light could still have been bright enough for her to write by, or perhaps she called to have the candles in the wall sconces and in the holders on the tables lit. Opening the tall casement windows that face the garden would allow for a breeze, but might scatter bits of wax on her papers, and cause the tapers to burn unevenly.

In this letter, thoughts came in no particular order, but turned around her need for her lover to be "in the same place" as herself. His military duties have kept him in Aroué. She has lived two days without any word from him. She can be patient about her condition when he is with her, "but when I have lost you, I see only black." She suggests that her long letter of yesterday will please him more than this one, not because "I was loving you better, but because I had more strength to tell you." She begins to write in smaller letters with less space between the lines to be sure she can finish her last thought by the end of the page. Only her heart is spared, she continues, by implication, spared in order to love him. The last sentence in even smaller script runs along the pale-green border: "I finish because I can write no more."[1]

In just a few days, mme. Du Châtelet completed the revisions of her commentary on Newton, and sent the original manuscript to abbé Sallier, the conservateur of the Bibliothèque Royale, keeper of the King's Library. In this same week, on the night of September 3rd, she gave birth to the baby, a daughter, Stanislas-Adelaïde, named for Du Châtelet's host and patron, King Stanislas, former King of Poland, and now Duke of Lorraine. Despite the ease of the delivery, six days later, on September 9th, she died—of "milk fever," according to the account of the valet and secretary, Longchamp. He made no mention of the baby's death.

This is one possible beginning for the biography of this brilliant, unorthodox woman. But, there are others. Mme. la marquise Du Châtelet can be introduced in a different time and place. Imagine Paris, a few months earlier, in June of 1749. She was then in residence in her grand three-storied house in the rue Traversière-Saint Honoré (now the rue Molière). Here, she and Voltaire each had their own suite of rooms, or *apartement*. The *hôtel* was only a few blocks from the busy government offices of the Louvre, and from the royal palace of the Tuilleries. In this second beginning Du Châtelet also sits at her work, in the middle of writing what would be an eleven-page letter to her young army officer, the marquis de Saint-Lambert, her current lover and the father of the child she carried. Although his letter has been lost, he must have asked her once again to join him in Lorraine where he was garrisoned, for the next pages of her answer both justify their separation and detail the sacrifices she has made in order to complete her grand scholarly project and to rejoin him before the baby arrives. She was in the sixth month of her pregnancy when a woman usually feels strong and the baby's size does not yet cause discomfort. Contemporaries described her as big-boned, perhaps 5'6", taller than many men, and this was her fourth pregnancy, so she probably carried the child easily until the last few weeks.

On this June evening, she explained to Saint-Lambert how she came to establish, what sounds today, a punishing regimen to complete her project of the last nine years, her translation of and commentary on Newton's *Principia*. In a characteristic show of intensity, self-discipline, bravado and common sense, she wrote that the imminence of her *accouchement*, or lying-in, gave her a clear deadline for its completion. She rose at 8 or 9 and worked straight through to 3 in the afternoon. A *café*, and then she began again at 4. Dinner alone at 10PM. Soon after that, Voltaire, her former lover and companion of fifteen years, came to her rooms for conversation. Work filled the rest of the night and the early morning hours, from midnight until 5AM.

The premonitions of death that understandably plagued the thoughts of an eighteenth-century French woman, pregnant well beyond the usual age of child-bearing, made the time even more precious. Death in childbirth with the manuscript unfinished, the page proofs unrevised, would mean, she wrote, that she had lost "all the fruit of my work." To avoid this unpleasant possibility, she had decided to profit from "mon voyage à Paris," and to "sequester myself absolutely, to risk all for all and to do nothing but complete my book."[2] As a result she refused all dinner invitations, was abstemious, and took her "dark syrup." "My health takes it marvellously," she announced. She only hoped that the child, who now moved frequently, took it as well.

In many ways this scene in Paris presents a more pleasing beginning, not so somber as the first one. Those few months earlier in June show the marquise at a more hopeful time with a future to imagine. However, there are yet other choices that can be made. The standard biographies—for example, by the popular historian of the 1950s, Nancy Mitford—usually start very differently, not with mme. Du Châtelet, but with Voltaire. In fact, the whole story of her death can be told from his perspective. And there are sound reasons for this approach. He is undeniably more famous, the reason why historians of eighteenth-century France and the Enlightenment usually bother to mention her at all. This more traditional introduction to the marquise's life explains that Voltaire and Du Châtelet probably first met when she was a little girl of eight or nine, and he was in his twenties. He frequented her father's salon in Paris and perhaps listened indulgently to her first translations of Virgil's *Aeneid*. As a young man, Voltaire achieved almost instant fame for the *Henriade*, his epic on the life of Henri IV. In 1733 when they remet at the opera, he was 42 and France's leading playwright; she was 28, appropriately married, mother of three young children, and already a student of mathematics.

The Voltaire sources for this third beginning are rich. He created many images of Gabrielle Emilie le Tonnelier de Bréteuil, marquise Du Châtelet, in these last months of her life. On August 29th, 1749 Voltaire composed an epistle to Saint-Lambert, a gift from the master in the arts of love and letters to his apprentice.[3] Portraying himself as the aged, displaced sexual partner, Voltaire offers the aspiring poet verses that will please "la belle amante de Newton." Busy himself since 1744 with a secret affair and a younger partner, his niece, mme. Denis, Voltaire could be both gracious and irreverent in his good wishes for his successor, characteristically facile with his amorous images and metaphors. He describes "nôtre heroine" leaving her studies, "her compass, her calculations and her telescope," for her boudoir. She is dressed in "an old black apron," her fingers, as always stained with ink. He tells the younger man to "take these flowers" to her and sing for her the pretty songs "rehearsed by love, and unknown to Newton."[4] Love, Voltaire suggests, is a time of "illusion," as is this poetic image of the marquise who in reality was now heavy with the final days of her pregnancy, in considerable pain and discomfort.

Voltaire alluded more accurately to her condition during these last weeks of August in his correspondence. After pages describing his own activities, he ended his letter to their friends, the comte and comtesse d'Argental, with a sentence of news about her condition. On an impatient note, he added: "Madame du Chastelet [*sic*] still gives birth to nothing but problems."[5] He remained self-absorbed. Even his light-hearted account of the baby's arrival, the night of September 3rd, dwelt as much on his own travails as on hers. He wrote to d'Argenson, his principal patron at Versailles, that while "at her *secrétaire*, scratching some 'pancarte neutonienne,' she felt a little need. This little need was a girl who appeared that instant. She put it on a geometry book," and then retired to her bed. He goes on to explain that he has also given birth to the tragedy of "Catilina" and that he is one hundred times more tired than she. Mme. Du Châtelet has merely given birth to a little girl who says not a word, while he must make men who speak, a Cicero, a Caesar.[6]

There are three possible introductions to the marquise Du Châtelet. Each is a "true," a "real" account of her last months. All are based on sources, on facts that make up the historical record, the official memory of her life. As an historian, I can choose the time, the place, when and where to begin the narrative. With these choices biographers decide which aspects of an individual's life and personality to expose, which part of a contemporary reputation to highlight. This is especially true for mme. Du Châtelet. The odd and incomplete assortment of letters, memoirs, published and unpublished writings from her and her friends and acquaintances, offers no clear narrative. What remains in the historical record of the marquise's life gives a wide range of often contradictory images and disparate accounts of her activities that sometimes make it hard to believe they all describe the same woman. Thus, there are few obvious choices to be made, and vast blank spaces to be filled.

The three alternative beginnings—at the palace of Lunéville, in Paris in mid-May, and during her last days as told from Voltaire's perspective—illustrate this process. Each uses different kinds of sources, different sets of facts. The different results are the product of judgment and imagination. They represent the range of choices open to me. I purposely focused each account on a different facet of mme. Du Châtelet's personality and her activities. All described her at work, however, because this is the first image I want readers to have: mme. Du Châtelet at the height of her career, the self-proclaimed "géomètre" and "physicien," the woman acknowledged in her own lifetime as a genius, accorded the title of "philosophe" by her contemporaries.[7]

At Lunéville, I introduced the marquise using information about her possessions and the royal palace where she died. This was done in order to set her in time and place, to show the privileged noblewoman and successful courtier. In addition to conveying the opulence of her surroundings and the perquisites of her rank, the description of the vista and her rooms in the ducal palace in Lorraine created a vivid picture. Every kind of information about the palace and what she might have had in the room where she worked was included, even experiences from my own life. I went to Lunéville in the summer of 1994 and felt the heat, saw the *allées* of trees and the flowered-borders of the gravel walks. Drawings from the eighteenth century show similar, if grander vistas. So I could assume there had been little change.

The scene of Du Châtelet at her writing comes from a number of contemporaries' accounts of the appearance of rooms she worked in. All marvel at the confusion of papers, books, and tables. Voltaire ordered "trimmed quills" in one of his letters. I liked the sharp neatness of the phrase and assumed she would have used them as well. Anyone writing in the eighteenth century would have had an ink pot, and sand to sprinkle over their writing. The sand would absorb the inevitable unevenness of the letters and figures on the heavy paper of the "cahiers," her notebooks, on the rough stock of page proofs, and on the thinner, glossy surface of her stationery. I have seen the manuscript at the Bibliothèque Nationale that she was working on that June evening. Ink spots the margins where she made notes to herself. Her words run closer together as she nears the end of the paper. She used the back of a letter to write an addition and fixed it to the page with sealing wax.

The same combination of reading and my own memories completed this first possible beginning of the biography. I have seen the breeze from an open window scatter the wax of the candles and make them burn unevenly. The description of her clothes is pure extrapolation. I have no idea what she was wearing; I do not know if she was hot. Historians who write on French fashion during her time provided names of styles and fabrics. The frontispiece of a previous book of hers, the *Institutions de physique*, her synthesis of metaphysics and science to explain contemporary understandings of the natural world, shows her dressed in the kind of loose gown described. I remember my own pregnancy, contending with the summer heat, sweating no matter how thin my clothing, when I sat, as she did, for long hours at my desk.

For the scene in Paris, the second beginning, I chose to rely on written, not material sources. In this account, Du Châtelet's own letters were used to reconstruct her state of mind, immediate aspirations, and her own speculations about her future. Here the focus is on her as the practical, independent, but sensual and affectionate lover with very little about the setting—partly because no clear description of her Paris hôtel exists.[8] One letter that she probably wrote in June, certainly from Paris in the middle of her pregnancy, made the narrative.

Du Châtelet's letters are among the richest sources for her and Voltaire's biographers. However, they fill only two published volumes and cover the years from 1733 to 1749. For example, after her death, the servant, Longchamp, and a government police informer mentioned seven bound volumes of her correspondence with Voltaire, but none have ever appeared. We have only one of Saint-Lambert's letters to her. The published collection is skewed in other ways. The marquise wrote to a wide circle of friends and acquaintances; this was how she maintained the network of influence and obligation that was part of her courtier's world. Yet, most of the published letters are to the men of Voltaire's immediate circle. Hundreds, perhaps thousands of others, wait to be discovered.

Even at their best, then, these letters tell only a small portion of what could be known. Like the material sources for the image of Du Châtelet writing on those summer evenings in June and in August, 1749, they are no more and no less than separate "facts," surrounded by vast spaces that biographers must fill in from their reading in the writings of other historians, from their own experiences and perspectives. Portions of letters can be quoted to draw attention to one sentence and not another. The words a woman writes acquire different meanings when presented in one order or another, in this and not that context. For example, Du Châtelet's love letters to Saint-Lambert have traditionally been used by her popular twentieth-century biographers and by Voltaire scholars to portray her as a foolishly passionate, semi-hysterical middle-aged woman.

And so they seem to read, as ordered by her editor, the Voltaire scholar, Theodore Besterman. They reveal frustration, rage, longing, impatience, sensuality, mistrust. Besterman himself acknowledges the tentative nature of the chronology he has set. Many of the most intensely emotional letters and notes have no date, or merely indicate the morning, the evening, or the day of the week. In fact, the originals, now carefully preserved in a red leather quarto volume at the Morgan Library in New York City, are bound in a completely different order. Besterman is a careful scholar. He used internal evidence whenever possible—references to a trip, to an event—to date the letters. Still, a third or more float free of time and place and can be used in an infinite number of sequences to make an infinite number of stories, to paint many emotions and thoughts.

The reconstruction of her emotions given in these pages relies on a different order, and a different emphasis. I see the passion, the impatience and frustrations, but not the foolish hysteric. I hear in the letters her hesitation and mistrust of attentions from an opportunistic young courtier, already known at Lunéville as lover to mme. Boufflers, the most prominent woman at King Stanislas's court. Du Châtelet can be annoyed and impatient with Saint-Lambert's absences one day and rapturous the next after a night together. As in all her letters to her intimate friends, the phrases and sentences reveal no apparent logic, as if after the long hours and the effort at clarity and precision in her scientific writing, she could now let her words come carelessly and spontaneously.

The second beginning presents emotions and attitudes that other historians have failed to mention. Although every biographer of Du Châtelet quotes from the letter describing her Paris regimen, not one connects her sense of urgency to her contradictory feelings about her work and her lover. Because of similar experiences in my own life, I know I want readers to hear the conflict she feels between her project on Newton and her desire to abandon it all for Saint-Lambert, the man she wants to make the grand passion of her life. In mid-May she had written from Paris and assured him "I love you," "à la folie," and "it's certainly folly, but it is for life."[9] A few days later, his impatience prompted, "don't reproach me for my *Newton*, I'm punished enough with it; I have never made such a great sacrifice to reason as to stay here in order to finish."[10] That letter from mid-June quoted by so many historians and popular biographers runs to many pages. In a later paragraph she imagined them in a play together and insisted that "I can love only what I share [with you], because I don't love Newton, at the least I finish it for reason and for honor, but I love only you and that which connects to you."[11]

In this way, I used my own preconceptions to interpret and recreate an individual's unspoken feelings from a letter she did not write for me and perhaps never intended for anyone else to read. This process of interposing my own interpretation of an individual's actions and attitudes is also evident in the third beginning. Yes, using Voltaire's writings to introduce the marquise offered the most conventional approach. Most of her biographers speak of her first in relation to the great man of French letters. But after that, I made different choices than those of other historians. Through my editorial comments his words were not allowed to represent the "facts" of her life but instead revealed his foibles and his attitude towards her.

The more we study the historical record, any historical record—sites and objects, letters, manuscripts, and memoirs—the more spaces we find, spaces between the "facts," that in turn pose questions defying simple answers. Gabrielle Emilie le Tonnelier de Bréteuil, marquise Du Châtelet, exemplifies such challenges. As a result of these challenges, I have chosen a different approach to biography. Instead of writing one chronological narrative, I am dividing the biography into three separate but complementary sections. Just as in this introduction, each presents the marquise from a different perspective, each comes from different kinds of sources, and includes speculations based on my own experiences. Each has a different purpose and answers different questions. The first set of chapters appears the most traditional. She is born to her privileged family, marries and gives birth to children. But the very conventionality of these first 20+ years of her life forces me to answer key questions. They are, in fact, questions every biographer must ask: How did the great woman come to be? What is the reason for her subsequent un-orthodoxy? What was the source of her "genius," of her passion for knowledge and for the glory she believed it would bring her?

In the second section her writings—her letters, her published books and unpublished manuscripts—take the reader through the next part of her life and suggest other questions. Why did the marquise Du Châtelet decide to write on so many different subjects, from a skeptic's critique of the Old and New Testament to her own version of the provocative *Fable of the Bees* by Bernard Mandeville? And then a question of particular importance for Du Châtelet, why did she decide to publish only her works on science? The sum total of these diverse writings demonstrates her gifted and multifaceted intellect and shows her as an active member of what she and her circle described as the "Republic of Letters." The biographer must then also consider how she achieved this status and reputation. How did she avoid having her work summarily dismissed simply because it had been written by a woman?

The third and final set of chapters explores the questions of why and how her history has been so neglected. Why, when it has been told, particularly the last months of her life, the story of her affair with Saint-Lambert, the completion of her commentary on Newton, and her death, has it been so skewed and fragmented? She is either the excessively emotional lover or the serious mathematician, never both. This part of the marquise's biography comes from past historians, those who have written her life and bequeathed to us her public reputation. In this section, I demonstrate how the same "facts" have been joined into many narratives and used to create contradictory, disparate images. Here I explore the truisms of historiography: that each century must write the narrative in its own way, that historians write within a framework bounded and crisscrossed with preconceptions. All of us have implicit or explicit agendas that determine what subject we have chosen to research and recreate. All historians have a particular story to tell that reflects our own questions about our own times, even about ourselves.

I first learned about the marquise Du Châtelet when I was thirteen or fourteen. I cannot remember exactly because the memory comes from a period in my life when I was learning all the time: how to dress, which fork to use, the names of classical composers, which authors to read and which to dismiss. My family had moved back to New York City from southern California, back to a culture that my parents knew, but I did not. No one considered bringing my bike, and and the Fifth Avenue hairdresser was instructed to cut off my long hair. That first summer of 1956, I spent much of my time with my cousin, Antonia, and her family. Antonia and I are the same age. Perhaps she told me, perhaps I heard talk at the dinner table. Her mother had a project, something for the radio about Voltaire, whoever he was. Everyone believed my aunt to be the most elegant, gracious woman in both appearance and gesture. She was a charming hostess for her lawyer husband, the editor of the newsletter for the City's Legal Aid Society, an attentive mother to her two daughters; she led a full and busy life. Yet, there was this project. Reading her letters after her death, I found an early reference to the marquise Du Châtelet. In her late twenties and newly married, my aunt assured her writer father that she had located Du Châtelet's published correspondence in a nearby library and would soon be working through them.

I never saw anything she wrote and forgot about her interest altogether. She died of cancer in the spring of 1962 with all of Voltaire's writings on the shelves above her desk—the plain French paperback books from the publisher Gallimard that leave the pages for the reader to cut. These books and all of her notes disappeared. I had to rediscover mme. Du Châtelet for myself. Almost fifteen years later, by chance, I found a popular account from the early 1970s, *The Divine Mistress* by Samuel Edwards, among the second-hand books at a Salvation Army Store, a few blocks from where I lived in New York City. It was months before I made the connection between this biography and the radio play my aunt had planned to write. It is as if this gifted eighteenth-century woman challenged us both: to tell her life in new ways that do justice to all aspects of her unorthodox interests and achievements, and that demonstrate how the marquise Du Châtelet could have been alternately admired, ridiculed and forgotten. As you can see, I, too, have an agenda.

Acknowledgments

Research for this biography was made possible by a fellowship from the National Endowment for the Humanities, time to write by a residency at the Camargo Foundation. I am particularly grateful to my Camargo fellows for their comments and encouragement. This portion of the as yet unfinished biography is published with the permission of Viking Penguin Press.

Notes

1 Du Châtelet to Saint-Lambert, "Samedi au soir" [31 August 1749], #485, (1958) in T. Besterman (ed.) *Lettres de la Marquise du Châtelet*, Geneva: Institutions et Musée Voltaire, 1958, vol. II, pp. 306–7. See also in the Morgan Library collection in New York City, *Autograph Letters to the Marquis de Saint-Lambert*, MA2287, #97.

2 Du Châtelet to Saint-Lambert, [around 15 June 1759 (*sic*)] *Letters*, #476, vol. II, pp. 293–6; Morgan Library Collection, MA 2287, #89.

3 Saint-Lambert would eventually complete a long poem entitled "The Seasons."

4 See Theodore Besterman's biography for the verses and for his translation, *Voltaire* New York: Harcourt Brace & World, 1969, p. 295 and fn. 9.

5 Voltaire to d'Argental, 28 August 1749, #D3995, *The Complete Works of Voltaire*, T. Besterman (ed.), Geneva: Institut et Musée Voltaire, 1970, vol. 95, p. 141.

6 Voltaire to d'Argenson, 4 September 1749, *Complete Works*, vol. 95, pp. 150–1. It is interesting to note, perhaps, that Catiline is the story of a younger man's treason and ambition, blocked through the efforts of one of Voltaire's heroes, Cicero. I am grateful to Robert Zaretsky for this insight.

7 In the *Encyclopédie* entry on "Newtonianisme" written by d'Alembert, Du Châtelet's commentary and translation are singled out as works that made Newton accessible. She is one of seven mathematicians and physicists mentioned by name. The others were: 'sGravesande, an early Dutch supporter; the English commentators, Whiston and Pemberton; Le Seur & Jacquier, the churchmen who published an annotated Latin edition in 1739–42; and the Scottish mathematician Maclaurin whose explication appeared in 1748.

8 Three different descriptions of the Paris hôtel where she lived with her family and with Voltaire exist. The inventory made at the time of her death goes from room to room as the notaries list her possessions. Voltaire's lease gives a description of his quarters. Longchamp, his valet, describes the floor where his master lived. Even so, I could not place her in a particular room. Together the three sets of "facts" made such a hodgepodge of bedrooms, cabinets (closets, sometimes as big as a dressing room, or small enough to just accommodate the equivalent of an eighteenth-century toilet), antechambers, and salons, that they defied synthesis. I simply could not envisage the floor plan, so I gave up and made only the most cursory reference to her surroundings in relation to the parish she lived in.

9 Du Châtelet to Saint-Lambert, n.d. [vers le 15 mai 1749], #470, *Letters*, vol. II, p. 283; Morgan Library Collection MA 2287, #86.

10 Du Châtelet to Saint-Lambert, 18 mai [1749], #471, *Letters*, vol. II, p. 284; Morgan Library Collection MA2287, #87.

11 Du Châtelet to Saint-Lambert, #476 *Letters*, vol. II, p. 295; Morgan Library Collection MA2287, #89.

AFTERWORD

When I first discovered Gabrielle Emilie le Tonnelier de Bréteuil, marquise Du Châtelet (1706–49), I was not yet a feminist. A decade later, my "consciousness" awakened, outrage, not theory, governed my approach to her life. How could such an important woman have been so neglected by historians of the Enlightenment and the history of science? And when included, so denigrated and ridiculed? I vowed that my research and analyses would be different: more complete, of course, more accurate, and thus the stuff of the first *true* biography of this remarkable woman. Only gradually did I realize how naive, simplistic and totally inadequate my approach was to the task of telling the life of this remarkable eighteenth-century French woman.

Feminists have been justifiably harsh in their criticisms of traditional history, not only for its omissions but also for its lack of any self-conscious awareness of the significance of gender in the shaping of our experiences. Long before Peter Novick discovered the flawed practitioners of *That Noble Dream* (1988), feminist historians, Natalie Zemon Davis, Joan Kelly Gadol, and Joan W. Scott, the first and most famous, had given their own proofs that history could never be the scientifically objective chronicle our nineteenth-century European and North American forefathers imagined. The biography of a single life seems to intensify these problems and challenges. If we had been blind or reluctant to reveal the interplay between research, writing and subjective predilections in broad histories of the past, biographers have been even more wedded to what the feminist theorist, Liz Stanley, calls "a realist fallacy."[1] Too many of us continued to believe, as I did so naively, that we could create seamless, uncritical narratives, linear progressions from birth to death. However, as Robert Rosenstone, the biographer and film historian, has warned us , critiquing existing histories is one thing, writing a "better" history is something else.[2]

When Catherine Drinker Bowen, wrote *Adventures of a Biographer* (1959 ed.), the telling of a life seemed a straightforward project. Bowen studied seventeenth-century English orthography, searched the archives, read letters and state papers. She made files of "Things that I need to know," and "Things that the reader needs to know," and then carefully "crafted" (to use her term) the story of the English Chief Justice, Edward Coke. Thus, she created a linear narrative. Narrative itself, "was the spine of history and the key to causation," according to her contemporary, the equally popular historian, Barbara Tuchman. Just arrange the facts in sequence, by month, week, day, Tuchman explained, and the relationships appear as if they had been written in "secret ink."[3] A few of the biographers of this generation admitted that the sheer number of facts necessitated selection and condensation, and that this could lead to distortion, or when there were too few facts, the necessity for invention. Some noted that this meant edging towards fiction and fabrication.

To traditional practitioners of the "craft," even more dangerous in its effect on biography than this need for "fabrication," was the bias arising from the attitudes and circumstances of the writer. If biography means "the interpretation of one mind by another, the attempt to understand and assess the values of one who lived in the past, by one who lives in the present," then how could the conscientious historian filter out needs and experiences belonging to the writer, not the subject?[4] Psychohistorians made a specialty of dissecting these relationships, but authors and critics, otherwise not known for their introspection, also used psychological language to describe their relationship with their subject: subliminal, projection, transference.[5] Sir Harold Nicolson, the great narrative historian, believed that "always there must be the reflection of one temperament in the mirror of another." André Maurois, one of the grand old men of biography, seemed to delight in the mixing. He assumed that in responding "to a secret need in his own nature," he would use his hero as "the medium" of his own feelings; "autobiography disguised as biography."[6]

Feminist biographers freely accept the reality and the consequences of this bias and personal involvement. The literary theorist, Felicity Nussbaum, calls the process "revisioning." Carolyn Steedman, an innovative biographer, described her *Childhood, Culture and Class in Britain: Margaret McMillan 1860–1931* (1990) as "done out of a set of preoccupations . . . a story about the present, using items from the past." Add to these standard preoccupations the "gender consciousness of a feminist biographer," and you have feminist historians eschewing objectivity not only because of shared attitudes and experiences with the female subject but also because of their perception of decades of historical neglect of women's topics. Writing the biography of a particular woman becomes "revisioning" with a sense of mission.[7]

In more ambitious experiments in biography that proudly identify with the postmodern "politics of representation," not the life, but the different versions of that life, both those presented by the subject, and those created by others, become the focus. From this perspective, according to the theorist Jane Flax, there is no "innocent knowledge to be had," all is "historically and culturally variable."[8] In Liz Stanley's radical model for "feminist biography" nothing separates fiction from the "actual," nothing separates the story from the storyteller or biography from autobiography. For, she explains, "each of them is dependent on the transforming creating medium of the writer and her states of consciousness."[9] I find myself saying "yes . . . yes, . . . but. . . ." Does this kind of self-conscious deconstruction actually replace the narrative? Make it seem impossible altogether? The biographer, Geoffrey Wolff, admits that inserting too much of himself and his quandaries "derails" the narrative.[10] I can easily imagine that happening. I can see my biography becoming a vast hall of mirrors: the marquise Du Châtelet constructed her own "identity," her own "representations" of herself; others did the same both at the time and later; I, in turn have constructed my persona as a biographer and my images of her, and so on. Is that what I want to do?

Clifford Geertz, sorting out these questions for his discipline, anthropology, identifies another hazard for the well-meaning scholar. Anthropologists do explain the personal factors that affect observation and the creation of an analytical narrative. They "tell all"—mention gaps in their reconstructions, admit imaginative leaps in their analyses, acknowledge the dangers of conscious preconceptions and prejudices to overcome (to say nothing of the subconscious unknowns of the creative process)—in an effort to give greater authority to the "knowledge claims" of their work. But, as Geertz points out, so much "honesty" has the reverse effect. For readers, this catharsis, however well-intentioned, "undermines our capacity to take any of those claims seriously." At its worst, our history, like his anthropology, becomes a "corrosive relativism in which everything is but a more or less clever expression of opinion."[11]

Geertz has described my ambivalence exactly. On the one hand, as an author, a biographer, I do want to confess; why did I choose this woman, from that era? What of her story is my story? But like the anthropologists, I still want to believe that despite my bias, psychological predilections, and so on, my version is the best, the truest. I want to write what Liz Stanley calls "accountable feminist biography," but at the same time, I want to change the public image of Du Châtelet; I want readers to remember what my biography says, not what others have said.[12]

The sum total sounds a contradiction in terms. You can perhaps imagine then, my excitement at discovering a writer who offered me a theoretical way out of my "postmodern anxiety": Donna Haraway in her essay, "Situated Knowledges: The Science Question in Feminism and the Privilege of Partial Perspective." A feminist critic of science, Haraway insists that "objectivity" is really about structures, established relationships, and efforts to control all the variables. This is the case whether science, her discipline, or the humanities, mine. She explains that no matter how diligently we try to find the "neutral ground," we are always standing somewhere, looking from some institutionalized, accepted vantage point, within some maze of preconceptions and learned memory, unable to know when and how all of these imbedded factors may have influenced either what we believe we know and or how we convey that knowledge to others. Thus, she offered me a model for "situating knowledge" even as I create it and ascribe authority to it.

As you can see in the prologue for *La Dame d'Esprit*, my biography of the marquise Du Châtelet, I constructed, I offered choices, so that the reader could participate in the process of "life writing" by making a "fusion" richer than any one of the images presented.[13] I situated myself, and made no claim to objectivity. I described the connections between subject and biographer, but I used my authority as the reader of archives, the fabricator of interpretations, and the storyteller, to privilege my view of my eighteenth-century heroine. Like the Latina activist author, Sandra Cisneros, I wanted to make you see this world, and this individual from my eyes, and that is real power. I freely admit that I am using this power to further my personal and political agenda. I want this biography to be my contribution to Haraway's grand project, the "transformation of systems of knowledge and ways of seeing."[14]

Notes

1 Liz Stanley, *The Auto/Biographical I: The Theory and Practice of Feminist Auto/Biography* (New York: Manchester University Press, 1992), p. 8.

2 Robert A. Rosenstone, "Rethinking History: Theory, Practice, and New Ways of Telling the Past," *Perspectives* 36 (4) (April 1998): 21–5.

3 Barbara Tuchman in *Telling Lives: The Biographer's Art*, Marc Pachter (ed.) (Washington, DC: New Republic Books, 1979), p. 144.

4 Paula R. Backscheider, *Reflections on Biography* (New York: Oxford University Press, 1999), n. 29, p. 241.

5 Samuel H. Baron and Carl Pletsch (eds) *Introspection in Biography: The Biographer's Quest for Self-Awareness* (Hillsdale, NJ: The Analytic Press), p. 22. One of the authors in this collection turned his biography of Nietzsche into a collaborative effort with his psychoanalyst.

6 Nicolson quoted in James L. Clifford, *Biography As an Art: Selected Criticism 1560–1960* (New York: Oxford University Press, 1962), p. 201; Maurois as quoted in Laura Marcus, *Auto/Biographical Discourses: Theory, Criticism, Practice* (New York: St. Martin's Press, 1994), p. 103.

7 Felicity A. Nussbaum, *The Autobiographical Subject: Gender and Ideology in Eighteenth-Century England* (Baltimore, MD: Johns Hopkins University Press, 1989), p. xxii. Carolyn Steedman, *Childhood, Culture and Class in Britain: Margaret McMillan 1860–1931* (London: Virago Press, 1990), p. 245; see also pp. 244, 246, 6–11.

8 Jane Flax, "The End of Innocence," in *Feminists Theorize the Political*, Judith Butler and Joan W. Scott, eds (New York: Routledge, 1992), pp. 447, 452. Joan Wallach Scott experimented with this approach in her collective study, *Only Paradoxes to Offer: French Feminists and the Rights of Man* (Cambridge, MA: Harvard University Press, 1996). Kali Israel made all sources "stories," grouping them together as "the production of a subject," *Names and Stories: Emilia Dilke and Victorian Culture* (New York: Oxford University Press, 1999), see pp. 8, 14, 16.

9 See for her definition of a "feminist biography," Stanley, *The Auto/Biographical I*, pp. 9–10, 253. See Liz Stanley and Ann Morley's *The Life and Death of Emily Wilding Davison: A Biographical Detective Story* (London: Women's Press, 1988), a biography written according to this definition.

10 Geoffrey Wolff in Pachter (ed.), p. 64. Diane Wood Middlebrook calls the strategy, "de-centered subjectivity," and the problem, "the postmodern anxiety about authorship: awareness that both author and subject in a biography are hostages to the universes of discourse that inhabit them." See her essay, "Postmodernism and the Biographer", in *Revealing Lives: Autobiography, Biography and Gender*, Susan Groag Bell and Mailyn Yalom, eds (Albany, NY: State University of New York Press, 1990), p. 164.

11 Clifford Geertz, *Works and Lives: The Anthropologist as Author* (Stanford, CA: Stanford University Press, 1988).

12 I understand that this may mean I am falling into the "woman worthy" trap, where I give value to a woman who succeeded in a male world, by male standards, and thus create more of the patriarchal historical narrative. On these issues see Bonnie G. Smith, "History and Genius: The Narcotic, Erotic and Baroque Life of Germaine de Staël", in *French Historical Studies*, 19 (4) (Fall 1996), p. 1079. Stanley also points out that the exceptional and "unique" woman is "unique" by default, because of all the constraints on women during her era. See Stanley, *The Auto/Biographical I*, p. 8.

13   On the idea of involving the reader in the creation and its choices as "fusion," see Vladimir Nabakov, *The Real Life of Sebastian Knight* (Norfolk, CT: New Directions, 1959 ed.), pp. 137, 95.

14   For this discussion, see Donna Haraway, "Situated Knowledges: The Science Question in Feminism and the Privilege of Partial Perspective," in *Simians, Cyborgs, and Women: The Reinvention of Nature* (New York: Routledge, 1991), pp. 191–6. Paraphrased from Cisneros as quoted in Ruth Behar, *Translated Woman: Crossing the Border with Esperanza's Story* (Boston: Beacon Press, 1993), p. 270.

10 Blackout

James Goodman

1.

Afterward everyone wanted to know why.

There had to be a reason.

People wanted to know what it was.

Or they thought they knew what it was. and they wanted to say.

Either way, they talked about it, talked in English, Spanish, Russian, and Korean: in Japanese, French, and German; in Italian, Arabic, Hebrew, and Chinese.

For weeks it seemed as if they talked about nothing else.

They talked about why, when the lights went out, people did the things that they did.

People also wanted to know why the lights went out in the first place.

Not everyone, but some: reporters. Mayor. Governor. City, state, and federal regulators. Certain customers. Even the president of the United States, who happened to have a keen interest in energy.

So they talked about it, and they asked Con Edison officials, who also wanted to know but would have preferred not to talk about it. They asked Con Edison to explain what went wrong.

There had to be a reason.

People wanted to know what it was.

Con Edison officials said it was lightning.

They hoped it was lightning.

Lightning is easy to explain, and there is no one, on earth, to blame.

Or they thought they knew what it was, and they wanted to say.

They thought there was a reason, one reason.

One reason for all the things those people did in the dark.

One reason for the things they do.

Electrical engineers said it was more complicated than that. Lighting may have played a role, but to say that lightning caused the blackout would be like saying the wind caused the capsizing of a poorly designed sailboat sailed by an inexperienced or even incompetent captain and crew.

Almost everyone agreed there was a reason.

There was lightning.

Not so much in the city, but just to north, in the rocky rolling hills of Westchester Country, the precious wedge of New York State that sits atop the Bronx. So much lightning that in Oradell, New Jersey, a budding scientist, nineteen years old, who climbed out on his roof after hearing severe storm warnings on the radio, could see it, great bolts in deep dark clouds. He stood thirty miles from the storm.

But people disagreed about what that reason was.

Half the city's power came through Westchester.

It traveled along conductors, thick transmission cables, each made up of many strands of wire hung on hundred-foot steel towers. The towers were laid out like a letter Y—albeit a Y drawn by a very young child. The top of the Y leaned so far to the left (which was west) that its right fork pointed due north.

The right fork brought power from upstate New York and New England.

The left fork brought it from three power plants along the Hudson River Roseton, an oil-burning plant in Newburgh; Bowline, another oil-burning plant, twenty-six miles to the south; and Indian Point, a nuclear power plant on the other side (the east side) of the river. Left and right forks met in Millwood, like busy lanes of southbound traffic, and merged into a congested corridor of towers, power lines, and substations in the west-central Westchester towns of Pleasantville, Eastview, Sprain Brook, and Dunwoodie. South of Sprain Brook and Dunwoodie, the lines went underground.

So they argued: raised their voices, shook their heads, waved their arms, pointed fingers, as if they were hammering invisible nails.

And argued.

It is not anyone's idea of a perfect system. If Con Edison had had more land at its disposal, it would have run its transmission lines over soil that was less rocky and therefore less resistant to electricity; it would have built more towers and put fewer circuits on each one. But Westchester is squeezed between the Hudson River, the southwest corner of Connecticut, and Long Island Sound. Land is expensive, wide-open space scarce. Rights-of-way are hard to come by.

They had strong feelings and opinions.

The stakes were high.

Lightning struck right in the middle of that corridor, at 8:37 in the evening, in the midst of a ferocious storm. It struck a tower carrying conductors between substations in Buchanan and Millwood, 345-kilovolt lines that supplied 1,200 megawatts of power from Roseton, Bowline, and Indian Point.

The arguments took some nasty turns.
It was New York.
It was July. It was 1977.
Many people were in sour moods to begin with.

2.

In the city, around the time of that first bolt of lightning, knowing nothing of the storm in Westchester or the shape of the power grid or the responsibilities of a system operator or even the source of all the electricity—6,000 megawatts—they consumed on a summer night, people did the things that city people do.

Some talked.
Some walked.
Some waited for buses.

Many worked: in hot kitchens and hotter subway stations: in cool, quiet offices after hours; in tire stations and precinct houses; in factories and warehouses; in bridge and tunnel toll-booths; in hospitals, machine shops, hotels, and stores of all kinds.

Some hailed cabs. Some drove them.

Firemen fought fires; policemen fought all kinds of crime.

There were a few signs but no warnings, and except for a few operators and dispatchers at a few power plants, substations, and control centers, no one knew anything was wrong.

At around nine o'clock, the time of the second lightning strike, people watching television might have noticed the picture on their sets contract.

Not many of them thought anything of it.

Not even those who knew, as one Queens man knew, that a shrinking picture was a sign of either a failing TV tube or low voltage.

The Queens man had much more faith in his television than in Con Edison, and though critics of Con Edison were more common than hot-dog carts in midtown, few of them knew as much about electricity as he did. He was an electrical engineer, and from 1958 to 1964, the chief engineer of the city's Bureau of Gas and Electricity.

People ate, on the late side: burgers and french fries; bagels, ribs, and baklava; pizza, plantains, and pork-fried rice; falafels, hot dogs, and shish kebabs; soggy soft pretzels and shaved ice; sausage bread on Arthur Avenue; striped bass in Astoria; dainty portions of veal and duck: oversize turkey-and-chopped-liver clubs.

The electrical engineer expected bad service and lame excuses from Con Edison, and he was rarely disappointed. In August 1959 a blackout had shut down the West Side from Columbus Circle to Columbia University, and a large part of the Upper East Side. Asked by the mayor to investigate, he found that the design of Con Edison's grid was at fault: too few feeders from too few substations, increasing the likelihood that small problems would lead to large ones. He conducted similar investigations after the mid-Manhattan blackout of 1961 and the Brooklyn blackout of 1962. Con Edison always blamed someone else, or something else. The electrical engineer always blamed Con Ed.

Some drank their dinners, in a mostly futile effort to beat the heat: frozen daiquiris, tequila sunrises, White Russians, Black Russians, banshees, and margaritas; frosty mugs of beer chasing shots of whiskey; seven-ounce bottles called ponies; twenty-five-cent quarts.

Some uncorked fine wine; others twisted the tin tops off Boone's Farm, Night Train, and Mad Dog 20/20.

When the lights went out in November 1965, the electrical engineer was in a tunnel beneath the East River on a Manhattan-bound D train. The train rolled to a stop. Four hours later, when the train's battery-powered emergency lights began to dim, he grabbed a trainman's lantern, climbed out of the rear of the train, and walked back to the Brooklyn station. His fellow passengers spent another nine hours underground.

Some sat on rocks or rooftops in the heights of the outer boroughs, marveling at the Manhattan skyline. Others hurried out of the city's big parks before dark, kicking soccer balls, bouncing basketballs, swinging golf clubs, tossing Frisbees and softballs, twirling bats like batons.

People sang in the shower. People played music in the street.

Some people prepared for bed. Others were already sleeping. Some people were married. Others decided to separate or get divorced. Thousands of people were out of work. Some of them pored over the classifieds; others found that work, for wages, it was not the only way to get by.

The 1965 blackout began when a surge of power, well within normal operating range, tripped an improperly set relay at the Beck power plant in Queenston, Ontario. The tripped relay opened the circuit on one of five lines carrying a 1.5 million kilo-watts of electricity north and west into Canada. The other four circuits overloaded, and the power from Beck reversed itself, sending a massive jolt of electricity south into New York. The surge overwhelmed protective devices. One feeder failed, then another. Within ten minutes. New England Power and Con Edison knocked themselves out trying to fill upstate New York's void.

Some listened to the game; the Yankees were in Milwaukee.

At Shea Stadium, twenty-two thousand watched the Mets.

Young men and women, in from Westchester, Long Island, and New Jersey, shopped for secondhand jeans, records, rolling papers, and marijuana. Many danced: to funk, to country, to punk, to Israeli music at the Ninety-second Street Y, and most of all, to disco.

People looked for prostitutes; prostitutes looked for johns.

Some watched *Beretta*, others said, "I've seen this one," before checking to see if anything else was on.

A relay in Canada, Con Edison said, caused the blackout.

Not quite, the electrical engineer replied. The relay certainly contributed to the blackout, but a precipitating event is not the same as a cause. A week after the blackout, he briefed reporters on the highlights of his twenty-two-page report. Con Edison, not Canada, was responsible for Con Edison's trouble. The utility needed to learn how to free itself from neighboring utilities when they threatened its stability, and it needed to install automatic load-shedding equipment, which would help its engineers manage the available load once New York, or some significant part of it, was on its own.

People stepped off trains: at Grand Central, at 125th Street, at Fordham Road in the Bronx.

People snatched purses.

People stepped onto trains, as a Long Island couple did at Penn Station, a few minutes after nine. They'd tried to take the 5:04, but when they learned that it would be delayed by a tunnel fire, they opted for dinner at the Steel Palace and tennis: Billie Jean King and Virginia Wade, playing for the New York Apples. As the 9:20 to Manhasset pulled out, at 9:20, the Long Islanders congratulated themselves on their city savvy.

And people had their purses snatched.

At around nine o'clock, the picture on his television set contracted.

The electrical engineer didn't think anything of it. Brownouts (tactical voltage reductions, intended to protect the system at times of extra-heavy usage) and mini-blackouts had become as much a part of summer in the city as smog. His lights often flickered and dimmed. It had been a 90-degree day, and it was a sultry night. There had been scattered electrical storms. Every air conditioner in the city was running on high.

The lights flickered. He didn't even get up from his chair.

Two dozen people stood in line outside a reasonably priced Italian restaurant.

A famous critic had recently raved about the food.

In newspaper offices and television and radio studios, people gathered the latest news.

The president defended his opposition to federal funding for health clinics that performed abortions even if it meant that only well-to-do women would have the right to choose.

Life, he said, isn't always fair.

Residents of Rockwood, Tennessee, returned to their homes a day after an overturned truck released a cloud of bromide gas. National guardsmen patrolled to prevent looting. Government officials said that one-third of the trucks on the highways were unsafe; without more inspectors and stiffer penalties, there would be horrible disasters.

At around nine-thirty, subway motormen began to report trouble with signals, the red, amber, and green lights that help ensure a safe distance between trains.

Some were flickering.

Others were out.

There was no pattern to the outages, nor obvious meaning.

The supervisor on duty at the Transit Authority's subway command center had heard nothing from Con Edison.

People went to mass; people went to minyan.

People played mahjong; people played bingo.

Sharpies played three-card monte with two or three shills, each of whom won hand after hand.

Tourists saw fistfuls of twenties, and on the cardboard-box card table they thought they saw the red queen the sharpies seemed to work so hard to hide. They put down twenties of their own, and lost them every single time.

Some complained about the heat; others said, "Why complain, you can't change it."

People played bridge, and people took bribes.

The subway supervisor, who had worked for the Transit Authority for twenty-nine years, had been on duty for his share of difficult nights and days, including the rush hour in November 1965 when the lights went out with half a million people underground.

He had also seen his share of changes, particularly since 1965.

The trains were ancient, covered with graffiti, horribly maintained. Stations were menacing: dilapidated, filthy, dark, and dreary. Panhandlers were everywhere. Ridership was way down.

But at the moment, with the signals on the blink, the city's curse was a system's operator's blessing. There were only forty-five thousand people on 175 trains along 714 miles of track.

A few people hid from Son of Sam.

Many people worried about him, including two sixteen-year olds who, spooked by their own speculation about the serial killer at an eerie moment just before dark, decided to return to their Co-op City apartments. They had to pass through a long walkway in the center of a shopping plaza; after sunset, it was like a tunnel without lights.

"He's in there!" one of them cried.

"But we're not with boys," the other said.

"And we're not in a car."

And who comes to Co-op City, anyway."

They took no chances. They pulled their bell-bottoms up to high-water level; drew their sweatshirt hoods around their heads until only their noses showed; locked arms; and walked with their stomachs sticking out as far as their stomachs would go.

Lots of people smoked pot; people with lots of money snorted coke.

"I could see it coming," said the supervisor, "from the first reports of temporary loss of power." There were too many for it to be a coincidence.

He did something that he'd never done—something no one, as far as he knew, had ever done in seventy-three years of subway service. He asked dispatchers to ask the motormen on all 175 trains to proceed to the nearest station and stop there.

People opened fire hydrants.

People swam in pools.

People worked for wages despite welfare rules.

Children ran under sprinklers; others played war with water guns to keep cool.

Parents kissed kids good night; people who hardly knew each other screwed; women waited in line for ladies' rooms; men walked right in and pissed.

The Transit Authority supervisor may have wondered why Con Edison had not warned him. But he had no reason to feel left out of the loop.

The police knew nothing. The fire department knew nothing. The mayor knew nothing.

The chairman of Con Edison himself knew nothing.

He had just finished dinner, at home in Bronxville. His work day was over. Despite the heat and the staggering demand, the system was humming along. He was on his way into the den.

Some shot heroin.

Some shot hoops.

Some ran from the police.

Some studied: for summer school, the real-estate-licensing exam, the LSATs.

Some stiffed waiters; some left huge tips.

Some burned abandoned buildings for landlord's cash.

Some burned them for kicks.

The chairman had come to Con Edison from LBJ's Department of the Interior in the shake-up after November 1965. The design of the system and much of the equipment, he immediately discovered, were outdated. Service was spotty. Management was cumbersome, with too much weight at the top. Con Edison was a company customers loved to hate.

The chairman promised reliability, efficiency, conservation, and clean air. He lowered the retirement age to sixty-five and breaking with company tradition, replaced retirees with executives from the outside. He saw to it that transmission lines were strengthened, plants modernized, control centers equipped with the latest load-shedding equipment, and emergency procedures streamlined. He worked especially hard to turn public opinion around, pulling the DIG WE MUST signs off excavation sites and opening an office devoted entirely to fielding customer complaints.

People planned weddings, people planned christenings.

People planned holdups, hits, bar mitzvahs.

Some read the ticker in Times Square: North Korea had downed an unarmed U.S. cargo copter, killing three.

Others read novels, billboards, air-conditioner-installation manuals, playbills, train schedules, maps, menus, concert programs, and poetry.

Politicians gave speeches.

People listening wanted to know what they proposed to do about crime.

Sidewalk preachers said Judgment Day was coming; wherever you looked, there were signs.

Despite the chairman's best efforts, the early 1970s were difficult years. Eighty percent of the company's generating capacity came from oil at a time when cartel and embargo contributed to price hikes as high as 400 percent. Clean-air regulations prohibited the company from switching to cheap crude, let alone coal. Energy consumption was rising, but steady inflation, cost overruns, and environmental concerns stalled the construction of new generating plants. The company's stock sank, and in 1974, for the first time in ninety-one years, Con Edison skipped its quarterly dividend.

The chairman sold two plants to the state and won approval for steep rate increases. By 1977 he had begun to turn things around. Revenues were up. Profits were up. The stock was on its way back up and once again paying a quarterly dividend.

Some jumped subway turnstiles or entered though broken exit gates; others decided to walk or take a cab; beneath city streets, nine o'clock was late.

People argued about welfare. People argued about the Middle East: Begin's ministers had approved a plan, but Sadat said that without justice for the Palestinians and a return of the occupied territories, there would be no peace.

Con Edison's customers were as unhappy as ever. They'd invested heavily in the company's revival ($700 million since 1975, in higher monthly gas and electric bills) without hope of interest or dividends. New Yorkers now paid over 10 cents per kilowatt-hour, twice what they had paid in 1972.

You couldn't please everyone. Overall, things were going well. Very well. On July 10, the chairman had been a guest on ABC's Sunday morning television talk show. "I can guarantee," he said, "that the chances of a brownout or a blackout are less than they have been in the last fifteen years, and that the chances are less here than in most other cities in the United States."

People woke for work, dressed, and grabbed a bite to eat.

Others returned, juggling briefcases, Chinese takeout, six-packs, and apartment keys.

Some got drunk.

Some got high.

A few teenagers in from the suburbs looked half-sick when two cops walked by. The cops shook their heads; one even smiled. They're cool, a kid said. They have bigger fish to fry.

These kids were a complete mystery to the cops. Not because of the 1960s hair, the beads, beards, or bandanas. Certainly not because of the marijuana. But because they could have been under a canopy of leafy trees. On a screened porch. In an air-conditioned room. By a backyard pool. At a place at the beach. Yet they chose to spend the evening on a stinking-hot city street.

The chairman walked into his den, turned on the hi-fi, which was tuned to WFCN, a classical-music station. He picked up a magazine and sat down in his chair.

The reception was terrible. He called to his son, all ready to "bawl him out." He assumed that the young man had once again been "fiddling" with the receiver.

Some stepped into elevators.

Others stepped out.

Strangers passed strangers.

Some said hi.

Others nodded, shrugged, wondered, sighed.

Some laughed. Some cried.

People were born. People died.

People asked questions: Who, how, what, when, where, and why?

3.

In sealed buildings, the first thing people heard was a deep, labored thunk, the dying breath of everything electric, all at once.

What was that?

"We aren't moving."

"Push it again."

One of the passengers pushed it again. Nothing happened. And again.

"Try to open the doors."

The large car was crowded. A passenger pried the doors open and the passengers spilled back into the restaurant, greatly relieved.

"The elevator's out," one of them said to the bell captain, pointing toward it with the impatience of an important person who has had a bit too much red wine to drink and red meat to eat.

The bell captain pointed, too, toward the window, the restaurant's main attraction, 107 floors above the street.

Moments before, the view had been a drunken expressionist's floor-to-ceiling canvas, a riot of electric light. Now all you could see was a line drawing so simple and sober on a canvas so hi and black that at first glance you couldn't even see it. Long white lines lay like moonlight on a large body of water. The headlights of cars driving into the city from Westchester and Long Island. Red lines of taillights showed the way out. Down in the harbor, out in the Upper Bay, up along the Hudson, the red, white, and green navigation lights of small boats, which on any other night might have been lost in the haze, suddenly looked bright. And the torch of the Statue of Liberty (which got its power from New Jersey) looked like a white fire in the sky. Across the river, in Hoboken and Jersey City, it was just another summer night.

"The elevator's out."

"So's New York," the bell captain said.

On a low floor of a high-rise in the middle of Harlem, a seventeen-year-old sitting by an open window heard a great roar—the stadium, after a Yankee hit a game-winning home run; the Garden, after an audience realized, a few bars into it, that the band had begun to play a favorite song—and then a cacophony of sighs, laughs, shrieks, cries, whistles, hoots, gasps, howls, curses, groans, and screams.

She thought the world was about to end.

She grabbed her fourteen-month-old son and her sister's babies.

Her mother turned on a transistor radio.

The anchorman was excited, but not alarmed. It was a blackout, not a bomb.

"Where's New York?" asked a pilot as he prepared to land a cargo plane, carrying crates of strawberries, at Kennedy Airport.

One second the city was there. The next it was gone.

The flight controllers had no idea.

"Proceed to Philadelphia," one of them said.

"What am I supposed to do with the berries?" the pilot asked.

"Eat them," the controller answered.

Subways slowed, stopped, sat, lurched forward, crept, stopped again. Lights flickered; some cars went completely dark. Air conditioning shut down, if it had been running to begin with. Conductors said nothing. Passengers on the trains that made it to a station—all but seven—or that crawled in on emergency power just after the system went down had no way of knowing, or reason to believe, that anything extraordinary was wrong. Especially if the station had a few emergency lights.

Some, fed up, walked out and up to the street.

But many stayed put, intending to wait out the delay. It's just another night, one man said, on the MTA.

Simon Hench, the lead character in *Otherwise Engaged*, was alone onstage when the lights went out and the music, a record playing on a turntable, skidded to a stop.

Had it been just the music, the audience might have thought it was part of the play. Hench's only desire was to sit, alone, and listen to his brand-new recording of Wagner's Parsifal. But every time he put stylus to vinyl, he was interrupted: first by his tenant, who had woman and money troubles; then by his brother, who had job troubles; then by a friend, who was having an affair with his (re-married) ex-wife; then by the girlfriend of the friend, who came by (braless, and before long blouseless) in search of a publisher for her book; then by an old prep-school mate, now the frustrated suitor of a young woman Hench had slept with on the sofa in his office a few days before; then again his brother, who informed Hench that Hench's wife was having an affair; and finally Hench's wife.

"What do we do now?" he asked.

"There was mass confusion," said a twenty-one-year-old who, at seventeen, had given up high school and hopes for a college football scholarship for the service. Now, four months out of the marines, and work, he was shooting hoops in Brownsville.

His friends hooted and hollered, dashed this way and that. A moment or two passed before someone realized it wasn't just in the projects that the lights were out.

"What have I done?" asked people who had just blown out birthday candles, shut heavy windows and doors, struck streetlight and utility poles with bats and sticks, slammed down telephone receivers, flicked switches.

"What did you do?" others asked them.

"What now?"

Others knew.

For them the question was not what or why but who, and when, and how.

Mayor Beame had been speaking about mortgages to a standing-room-only crowd in a Co-op City synagogue when, in the words of a reporter, the lights "flickered, dimmed, and died."

As aides and synagogue staff tried to figure out what had happened, the mayor kidded his audience about the importance of paying bills on time.

He had many enemies. But even allies acknowledged that the lights had dimmed on his administration two years earlier, when investors (suddenly purporting to be "shocked" at the sleights of hand by which the city balanced its books) stopped bidding on its bonds. With the city on the brink of bankruptcy, the mayor's fiscal powers passed to two state agencies, the Municipal Assistance Corporation and the Emergency Financial Control Board. As those agencies pressed the city to freeze hiring and salaries, cut spending, and dramatically reduce services, the boss became a broker, a go-between among labor unions, state and federal officials, fiscal overseers, bankers, and other powerful money men.

By July 1977 the worst was over.

But the city, like the nation, was still mired in troubles, material and spiritual, and many people had concluded that the seventy-one-year-old Democrat was not up to the job. He had six challengers for his own party's nomination, and the primary was two months away.

All kidding aside, the mayor assured his audience that despite the recent wave of foreclosures at the fifteen-thousand-unit middle-class housing project in the Baychester section of the Bronx, neither the city nor Con Ed had turned off their lights.

A Brooklyn couple, on their way home from the movies, had just stepped onto a Bushwick-bound bus.

The ride was slow, but steady.

On the walk between bus stop and home, he decided to go back out.

Why? she asked. She didn't understand.

She pleaded with him.

They argued.

But his heart was set.

"How will I ever identify Mr. .44 now?" a Bronx woman wailed.

He was Son of Sam, the .44-caliber killer. She fit the profile of his victims perfectly: eighteen, long brown hair, hanging out on the steps of her friend Theresa's house, across the street from Westchester Square Hospital, with her boyfriend, Tony. Police had warned young couples to stay off the streets, and especially out of parked cars. At least they weren't in a car.

She'd seen him again, she had just told her friends, who were tired of hearing it, seen him on the subway ride home from her class at the Eastern School for Physicians' Aides. "I knew it was him," she said. "I was positive. I've seen enough composites to be able to pick him out of a crowd."

Now she could not see a thing.

"What did you do?" a young woman asked her boyfriend.

It was a rhetorical question.

The television had died, and she assumed he hadn't paid the bill.

He went to the window. For a few moments, people stood still, as if stunned or frozen by the great patches of darkness that had fallen on them. Slowly at first, then faster, they began to move, en masse, toward Broadway.

The Cubs's Ray Burris was in mid-windup.

The Mets' Lenny Randall, at the plate.

The arc lights above the field and seats went off, along with the lights in the corridors, concession stands, and ramps.

Burris held on to the ball.

Randall thought the game was over: "God. I'm gone. I thought for sure He was calling me. I thought it was my last at-bat."

Con Edison's acting vice president for public affairs had just returned home, "horribly hot" and bothered, from a class at Columbia, where she was working, virtually full-time, toward an MBA.

Home was a sublet on West Sixty-sixth Street, around the corner from the utility's Energy Control Center. She'd taken the place a week before, shortly after leaving her husband.

Wanting nothing more than a shower and some sleep, she turned on the radio, took off her clothes, and turned on the water. She was about to step in when the newscaster began to slur his words and the lights went out.

"Oh shit," she said

She managed to find her way to the phone and dial the number of Con Edison's Central Information Group. "CIG," a colleague answered.

"This is Joyce. I'm here in Manhattan. The lights just went out. What's going on?"

"We lost the system," he said. "Lightning."

"I'm two blocks away," she said. "I'll run over as soon I get dressed. Tell security if any media show up, keep them down on the sidewalk until I get there."

She had hung up the phone and started to get dressed when it occurred to her that if she hadn't known what was going on until she called, perhaps the chairman didn't know. She went back to the phone.

"Chuck, it's me, Joyce, in New York."

"Joyce," he said. "I am sitting here in the dark, in my den, in Bronxville. Bronxville's dark. And can't get through to the Westchester control room to find out what's happening here in Bronxville."

"'Forget about Bronxville," she said. "Forget about Westchester. I just got off the phone with CIG, and we lost Manhattan. We lost the whole system."

Part III

Miniatures

There is an impossible to resist temptation to keep our comments introducing this section short. In her short miniature 'Dictator in a dumpster: thoughts on history and garbage' Maureen Healy asks historians to consider the similarities between what ends up in an archive and what ends up in the dump. The figure of the dustbin-cum-dumpster, the Albanian embassy in a posh district of Vienna, and the collected works of the dictator Enver Hoxha serve Healy to explore the parallel between making history and making garbage. As always with Miniatures, it never quite turns out as you might imagine.

William Deverell and David Igler in their 'The abattoir of the prairie' describe the history of the organized rabbit drives that took place throughout the rural American West during the late nineteenth and early twentieth centuries. Through their brief description of the small farming town of Huron in California's San Joaquin Valley in 1891and its winter rabbit drive, they argue that the mass killings of prairie rabbits represented a community ritual as well as an organized response to an agricultural pest. Deverell and Igler offer a succinct yet redolent insight into a little known aspect of western life. There is also a rather dramatic photograph – be warned.

Jesse Berret's 'Liberace: behind the music' is a deft, funny and scholarly study of the entertainer Liberace. As Berrett says, Liberace may appear an antique figure of pre-Stonewall self-hate, but his performances reveal a fascinatingly shaded dance that took place in plain view of the most conservative audiences. Using insights provided by queer theory, Berrett's brief biography illustrates how Liberace's flamboyance and innuendo-laden patter enabled both revelation and concealment.

As Janet Golden and Elizabeth Toon argue in their three-act rendition called 'Rethinking Charles Atlas' from the 1920s on, Atlas, the former '97 lb weakling', offered his own story of personal transformation – humiliation, inspiration, anointment – as testimony of his 'Dynamic Tension' bodybuilding system's values. Viewing Atlas's system in its historical context, Golden and Toon maintain, helps illuminate the disjuncture between earlier body culture and our own. Their history demonstrates – using the regimen of physical fitness – how history can teach without pain.

11 Dictator in a dumpster
Thoughts on history and garbage

Maureen Healy

While readers of Hegel know that a latter stage of historical consciousness contains within it elements of a former, perhaps they, like me, have wondered about the mechanics of such a transition. I have often imagined that in the wake of an epic Hegelian transformation, there remains an empty conference room littered with the cigarette butts and coffee mugs of those thinkers who didn't make it to the next stage. In 1917, Leon Trotsky took up the issue of litter and historical change. When he made the famous declaration to Mensheviks: "You are pitiful isolated individuals; you are bankrupts; your role is played out. Go where you belong from now on—into the dustbin of history," the dustbin to which he referred was metaphoric.[1] It was a figurative resting place for discredited political systems and personalities. This dustbin contained the debris left behind when one historical era progressed to the next, as inevitably dictated by the laws of history. A recent encounter on the street prompted me to further probe this relationship between history and the garbage bin. What if it wasn't a metaphoric link at all? What would it mean for historians if we actually trashed the losers of history?

I was walking in a posh district of Vienna, where stately turn-of-the-century mansions have become manicured embassies of foreign states, when a dumpster caught my eye. It was full of books. We have all "gotten rid" of books, but usually by the conventional methods of passing them to friends, selling them to a used book store, donating them to a library or, as a last alternative, abandoning them in the night in front of a Goodwill. But loading them into a dumpster seemed an audacious choice, and I moved closer. The dumpster was outside of the Albanian embassy, a building in need of a paint job, a slightly dilapidated symbol of a poor country trying to keep up diplomatic appearances in a very expensive city. It became apparent that employees had decided, or been instructed, to throw away the embassy's library, which contained, along with some outdated tourist brochures on Albania's forgotten coastline, the collected works of Enver Hoxha.

Hoxha, the communist dictator who ruled Albania for four decades until his death in 1985, had a publication record that would boggle the minds of young scholars trying to round out their c.v.'s. But this is not surprising from a one-man cabinet who once simultaneously held the posts of prime minister, foreign minister, defense minister and commander-in-chief of the armed forces.[2] Books by Hoxha, about Hoxha, or carrying a frontispiece endorsement of Hoxha were the staple of the embassy library, and perhaps of all libraries in the home country. The books were printed on the prematurely aging, yellowish newsprint of communist-era state-run publishing houses, precisely the kind of paper that librarians of the international acid-free movement are out to eradicate. Hoxha's works left me in a quandary: Wasn't this a living archive? An "archive of the street" discovered by a historian who likes to think she is committed to the nitty-gritty, forgotten history of the everyday? I was in Vienna on a research trip anyway, and wasn't this dumpster an archive that needed to be excavated—and quickly—before the garbage truck came along and obliterated it?

I thumbed through the materials and decided, for two reasons, that the Hoxha library would remain in the dumpster. First, high-brow Vienna is not the kind of place one wants to be seen dumpster-diving. While not legally *verboten*, it simply *isn't done*—which in Austria amounts to the same thing. Second, and more decisively, I don't read Albanian. Taking the books would have been the act of a souvenir collector rather than a historian, the equivalent of buying an "authentic" Red Army cap or Stasi badge from street vendors near the demolished Berlin Wall. It made me feel sorry for Hoxha, a figure whose writings hadn't even acquired any of the kitsch value of other post-cold war artifacts. He was not the first communist-era figure to be "thrown away" by his own people, but I would argue that many of the other recent acts of post-communist discarding rather aspired to Trotsky's *metaphoric* dustbin. We saw a few years ago the ritual lifting, by industrial crane, of Marx and Lenin statues that had once graced town squares. The spectacle of the great men in stone tipping off of their pedestals to the roar of cheering crowds did not create garbage, however, but relics. The grandness of the gesture marked the transition to a new historical era.

Cultural critic Greil Marcus writes, "'The dustbin of history' is one of our terms for finality, for putting history behind us, where it seems to belong."[3] In the Hoxha incident, the dumpster challenges this dustbin-as-metaphor. Sometimes, "pitiful, isolated individuals" who are bankrupt and whose "role has been played out" go to the dustbin as symbols of historical transformation, as in Trotsky's Mensheviks; sometimes equally menacing individuals just end up in the trash. Many historians have confronted the paradox of garbage; as researchers, we know the frustration of being told that certain documents once held by an archive and listed in its catalogue have since been "removed" during an archival culling. The Viennese call this action *skartieren*—the periodic clearing out of space to make room for different, perhaps more "valuable" papers. Documents that are *skartiert* stand in even more perplexing relation to history than the Hoxha library because they were so close to making the cut. Wiggling their way into an archive, they were practically guaranteed to be accorded "historical significance" by someone, sometime, when an archivist's whim turned them ignominiously into trash. Hoxha wasn't rescued this time, but in future research trips, perhaps we should consider excavating the contents of the city dump, for the making of history runs parallel to the making of garbage.

Notes

1 Cited in Elizabeth Knowles (ed.) *Oxford Dictionary of Phrase, Saying and Quotation* (Oxford and New York: Oxford University Press, 1997), 421. Thanks to Jon Bone for pointing out that translators have alternately settled on rubbish can, trashcan, trash heap and garbage can.

2 See Miranda Vickers, *The Albanians: A Modern History* (London and New York: I.B. Tauris, 1995), 168.

3 Greil Marcus, *The Dustbin of History* (Cambridge, MA: Harvard University Press, 1995), 4.

12 The abattoir of the prairie

William Deverell and David Igler

Imagine this place: just outside the small farming town of Huron, in California's San Joaquin Valley. It is a cold February morning, a few moments before dawn. It is 1891.

Sixty, seventy, one hundred men, women, and children gather in eager anticipation on the flat farmland and plains. Some come on horseback or in buggies. Most walk from nearby homes. Boys and men carry clubs, big sticks, rifles, pistols, shotguns, and planks; the smaller boys grasp fist-sized rocks.

Imagine the shape of a huge baseball diamond. Where the first and third base lines run at right angles to one another is a hastily constructed fence. Huron farmers built it during a week or two of shared spare time. The fence is flimsy, but long strips of wire running from fence post to fence post make it a bit sturdier. Chicken wire hangs in ten or twelve-foot-long sections here and there. This fence is one-half mile long in either direction, stretching out into open fields of low-lying brush and wild scrub grass.

Think of centerfield. Here the people of Huron have gathered, maybe a mile away from homeplate. Here they share small talk as the sun rises. They talk of the weather. Of children and livestock and soil. Someone gives a signal. Maybe it is the county sheriff, or perhaps it is one of Huron's wealthier farmers. Someone blows a whistle or rings a bell or shouts the right phrase. The people stretch themselves out into a long line, leaving about a ten feet between one another. This takes several minutes.

Then another signal. In unison, the crowd begins to move toward homeplate, a few thousand yards in the distance. They move slowly, deliberately, attempting to keep their line in formation. Most are now on foot, and most of the women hang back and do not move with the group. The children run, too excited to keep the methodical pace of their fathers and brothers. At homeplate, where the foul line fences nearly converge, a circular corral has been built. The fences make a doorway into the corral. The corral is sturdy.

The first rabbits appear before the phalanx. They are startled, but they do not panic. Plenty of open space yawns in front of the crowd. The rabbits scamper away. At the sight of the first flushed rabbits, the teenagers start to run. Men fire guns into the air. They cheer and shout, dogs bark, and the line presses forward.

Lewis and Clark "discovered" the prairie rabbit. Their leaping ability aston-
ished Meriwether Lewis. He measured the average prairie rabbit's leap at twenty
feet. Lewis and Clark did not witness a rabbit drive, but some of the Indians
they encountered certainly drove rabbits. By the 1880s rabbit drives regularly
took place in many communities across the American West. Most occurred in
the San Joaquin Valley, where jack rabbits (*Lepus californicus*) multiplied at
a furious rate. Rabbits endangered farmers' crops. The rabbit drive became a
community ritual, waged against this four-legged threat.

On this winter morning in 1891, the human line continues forward and they
close the spaces between them. Some rabbits zigzag their way to the edges of
the crowd and leap over men and boys and fence. Most are too tired to clear the
high fence. Some bounce against the wire strung between fence posts but cannot
escape.

The line continues to move forward. The rabbits are frightened now. There
are several hundred of them, they seem to appear out of nowhere. They swirl
the dust and trample the grass between the crowd and the corral. Their eyes
bulge as they run to and fro. Boys start to swing their clubs. Someone sets loose
a dog. Everything speeds up. Rabbits run like lightning, boys chase them, men
pant along as fast as they can. Another dog is let go. The sun is up, well above
the horizon.

Figure 12.1 The abattoir of the prairie

The mile-long line begins a flanking maneuver, tightening into an inverted U that neatly fits atop the mouth of the corral. The men and boys of Huron drive one thousand terrified rabbits before them.

The rabbit corral is the abattoir of the prairie.

Huron farmers, their sons, and hired hands all swing their clubs and sticks and planks. They sweat. They shout. They smash rabbits to death. Dogs tear rabbits apart. Blood is everywhere: on clothes and sticks and boys and dogs. Rabbits screech as they die. Some people weep as they watch and listen to the slaughter. Others cheer.

After it is all over, and the men and boys have caught their breath, they pose. They gather up the dead rabbit trophies. They stretch rabbit carcasses out lengthwise. They hang them from the corral posts. They drape rabbits from their shoulders, attach them to their waists. Men and boys insist that their mothers and sisters and wives share in their pride. People smile and laugh as they gather amidst the ocean of dead rabbits.

Someone has brought a camera, and a photograph is taken.

13 Liberace
Behind the music

Jesse Berrett

You're barely a minute into Liberace's 1978 TV special, *Leapin' Lizards, It's Liberace*, before you're wallowing in it. Wouldn't do to keep the customers waiting. We first meet Lee, as his friends called him, plinking the ivories throughout his mansion—in his bedroom; in the tub; along the wall of his pool; on a cake; even in the center of his walk-in closet—before he's whisked off to the Hilton in that diamond-encrusted, *88 Keys*-plated limo that delivers him onto the stage. His driver, "piano virtuouso" Vince Cardell, winged perm frosted with gray, exudes aging gigolo—handsome, with a very 70s hot-tub/Mac Davis chic.

Springing out of the car, Lee confides to the crowd in best folksy manner that his ridiculous automobile "really stops traffic when I shop at Safeway." And then . . . then it's time for what we've all been waiting for, the real show-stopper, the talent that shot him from New York drag bars to stardom on the budding Vegas strip in only four years: Yes, it's the first costume change, before he's even broken a sweat! It's spectacle as artistic principle, excess as world-view, fabulousness for the joy of fabulousness. "Let me slip into something more spectacular," he purrs, and damned if it isn't so.

But to inquire politely, just what the hell is going on here? Dead since 1987, Wladziu Valentino Liberace bangs and grins all over again on a three-videotape collection that allows you to soar as close to his finery as you dare. In addition to *Leapin' Lizards*, there's a Valentine's Day special and a concert with the London Philharmonic. The box set comes in a sparkly case with a nifty fold-out Lee dancing atop a keyboard; over the top is the only way to go. But what's really for sale is a fascinatingly archaeological glimpse at the vagaries of mass-cultural gayness well before the age of *Ellen*.

The earliest of these concerts takes place nine years after Stonewall, but to the leisure-suited armies who made the Vegas pilgrimage, drag queens rioting in Greenwich Village might as well have been walking the runway in Moscow. The segments of the audience we can see suggest that even the crowd's hippest members weren't having much truck with this whole '70s thing. (It's no stretch to figure out why the world's supreme blue-haired granny, England's Queen Mum, was a devoted Liberace cultist from his first UK tour in 1956.) And the mob bosses who paid Lee's salary certainly didn't want any of that fairy stuff messing with the bottom line. So the whole product sounds unpromising, to say the least: Liberace as the gay Uncle Tom, bowing and scraping for the straights' delight.

But little hints of queerness keep shining through. "I'll tell you one thing about this outfit," Lee smirks while done up in full regalia: "You'll never see anything like it on *Grizzly Adams*." With the famous Dancing Waters ejaculating mechanically away behind him, he expertly treads the line between in-joke and self-parody, revelation dancing into sight but slipping away before you can pin it down. He plays a stripper's bump-and-grind while taking off his robe; tells Lola Falana and Sandy Duncan to "come in with your big cadenzas"; asks older women to feel the fine cut of his pant leg, then pleads "do the other one; I don't want to be frustrated"; and boasts that Lee "is one of my nicer nicknames—I have others." What are they? What does innuendo mean when it's never going to be followed up? Only his hairdresser knows for sure.

There's a real expertise here, one honed over years spent calibrating just how much you can imply without bringing down the wrath of bigots and homophobes. Sure, he's different, his fans argued in the face of 30 years of bachelorhood, the odd prospective marriage, two successful libel suits against tabloids that insinuated he was gay, a palimony suit by his male lover (settled out of court, and the subject of a tell-some autobiography, *Behind the Candelabra*), and posthumous AIDS diagnosis. But Liberace's not, you know, weird or anything— just sort of . . . odd, like (insert bachelor uncle). And seeing him toe that line is heartbreaking and enthralling at once: heartbreaking because you grieve for a career, for an emotional life spent orbiting such a limited space; enthralling because the world rarely requires such a degree of expertise anymore—it's as quaint as watching an ace telegrapher tap out his lost trade.

Exploding into dimensions beyond bathos, Liberace is the Columbus of camp, a discoverer of worlds where cheese, sincerity, and parody merge into some unholy trinity in which no one, not even Lee himself, can tell joke from truth. As his favorite Mae West quip had it, "Too much of a good thing . . . is wonderful!" (By the by, the Liberace Museum in Las Vegas, which documents how thoroughly he lived that philosophy, will happily sell you a shirt bearing that motto for a mere $20.) What is too much? Put it this way: He dares to start a medley with "Send in the Clowns," a strong contender for corniest song of all time, then adds insult to injury by having a little clown mannequin walk out onstage, blow up a balloon, laugh, cry, and, most horrible of all, cavort. And, well, it works . . . or you surrender, which amounts to the same thing. By show's end, he's pretty much had his way with you.

Of course, no one would willingly revert to "Friends of Dorothy" codes and innuendo today. (Which is not to say that such skills have been rendered utterly irrelevant: What is *Frasier*'s Niles Crane but an upper-middle-class Liberace, invisible Maris, opera queendom, and all? Or *Will & Grace*'s Jack, a Lee who dares speak the name of his love?) But before—or even after—we glory in being here, queer, and used to it, attention must be paid. There's an art and a nerve to Liberace's performances that demands respect. After all, he survived Anita

Bryant's America, not Ellen De Generes's (much less Gregg Araki's). His world hadn't traveled far from the one where reputable newspapers printed the names of men nabbed in raids on gay bars, or where more government employees were hounded from their jobs for being gay than for being Communists.

But don't take my word for it. Consider Liberace in the light of a surprising booklet for the culture of closeting written by its survivors. In his 1997 book *The Rise and Fall of Gay Culture*, essayist Daniel Harris mourned the passing of old-style gay porn; recognizable humans getting it on, he argued, have been supplanted by robotic constructs like Jeff Stryker going at it with mechanical efficiency. Literary critic D.A. Miller's *A Place for Us*, an elegant little hymn to the grand subtextual tradition of classic Broadway musicals, observes that these shows offered hiding places for "a somehow gay genre, the only one that mass culture ever produced"—words that could just as well describe Liberace's one-man theater of closeting. That culture "denominates those early pre-sexual realities of gay experience to which, in numerous lives, it became forever bound: not just the solitude, shame, [and] secretiveness by which the impossibility of social integration was at first internalized; or the excessive sentimentality that was the necessary condition of sentiments allowed no real object; but also the intense, senseless joy that, while not identical to these destitutions, is neither extricable from them."

So give Liberace his due. Today he may read as painfully old and tired, an extinct species fighting a battle that's been mostly won. Seeing him sing "I'll Be Seeing You" for what must be the 10,000th time, winking and smiling at an audience that would be horrified to admit what "you" actually meant to him, tastes of purgatory. But think of Liberace instead as a spy in the enemy's camp and your view brightens. Going onstage every night must have felt like that to him: simultaneously a dance with career death and an exercise in speaking up, even if no one could say out loud that they heard.

When you enjoy the plethora of gay characters mobbing mass culture these days, spend a minute honoring those whose struggle helped win the airwaves. Luxuriant, fabulous, and everything else, Liberace did as much as anyone to boldly go where no (gay) man had gone before—and all without ever leaving his closet.

14 Rethinking Charles Atlas

Elizabeth Toon and Janet Golden

In 1947, 18-year-old New Yorker Donald Trill (pseudonym) signed his application for the Charles Atlas Championship Trophy.[1] He listed his measurements before and after completing Atlas's "Health, Strength and Physique Building System" and described his improved appearance: "Have developed rosy cheeks. My vests have become so tight that I think a few buttons will pop soon". In response to the question regarding "Health (constipation, etc.)", Trill wrote "Am in good health, no constipation, or any suspicion of it". His strength had also improved: "Can now play bass fiddle and get a much stronger and fuller tone out of it. My fingers and arms no longer get tired after an orchestra workout, but instead I feel fresh as a daisy". Finally, he stated, "I can now go swimming and not be afraid that fellows and girls will laugh at my physique". His response mirrored the plot of the famous magazine advertisement for the Atlas System, the comic strip story of "Mac", who redeemed his honour and recaptured his girl by remaking his physique.

In the late 20th century, as "iron" men and women compete in weekend triathlons, joggers crowd the streets at dawn and dusk, and those in search of "hard bodies" affix themselves to exercise machines calibrated to their individual needs, both Trill's self-depiction and Atlas's regimen seem touchingly innocent. This innocence, we believe, is a reflection of a shifting 20th-century body culture in which "fitness" has become a new form of work and a source of status for the bourgeoisie (Green 1986; Gorn 1986; Mrozek 1989; Kimmel 1994). Our exploration of the career and meaning of the Charles Atlas System will examine this shift and its importance.

Charles Atlas himself lived a life in three acts, finding redemption not by faith but through fitness (Dougherty 1972; Gaines and Butler 1982; Gustaitis 1986; Graebner 1994). His saga opens in Brooklyn, where the teenaged Angelo Siciliano is humiliated by a Coney Island tough. Act 2 takes Siciliano on a journey. He views the Greek and Roman statuary in the Brooklyn Museum and he visits the Prospect Park Zoo, where he observes a lion flexing its muscles and is inspired to develop his own system of isometric exercise. In Act 3, Siciliano's friends dub him "Atlas" and the famous physical culturist Bernarr Macfadden anoints him "the World's Most Perfectly Developed Man". Angelo Siciliano renames himself Charles Atlas and uses prize money to hire a naturopath to write his Dynamic Tension lessons. Atlas then teams up with advertising genius Charles Roman, who creates what has been called "the single greatest mail order ad of all time"—the comic strip advertisement featuring Mac, the former 97-pound weakling who would have sand kicked in his face no more (Schultz 1988: 44). Thereafter, Atlas lives a life of fitness, entertaining visitors to his company's headquarters by bending railroad spikes and advising them: "Live clean, think clean, and don't go to burlesque shows" (Zolotow 1942: 21).

Did Atlas devotees follow this advice? How many "dear friends" purchased and/or used Atlas's system? Who were they: pre-adolescents, adolescents, young adults? Did older men subscribe as well? Did women? Did the sexually suggestive images and discussions of nude bathing with a "friend" give the Atlas system a particular appeal to gay adolescents? Was Atlas's dietary advice— which eschewed white bread and fatty meats—followed? Did his suggestions for avoiding worry and anger (which Atlas deemed "mental and physical poisons") and his directions for cultivating happiness help subscribers overcome feelings of self-doubt? Finally, how did readers respond to Atlas and his system? Playwright David Mamet wrote of the shame he felt at receiving the lessons in a "plain brown wrapper", while Mahatma Gandhi's grandson Arun—now a spokesperson for non-violence—told of subscribing to the Atlas system after beatings suffered while he was a youngster in South Africa (Mamet 1989: 15–16; Culver 1998: B1).

Atlas's lessons are filled with references to late 19th- and early 20th-century health practices, some mainstream and some faddish. Atlas recommended constant exposure to fresh air, echoing the advice of anti-tuberculosis crusaders. He encouraged frequent cold water baths, as did reformers anxious to dampen youths' interest in masturbation or sexual engagement. Wary of "autointoxication", he urged a diet heavy on roughage—a complaint and a cure made famous by John Harvey Kellogg in the late 19th century and further popularized in early 20th-century food advertisements (Whorton 1989: 102–8). The persistence of such advice demonstrates the power of popular health ideology in a society seemingly dominated by scientific medicine.

Atlas's cultural genealogy extends back to his mentor, Bernarr Macfadden, and to earlier fitness advocates such as Eugen Sandow (Hunt 1989; Ernst 1991; Chapman 1994; Budd 1997). Also visible are the connections and disjunctures between Atlas and late 20th-century fitness advocates such as Jack LaLanne and Richard Simmons. Textually, the Atlas lessons demonstrate discursive, narrative, and metaphoric ties to such recent fitness tomes as *Jane Fonda's Complete Workout* [videorecording] (1989) and *Arnold: The Education of a Body Builder* (Schwarzenegger and Hall 1977).

Placing Atlas's fitness regimen in its historical context suggests the distance between the modern body building movement and an earlier body culture which promised to democratize fitness.[2] Atlas believed any man could become healthy, strong, and successful if he practiced the Dynamic Tension exercises, followed dietary guidelines, and believed in his own virility, today's bodybuilders, by contrast, are steeped in a culture of pain (and pharmacology) and tied to sophisticated, expensive technology. One example of the cultural chasm between Atlas and his successors can be found in Samuel Wilson Fussell's memoir, *Muscle: Confessions of an Unlikely Body Builder*, when the newly pumped-up Fussell sneers at the fitness regimens of the past:

> Gone were the days of Indian clubs and Charles Atlas. I had seen a photo of him once, smiling and flexing on the beach, supporting a pair of bathing beauties on his broad shoulders. He made lifting seem as easy and pleasant as a Sunday afternoon stroll in the park.
>
> (Fussell 1991: 30)

It is our intention to explore why "easy and pleasant" has become, in our postmodern world, a pejorative phrase.

A final note: Atlas lives.[3] Charles Roman, Atlas's recently deceased publicist, business partner, and devoted follower of the regimen, sold the company in 1997 (Pace 1999: B9). New owner Jeffrey Hogue has moved the company into cyberspace (www.charlesatlas.com), where the story of Mac promotes the Dynamic-Tension® system to a new generation (Donald 1997: 1D). That this advertisement lives on in a new medium appropriate, given the metaphoric vigour of this account of personal transformation. One example of this will suffice: during the Gulf conflict, then-President George Bush motivated the troops by calling Saddam Hussein "a classic bully, kicking sand in the face of the world" (quoted in Bierman 1990: 24).[4]

Notes

1   Trill's trophy application and copies of the Atlas lessons are in the possession of the authors.
2   The Boy Scouts, for instance, made fitness central to their programme for making boys into men (Fisher 1918).
3   Although Charles Atlas the man died in the 1970s, his name, his Dynamic-Tension® system, and even the phrase "97-pound weakling" live on in part as registered trademarks of Charles Atlas, Ltd., the firm that currently markets his lessons and related products.
4   The authors request that any one who had experiences with Atlas or the Charles Atlas Dynamic-Tension System write to them at: Janet Golden, Department of History, 316 Armitage Hall, Rutgers-Camden, Camden, NJ 08102, USA; e-mail: jgolden@crab.rutgers.edu

References

Bierman, J. (1990) "Talking Turkey: Bush Celebrates Thanksgiving in the Desert and Steps up the Pressure against Saddam Hussein," *MacLean's* 3 December p. 24.

Budd, M. A. (1997) *The Sculpture Machine: Physical Culture and Body Politics in the Age of Empire*, New York: New York University Press.

Chapman, D. L. (1994) *Sandow the Magnificent: Eugen Sandow and the Beginnings of Bodybuilding*, Urbana: University of Illinois Press.

Culver, V. (1998) "Grandson in Gandhi Tradition; Offspring Brings Teens Indian Leader's Message," *Denver Post* 18 January, p. B-01.

Donald, L. (1997) "Arkansan Gets Grip on Charles Atlas: Firm and Trademark," *Arkansas Democrat-Gazette* 26 September.

Dougherty, P. H. (1972) "Atlas at 70, Still Reigns as a Tower of Strength," *New York Times* 20 August, p. 112.

Ernst, R. (1991) *Weakness is a Crime: The Life of Bernarr Macfadden*, Syracuse: Syracuse University Press.

Fisher, G. J. (1918) "Chapter seven: health and endurance," in Boy Scouts of America, *Official Handbook for Boys*, 18th edn., New York: Boy Scouts of America.

Fussell, S. W. (1991) *Muscle: Confessions of an Unlikely Body Builder*, New York Poseidon.

Gaines, C. and Butler, G. (1982) *Yours in Perfect Manhood, Charles Atlas: The Most Effective Fitness Program Ever Devised*, New York: Simon and Schuster.

Gorn, E. J. (1986) *The Manly Art. Bare Knuckle Prize Fighting in America*, Ithaca, NY: Cornell University Press.

Graebner, W. (1994) "Charles S. Atlas," in *Dictionary of American Biography Supplement 9, 1971–75*, New York: Charles Scribner's Sons, pp. 51–3.

Green, H. (1986) *Fit for America: Health, Fitness, Sport, and American Society*, New York: Pantheon.

Gustaitis, J. (1986) "Charles Atlas: 'The World's Most Perfectly Developed Man'", *American History Illustrated* September, pp. 16–17.

Hunt, W. R. (1989) *Body Love: The Amazing Career of Bernarr Macfadden*, Bowling Green, OH: Bowling Green State University Popular Press.

Jane Fonda's Complete Workout [videorecording] (1989) Burbank, CA: Warner House Video.

Kimmel, M. S. (1994) "Consuming Manhood: The Feminization of American Culture and the Recreation of the Male Body, 1832–1920," in L. Goldstein (ed.) *The Male Body: Features, Destinies, Exposures*, Ann Arbor: University of Michigan Press, pp. 12–41.

Mamet, D. (1989) *Some Freaks*, New York: Viking.

Mrozek, D. J. (1989) "Sport in American Life: From National Health to Personal Fulfillment, 1890–1940," in K. Grover (ed.) *Fitness in American Culture: Images of Health, Sport, and the Body, 1830–1940*, Amherst and Rochester: University of Massachusetts Press, and Margaret Woodbury Strong Museum, pp. 18–46.

Pace, E. (1999) "Charles Roman, the Brains Behind the Brawn, Dies at 92," *New York Times* 20 July, p. B9.

Schultz, R. (1988) "The Two Faces of DM," *DM News* 15 November, p. 44

Schwarzenegger, A. and Hall, D. K. (1977) *Arnold. The Education of a Body Builder*, New York: Simon and Schuster.

Whorton, J. C. (1989) "Eating to Win: Popular Concepts of Diet, Strength, and Energy in the Early Twentieth Century," in K. Grover (ed.) *Fitness in American Culture: Images of Health, Sport, and the Body, 1830–1940*, Amherst and Rochester: University of Massachusetts Press and Margaret Woodbury Strong Museum, pp. 86–122.

Zolotow, M. (1942) "You, Too, Can Be a New Man," *Saturday Evening Post* 7 February.

Index